Real Estate Brokerage:
A Guide to Success

Dan Hamilton

Real Estate Brokerage: A Guide to Success

Dan Hamilton

VP/Editorial Director:
Jack W. Calhoun

VP/Editor-in-Chief:
Dave Shaut

Executive Editor
Scott Person

Assoc. Acquisitions Editor:
Sara Glassmeyer

Developmental Editor:
Arlin Kauffman
LEAP Publishing Services, Inc.

Sr. Marketing Manager:
Mark Linton

Assoc. Marketing Communications Manager:
Sarah Greber

Sr. Content Project Manager:
Emily S. Gross

Director of Professional Marketing:
Terri Coats

Manager of Technology, Editorial:
Vicky True

Sr. Technology Project Editor:
Matt McKinney

Manufacturing Coordinator:
Charlene Taylor

Production House:
Interactive Composition
Corporation

Printer:
West Group
Eagan, MN

Art Director:
Linda Helcher

Internal and Cover Designer:
c miller design

Cover Images:
© Getty Images

Library of Congress Control
Number: 2006923588

For more information about our products, contact us at:

Oncourse Learning
Customer & Sales Support

1-855-733-7239

OnCourse Learning
3100 Cumberland Blvd Suite 1450
Atlanta, GA 30339
USA

BRIEF CONTENTS

CONTENTS

CHAPTER 13

Real Estate Business Planning   283

CHAPTER 15

Starting Up a Real Estate Business 329

INTRODUCTION

The field of real estate brokerage management is undergoing a revolution. Demands on today's brokers and managers go well beyond the techniques and ideas traditionally taught in real estate courses. The traditional management paradigm assumes the purpose of management is to control and limit people, enforce rules and regulations, seek stability and efficiency, design a top-down hierarchy to direct people, and achieve bottom-line results. Today's brokers and managers need different skills to engage workers' attitudes and efforts, and today's management systems must focus on leadership, creativity, and enthusiasm. The broker must find a shared vision and values to engage his or her salespeople and bring them to peak productivity. Cooperation, collaboration, contribution, and education are guiding principles that help brokers, salespeople, and employees through today's complex business environment. Brokers focus on developing, not controlling, people to adapt to the current business environment and achieve total business success.

My vision for this book is to explore the brokerage business in a way that is interesting and valuable to readers and students. To achieve this vision, I have included the most recent management theory and research, as well as the contemporary application of management ideas in organizations of all types. The combination of traditional views, new ideas, and real-life applications gives the reader a glimpse of the excitement, challenge, and quest inherent in the dynamic field of real estate brokerage.

The group at Cengage Learning and I have worked together to provide a textbook better than any other at capturing the excitement of real estate brokerage management. In writing this text, I sought to provide a book of utmost quality that will create in readers both respect for the changing field of brokerage and confidence that they can understand and master it. The textual portion of this book has been enhanced through its engaging, easy-to-understand writing style.

Focus on the Future

The Real Estate Brokerage: A Guide to Success is directed toward anyone who is or would like to become a real estate manager, real estate broker, or real estate business owner. The principal difference among these positions is the degree of authority and ownership in the organization. This book focuses in particular on the future of brokerage education by identifying and describing emerging elements and examples of the way real estate brokerage is conducted in today's marketplace. The book is divided into fifteen chapters, each having an introduction that explains the content of each chapter, a body that explains how to operate and manage a real estate brokerage business, and a conclusion with questions to test the reader's comprehension and understanding. The following is a brief summary of the chapters:

- Chapter 1: The Real Estate Industry—This chapter gives an overview of past and current real estate markets. The information points out the important clues the past reveals to the future of real estate brokerage. It shows the reader the future and how to adapt to lead the pack. The chapter delves into the legal and ethical side of real estate brokerage and how it can positively or negatively affect a real estate business.

- Chapter 2: The Real Estate Broker and Owner—Chapter 2 asks the relevant questions as to the character of a qualified real estate broker. The chapter looks at the traits necessary to become a success as a broker and how those traits should be used to turn a profit. The chapter also analyzes the types of management styles and the advantages and disadvantages of each.

- Chapter 3: The Real Estate Brokerage Office—Chapter 3 addresses the factors that make up a successful real estate office. There is a comprehensive discussion of the types of real estate offices and their risks and rewards. The chapter reviews the rooms that should make up an office, the layout of those rooms, and the equipment in those rooms.

- Chapter 4: Real estate brokerage operations—Real estate brokerage operations include all the day-to-day operations of a real estate office. These operations include salesperson operations, recruiting operations, marketing operations, and accounting operations. This chapter analyzes these factors and many others.

- Chapter 5: Real Estate Brokerage Marketing—The marketing of a brokerage business begins with identifying the type of real estate to be practiced, such as residential, commercial, property management, farm and ranch, fine homes and estates, and/or vacation properties. A broker must also determine the geographic area the office will operate. Chapter 5 discusses marketing strategies, marketing plans, marketing campaigns, and the marketing budget.

- Chapter 6: Additional Marketing Ideas—Chapter 5 introduced the marketing concepts, and Chapter 6 looks at a multitude of additional advertising and marketing ideas. The ideas range from shopping mall kiosks to sponsoring events.

- Chapter 7: Real Estate Brokerage Compensation Structures—Chapter 7 describes several types of compensation structures and the advantages and disadvantages of each. The chapter also looks at alternative ways to compensate a salesperson.

- Chapter 8: Real Estate Staff Brokerage Operations—This chapter deals with employment law, management development programs, and the types of salespeople a brokerage firm should hire. The main focus of Chapter 8 is describing the perfect office and how to develop it.

- Chapter 9: Recruiting Real Estate Salespeople—Recruiting is a broker's most important function; it is constant and never-ending. Chapters 9 and 10 are devoted to discussing recruiting activities. Chapter 9 covers the differences among types of possible recruits and the best ways to capture those recruits. The chapter looks at the wants and needs of the recruit and describes ways for the broker to give the recruit what he or she desires. This chapter is full of ways to prospect for recruits.

- Chapter 10: Recruiting Interview—The key event in recruiting a real estate salesperson is during the recruiting interview. Chapter 10 examines the interview process in its entirety. The chapter sets the interview parameters and includes scripts and dialogues. The chapter concludes with objection handling and closing techniques.

- Chapter 11: Retention of Real Estate Salespeople—The second greatest function for a broker is to be able to retain the real estate salespeople already recruited. Chapter 11 provides insight on the best ways to motivate and retain real estate salespeople. The chapter defines handling of company events, training, and ancillary business.

- Chapter 12: Real Estate Business Development—Relocation and referral business is frequently overlooked by real estate brokers. This chapter describes the arrangement of a business development segment in a brokerage. It encompasses all aspects of relocation and referral business and provides interviewing techniques and scripts.

- Chapter 13: Real Estate Business Planning—The best way to be sure of running a business successfully is to have a business plan. Chapter 13 takes an in-depth look at business planning and provides an outline to develop a business plan.

- Chapter 14: Financing a Real Estate Business—Chapter 14 gives details on financing a real estate business, including the necessary paperwork and requirements for obtaining a loan. This chapter also explains alternative and creative financing options.

- Chapter 15: Starting Up a Real Estate Business—Chapter 15 wraps up brokerage and details the actions necessary to open a real estate brokerage.

Organization

The Real Estate Brokerage: A Guide to Success is organized around the two main functions of a real estate broker: recruiting new and experienced salespeople and then retaining them once they join. These two functions are the basis of real estate brokerage success.

Brokers in today's real estate companies have a multitude of exhilarating and challenging roles simply because of the way the industry is evolving. Technology and the Internet, which has touched virtually every aspect of the business, are constantly changing and evolving. Additionally, economic, geopolitical, social, and legal climates create opportunities that challenge the management skills of today's brokers. Running a brokerage in this environment most likely means an attitudinal shift to move away from traditional practices.

Becoming a real estate broker appeals to individuals' desires to be imaginative and to influence, lead, and inspire others. The reward is that the brokerage does more than simply exist; rather, it thrives. Most gratifying of all for brokers is the exhilaration of seeing the people they manage grow in their professional successes.

Operating a real estate brokerage firm can be an intimidating and humbling experience. *The Real Estate Brokerage: A Guide to Success* helps brokers with their responsibilities, as everything that happens in an organization rises or falls on their decisions. Today's brokerages are complex sets of systems, processes, and people that function in a fluid or changing business environment, an understanding of which requires the education provided by this book.

Perhaps the most significant word in this book's title is *guide*. Today's real estate companies don't fit into one model. Each company is unique, and each broker is an individual. There are, however, certain basic principles for running a real estate company and coaching salespeople that are the foundation of a well-run brokerage. The purpose of this book is to help brokers understand the fundamentals of management and develop the ability to apply those fundamentals in ways that best fit their situation and company.

The Real Estate Brokerage: A Guide to Success provides a framework within which to manage in any environment. Whether the book is used for classroom study and certification or as preparatory reading prior to opening a brokerage, the book is an indispensable resource in any real estate library. The book is well designed and formatted for easy reference during challenges and expansion of any real estate company.

You may be embarking on a new career or already have real estate brokerage experience. You may be a salesperson, not yet involved in management but seeking an inside look into the operation of a brokerage company. In any case, *The Real Estate Brokerage: A Guide to Success* is useful for gathering the tools of today's management trade and seizing new opportunities that are on the horizon.

To most people, the real estate brokerage business seems concerned largely with salesmanship, with success depending only upon the listing and selling abilities of the sales force. While these activities are important, and they have a lot to do with individual success, real estate brokerage is also a business and must be run with profit in mind. In today's competitive market, the ability to operate a brokerage firm as an efficient business is just as significant as the quality of the service the firm provides. It is this aspect of the real estate brokerage business that this book addresses.

These pages contain little about the activities of salespeople. Rather, we are concerned here with the management of the business: planning, organization, control, and financial well-being. In every field, a great many new businesses are formed every year, and most of them eventually fail. While the reasons for failure are many, much of the time it is because of improper management and the confusion, inefficiency, and money troubles that result. For the same reason, many that are able to survive do so far below their potential.

This book is arranged as a text, but it is not intended only for classroom use. The working broker and sales manager will be able to find plenty of use and value in these pages. Furthermore, anyone considering owning and/or operating a real estate brokerage business should learn and apply the ideas and concepts contained here. Because most states require that an individual's broker's license be preceded by a period of licensure as a salesperson, this book assumes that someone interested in the operation of a brokerage company will have acquired some knowledge of the real estate selling process. This allows the book to concentrate upon the management and organization aspects of the real estate brokerage business.

ACKNOWLEDGEMENTS

I would like to thank several people for their help on this book. My publication crew at Cengage Learning have worked with me and held my hand through a process I knew little about. They include Sara Glassmeyer, who has believed in me from the beginning, Scott Person, Mark Linton, Emily Gross, Arlin Kauffman, Ruchika Vij, Heather Dubnick, and the newest member of the team, Jean Buttrom. In addition to being invaluably helpful, all have generously given their time and knowledge. Special thanks to my family, who has given me the time and space to complete this project. And all my gratitude goes out to all my students who have let me "experiment" on them in class as I perfected this material.

ABOUT THE AUTHOR

Dan Hamilton has been working in the real estate business for over eighteen years. His successes and accomplishments are vast, including owning and operating a multiple-office real estate company. He has been a certified real estate trainer for fifteen years. He has written many real estate training courses, culminating with the publication of his book *Real Estate Marketing and Sales Essentials.*

Dan is currently the director of a real estate school in Texas that he founded, while also continuing to work as an active broker and investor in real property. He has a beautiful wife, Kimberly, and a remarkable daughter, Brittany, who happens to be the best salesperson in the world.

1 The Real Estate Industry

Introduction

Real estate brokerage is the business of real estate sales in its many forms. The real estate industry is an exciting business in general. Everyone wants to talk about real estate—it is the "American Dream." People are interested in buying and selling their homes, in investing in rental property, and in purchasing vacation property. The list is endless. Buying a place to live can be one of the most complex and important financial events in one's life. Buyers and sellers want help with these important decisions and that is why and how the real estate industry has evolved.

Most people entering the real estate field as a career want to become brokers and have their own company. They get their broker license and buy some yard signs, and "BAM!"—they have their brokerage, without training, financial backing, or experience. That is what I did, and that is what I have observed during my career. My experience is that they call us "Broke-ers" for a reason. I made more money selling real estate as an agent than I did when I owned and operated three real estate companies—that is, until I figured out how to be a broker through the "School of Hard Knocks." I don't want to talk you out of real estate brokerage, but I do want you to understand what is ahead for you if you choose brokerage as a career path: I wrote this book to help *you* be the best broker you can be.

Real estate brokers are independent businesspeople who sell real estate owned by others. Brokers supervise real estate salespeople, who also sell real estate owned by others. Brokers hire office managers or manage their own offices, advertise properties, and handle all other business matters. Some combine this with other types of work, such as leasing, property management, mortgage, and insurance.

Most real estate brokers and salespeople sell residential property. A much smaller number sell commercial, industrial, agricultural, or special-purpose real estate. Every specialty requires knowledge of that particular type of property and that particular type of client. Leasing property requires an understanding of leasing practices, business trends, and available property locations. Salespeople who sell or lease industrial properties must understand the region's infrastructure, transportation, utilities, laws, regulations, and labor supply. Whatever the type of property, the salesperson or broker must know how to meet the client's particular requirements.

Once you become your own broker, it feels great to hold your first sales meeting and to know that all the salespeople are looking to you for leadership; to walk in front of several hundred of your peers and receive an award for a top-producing real estate office; to mentor a rookie real estate salesperson and create a star! Money is a reward in and of itself, but the great brokers want to see others succeed as a result of their efforts rather than claiming all the limelight for themselves.

Brokerage History

The real estate industry was ultimately developed to fulfill a need of buyers and sellers of real property. The need developed because real estate can be a complicated business, and without the help of experienced real estate professionals, the ordinary consumer could be at a disadvantage. Real estate has been around since dirt, and I mean that literally. Real estate has had to adapt to keep up with current changes and demands, and these changes and demands have had a profound effect on the real estate brokerage business: regulators began limiting the role of the broker; the age of information changed the role of the broker; and the advent of the computer completely changed the direction of the real estate industry. The formation and prevalent use of the Internet changed the way the real estate industry found clients and moved information. Many brokers have changed their entire philosophy because their salespeople no longer need a "brick-and-mortar" office to work from. These salespeople now work from home or from their vehicle. Despite these changes, however, a real estate salesperson still makes money by connecting buyers and sellers, and that will never change.

Most real estate firms are relatively small; some are one-person businesses. By contrast, some large real estate firms have several hundred real estate salespeople operating out of numerous branch offices. Many brokers have franchise agreements with national or regional real estate organizations.

Real estate brokers deal frequently with other specialists in the real estate business: competing brokers, investors, property managers, commercial brokers, leasing agents, appraisers, surveyors, engineers, financial institutions, title companies, architects, contractors, inspectors, attorneys, and accountants. A broker should establish and maintain good working relationships with these professionals.

Real estate brokers and salespeople have a thorough knowledge of the real estate market they serve. They know how to find the right neighborhoods that will best fit their clients' wants and needs. They are familiar with the laws and regulations affecting a real estate transaction. They know where to obtain the best financing options.

Brokerage Outlook and Trends

The outlook for real estate and the real estate brokerage business is continually improving. The economic fundamentals of the real estate climate are strong, but rising technology costs are putting pressure on the profitability of real estate brokerage offices.

The competition in the real estate sector is increasingly stiff and harsh. As more and more real estate salespeople enter into the real estate industry, the competition for the sale will also increase. The brokerage firms must provide the services demanded by the consumer and the real estate salesperson.

Consistent growth in population and economic production, along with low mortgage rates, has produced a strong base for home sales. This trend should continue well into the future. Interest rates are creeping up, but the overall twenty-year average is still extremely affordable. Because interest rates are at such a low level, investments in real estate have been increasing for the past five years.

The business is breaking into two main segments. The first segment is the Mom and Pop shop, a single broker working from home. Overhead is so small that the Mom and Pop shop will survive any change in the real estate market.

The second segment is the mega-firm. This type of company is so large that it operates on the Sam Walton belief that you can make money on anything if you can sell enough of it. The mega-firm has hundreds of real estate agents and several offices. The ability to buy large quantities of supplies at a discount and to negotiate large discounted contracts with service providers allows this company to survive any change in the real estate market. Watch for the consolidation of middle real estate companies for many years into the future.

I believe these are the only two types of real estate brokerage firms that will survive and thrive in the near future. The middle firms, the ones with one or two offices with ten to fifty real estate salespeople, will get squeezed until they cannot continue in business. The real estate salesperson is demanding more on a commission split and expects the broker to pay for all the necessary services associated with selling real estate. The profit margins in the real estate industry have been shrinking for the last fifteen years and will continue to dwindle until all the middle firms are gone. The problem with this approach to business is that "everyone" wants to be the owner of his or her own real estate company, and the most frequent type formed is the middle firm. These middle firms will form and dissolve many times in the next several years.

A new concept is the purchase of residential real estate brokerage firms by non-brokerage real estate or financial services companies, such as title insurance firms or banks. The entry of non-brokerage firms with unlimited capital could change the brokerage industry quickly because they can acquire existing brokerages with the largest market share and broadest reach. However, in some cases, regulatory approval would be required.

Some soothsayers believe that the Internet will replace the need for real estate professionals. No chance. The Internet can do a lot of things, but it cannot give the feel of actually walking through a house. Even a 360° virtual tour cannot duplicate the feel of a buyer's first walk-thru of a house. We (in the real estate profession) like to say that the house "talks" to the buyer. I truly believe that. I have seen it. A buyer walks through a house and simply pauses for a second in complete silence, then smiles. I then realize the house just "talked" to the buyer and the buyer listened. How can the Internet "talk" to a buyer—it can't!

- A Pew Internet & American Life study found that 40 million Americans, or one-third of all Internet users, have used the Internet for information about a place to live. On average, more than three million people are searching online for a new place to live on any given day.[1]

- An Inman Real Estate article reported that the paid-per-click search engine Overture records about 1.1 million monthly searches for the phrase "real estate," and the number one search engine, Google, will record about 500 million real estate-related searches per year.[2]

---

[1] "Pew Internet & American Life Project Data Memo," Angie Boyce and Lee Rainie, August 2002, http://www.pewinternet.org/pdfs/PIP_Housing_Data_Memo.pdf.

[2] "Real Estate Marketing," David Erickson, http://e-strategy.com.

- The NATIONAL ASSOCIATION OF REALTORS® found that Internet homebuyers were more likely to use a real estate agent to complete the home search and close the transaction. Internet users purchased more expensive homes than their offline peers.[3]

The Internet is about the biggest thing that has hit the real estate business in the last ten years. It has revolutionized the way real estate salespeople communicate. But the biggest trend that has surfaced is the way a real estate brokerage business uses the Internet to advertise for clients. Many real estate brokerage businesses have rerouted their advertising funds from print media to the Internet, and this trend will continue.

The real estate industry is evolving and creating a multitude of opportunities for today's real estate brokerages and tomorrow's business leaders. As NATIONAL ASSOCIATION OF REALTORS® Vice President Mark Lesswing has said, "The changes in technology usage suggest an increased reliance on the Internet and new consolidated technologies in the conduct of Realtor business over time." (http://www.rismedia.com/index.php/article/articleview/3828/1/1/RISMedia, Realtors Are Increasing Use for Internet, Web Technology)

Another recent trend is low interest rates, which should continue to stimulate sales of real estate and result in the need for more agents and brokers. Growing families will be in a better position to buy a new home. The baby boomers are now retiring and seeking alternate living arrangements. All of these changes are opportunities for the real estate company that is alert, aware, and willing to adapt. While the future is never certain, the willingness to adapt to change will help the pioneers in this business grow and prosper.

Brokerage Regulations and Laws

All real estate business falls under the state's real estate commission. The commission regulates the operation and activities of real estate brokers and their salespeople. The regulations have become more stringent because of the pressure of the consumer to be treated in an honest manner. Agency laws have defined the relationships of the real estate brokerage business. The agency laws spell out how a broker and a salesperson should represent their client and the duties they should perform. The real estate broker must know these laws and how they can affect the real estate business.

---

[3] "NAR Survey Shows Growing Web Use," http://houstonrealtor.har.com.

Real Estate License Law

Every state has some type of real estate license law. These laws were enacted to protect the public from unscrupulous real estate practitioners. Each state will have certain laws for that particular state, but in general the laws limit the activities the real estate broker and salesperson can perform. The laws generally prohibit a list of activities, such as

- Payment of fees to unlicensed persons
- Material misrepresentation of a significant property defect
- Felony conviction—especially for fraud
- Fraudulent procurement of real estate
- Dishonesty
- Failure to cooperate with their real estate commission
- False advertising
- Maintaining undisclosed agency relationships
- Commingling, or mixing of personal funds with those of another
- Conversion, or using funds of others for a use other than that intended
- Negligent or incompetent behavior

These activities are prohibited to protect the consumer. The broker should obey these laws and make sure the office personnel understand and act in accordance with them.

National Regulations

There are few national regulations for individual real estate offices. The laws passed on a national level include the Real Estate Settlement Procedures Act and the Federal Fair Housing Act. These laws apply to all that engage in the real estate industry and overrule any laws and regulations on the state and local level.

State Regulations

Most major laws and regulations for individual real estate offices are passed on the state level. These laws include abiding by the state real estate commission.

Local Regulations

Again, there are few local real estate regulations that apply only to real estate brokerage and no other business. Those laws are usually formed on the state level. Regulations like zoning laws apply not only to a real estate company but also to all businesses in that specific area.

Agency Law

Agency law is derived from common law. That simply means that agency law applies to everyone. An agent is one that acts for and on behalf of another. The real estate broker/owner needs to establish an office policy for agency law, put it in writing, and make sure all the salespeople associated with the company are aware and abide by those rules. The best way to protect the traditional real estate company is to have all real estate salespeople associated with the company sign a notice stating that they have read and understand the agency policy manual.

There are several types of office policies that an office could adopt:

SELLER ONLY

The *seller only* office is referred to as a traditional office because for years real estate brokerages represented the seller only. With this type of agency policy, company salespeople cannot represent buyers. This doesn't mean the salesperson cannot "work with" a buyer, but it does mean they cannot "work for" the buyer. I remember selling real estate during the time of seller only agency; we never even thought about representing the buyer. We could show property, help with the paperwork, and monitor the closing process, but at all times we still represented the seller's best interest. Times have changed, however, and in today's market it is expected that the buyer will be represented.

Buyers have figured out the system of representing sellers only and are seeking representation for themselves. Because of this trend, seller only real estate companies had to adapt or lose business. Very few real estate offices today practice seller only agency.

BUYER ONLY

Buyer only offices represent buyers only. Under such an arrangement, the office must refuse seller representation. Just as with seller only offices, buyer only offices miss half of the market. These offices specialize in representing buyers. They provide advice and advocacy to the buyers and help them make the correct decisions in a real estate transaction.

Buyer only offices tend to be smaller Mom and Pop operations because of the reduction of the potential market. Again, very few real estate offices today practice buyer only agency.

SELLER ONLY WITH BUYER REPRESENTATION

Seller only with buyer representation is a type of agency policy that I believe is quite dangerous. With this type of policy, the real estate company represents sellers only. If a buyer wants to buy an office listing, the company must represent the seller and can only work with the buyer. However, if a buyer wants to buy a property not represented by the company, they can be represented.

Confused? Just think about the buyer prospect. A couple decides they want to buy a home and walk into an office that practices seller only with buyer representation. They look at the company's listings in which the real estate salesperson is representing the seller only. They do not find anything they want to buy, so the salesperson shows them listings from other offices. The buyer wants to make an offer on one of those properties. The salesperson (now representing the buyer) completes a competitive market analysis (CMA) to determine a fair price to offer to the seller and advises the buyer on what type of repairs to request. The offer is negotiated but never consummated. The buyers now want to make an offer on a listing that is in-house. The salesperson now represents the seller. The buyer asks for a CMA. The salesperson must refuse because that might not be in the seller's best interest. The buyer asks the salesperson what he or she should offer, and the salesperson can only state the list price. Think the buyer is frustrated? My only advice for choosing the agency policy is to stick either with representing the seller or with representing the buyer or an intermediary (explained later), but not to switch hats. I know of no real estate company practicing seller only with buyer representation, but it must be discussed because it is a legal option.

BUYER ONLY WITH SELLER REPRESENTATION

Buyer only with seller representation is the opposite of the previous agency policy. If you believe, as I do, that seller only with buyer representation is crazy, just consider buyer only with seller representation. We will not discuss this one in detail because by taking the previous discussion and substituting "buyer" for "seller" you will grasp the concept. Again, I know of no real estate company practicing buyer only with seller representation.

INTERMEDIARY

An *intermediary* office represents buyers and represents sellers. The only time there is a change is when a represented in-house buyer wants to buy a represented in-house seller's property. At this time the broker of record becomes an intermediary. An intermediary's position is to remain neutral and not favor either the buyer or seller. The salespeople involved still represent their respective clients 100 percent.

The advantages for a real estate company are many. First, the company can represent both buyers and sellers, thus appealing to more potential clients. Second, the broker remains neutral, which should be easy because a broker typically does not know confidential information about any one client. The disadvantages are for the smaller companies where the broker lists and sells. The broker cannot represent one party and also be the intermediary. In these cases, the broker must appoint a salesperson to represent the client, and then the broker moves to the position of the intermediary. Most real estate brokerages in this market are intermediary.

DUAL AGENCY

Dual agency had its time, and that time has passed. When the real estate industry was going through the change from seller only to representing buyers, dual agency reared its ugly head. Dual agency is representing both parties in one transaction. It is not illegal, but it is extremely dangerous.

As mentioned in my previous book, *Real Estate Marketing and Sales Essentials,* when a broker represents a seller, it is the broker's duty to obtain the highest price and the best terms possible for the seller. If a broker represents a buyer, the broker's duty is to obtain the lowest price and best terms for the buyer. When the same broker represents two or more principals in the same transaction, it is a dual or divided agency, and a conflict of interest results. If the broker represents both principals in the same transaction, to whom is the broker loyal? Does he work equally hard for each principal? This is an unanswerable question; therefore, the law requires that each principal be told not to expect the broker's full allegiance, and thus each principal is responsible for looking after his or her own interest. If a broker represents more than one principal and does not obtain their informed consent, the broker is in violation.

Dual agency is dangerous—how can a person *truly* represent both parties in one transaction? Answer: no one can. Dual agency is *restricted agency,* meaning that the agent must not represent one party over another or disclose confidential information between the parties. It can be done, and that's why it is still legal. The only problem is that in practice it is difficult to perform, and one mistake can lead to a legal nightmare. Intermediary allows the representation of both parties without the liability of dual agency, which is why most real estate companies practice intermediary as their agency policy.

NON-AGENCY

Non-agency is a dream world where real estate brokerages get paid millions of dollars to make real estate transactions happen without the liability of representation. Not a realistic scenario—if for the same amount of money you had a choice between one person who would represent you and give you advice and another person who would help but cannot give any advice, which would you choose? Yes, brokers love this one, but consumers don't. Who do you think will win this debate?

Non-agency is simply not representing anyone in the transaction. I do see a place for non-agency in limited service. For example, to do a fee-for-service type transaction one must be a non-agent. I was a non-agent once. I received a call from a "For Sale By Owner" who disclosed that they had found a buyer and was wondering if I would do the paperwork for a percent of the transaction. I agreed. I met the buyer and seller at the seller's house. I brought out the purchase agreement and looked at the buyer, "In what name would you like to take title?" Twenty minutes later I had signatures on the agreement and was out the door. I made about $800.00 for twenty minutes of work—not bad. In this case, I represented neither party and only did the paperwork. I could not represent the seller because that representation meant more than I agreed to do. Some other terms synonymous with non-agency are *consultant, counselor, facilitator,* and *transactional broker.*

Non-agency is also appropriate for the real estate counselor, who represents corporations buying property in the hundreds of millions of dollars. No one cares about paying 100 thousand dollars for the advice of a real estate counselor on a 400-million-dollar housing complex. But there might be trouble paying the same $1,00,000 on a single-family property valued at $75,000.

License Law

All states have some type of real estate license law. The laws vary, but most are there to protect the consumer from the unscrupulous business practices of real estate brokers and salespeople. The laws regulate the relationship between agents and principals, as well as the duties that are to be performed. The laws regulate the brokerage companies and the registration process to practice real estate.

Contract Law

Contract law regulates the action of an agreement between two parties. In real estate, contracts and contract law are a main part of business. Without contracts, how could we be sure of the terms of a real estate purchase? And even more important, how could we be sure we will get paid? As the broker, you are responsible for your salespeople's authorized acts. As such, you or someone you trust should review each and every contract and agreement that your salespeople are participating in. Too often a broker feels that the salesperson with a prelicense course on contracts is prepared for real estate. Believe me, as a trainer I have learned that this is far from the truth. Everyone needs ongoing training for changes that inevitably occur.

Deceptive Trade Practices Act (DTPA)

The Deceptive Trade Practices Act is probably the best protection available to consumers in business transactions. Its provisions insure that real estate professionals deliver to our clients professionalism, knowledge, and honesty. The DTPA is a means of eliminating the real estate salespeople who seek to take advantage of consumers of real estate services. However, the DTPA applies to anyone, not just to real estate licensees.

The provisions of the DTPA are believed by many to unfairly disadvantage real estate salespeople by making them responsible for things not always under their control. A real estate salesperson could be in violation of the DTPA by failing to disclose property defects that they should have known were present. The DTPA asks two questions:

> *Did you know?*
>
> *Should you have known?*

If the answer to either question is "yes," then the salesperson could be in violation of the DTPA. The law also protects the consumer when the salesperson has made a misrepresentation concerning a transaction. Misrepresentation is a false statement. Misrepresentation can occur by commission or omission. Commission is making of a mistake or error, and omission is the leaving out of information. Misrepresentation can also involve fraud. Fraud is the intentional misleading of a person. Certain factors must be in place for fraud, including

> ### *Reliance (on the information)*
> ### *Intent (to fraud)*
> ### *Damage (to the individual)*

The Act provides for a consumer who prevails in a DTPA action to receive actual damages. If it is found that the conduct of the salesperson was committed knowingly (fraud), the award may be three times the amount of actual damages, called punitive damages. Punitive damages have been awarded even though the buyers would have discovered the misrepresentations had they exercised reasonable diligence. A buyer does not have to do anything; the salesperson should have disclosed the information.

There is no defense from the DTPA that will work every time, but the next three will "probably" work most of the time; "probably" is inserted here because most DTPA cases are settled without a ruling. These defenses should be used to protect you as much as possible:

Inspections by licensed inspectors. It is the job of licensed inspectors to find out what is potentially wrong with a property. Once they give their professional opinions on an inspection report, they are liable for their opinions.

Written seller's disclosure statement. A seller's disclosure statement is a document that describes the property in detail. It allows the seller to note anything about the property and whether or not it is functioning properly.

Information from the government. Information is given by the government that you have no reason to believe is false.

The following three defenses under the DTPA will not work even though those in the real estate profession always try to use them:

1. Waiver. You cannot waive your right to sue before the event happens.

2. "As-Is." This phrase means the buyer is stating that he or she will not sue the seller even though the buyer is not fully aware of the property

and any problems the property could have. The law says problems must be disclosed; it doesn't, however, require that you repair the problems.

3. *Caveat emptor* (let the buyer beware). Under DTPA, the buyer does not have to show due diligence.

The Deceptive Trade Practices Act applies to all business transactions. We are especially concerned with how the DTPA applies in transactions involving the sale or rental of real estate, including the actions of real estate licensees engaging in the practice of real estate brokerage. The DTPA provides a "laundry list" of deceptive practice that the real estate broker should be keenly aware of. Here is a partial list of practices that are clearly deceptive:

- Passing off goods or services as those of another

- Causing confusion or misunderstanding as to the source, sponsorship, approval, or certification of goods or services

- Causing confusion or misunderstanding as to affiliation, connection, or association with, or certification by, another

- Using deceptive representatives or designations of geographic origin in connection with goods or services

- Representing goods or services that claim to have sponsorship, approval, characteristics, ingredients, uses, benefits, or quantities but do not; or claiming to have a sponsorship, approval, status, affiliation, or connection but not having them

- Representing that goods are original or new if they are deteriorated, reconditioned, reclaimed, used, or secondhand

- Representing that goods or services are of a particular standard, quality, or grade, or that goods are of a particular style or model, if they are of another

- Disparaging the goods, services, or business of another by false or misleading representations of facts

- Advertising goods or services with intent not to sell them as advertised

- Advertising goods or services with intent not to supply a reasonable, expectable public demand, unless the advertisement disclosed a limitation of quantity

- Making false or misleading statements of fact concerning the reasons for, existence of, or amount of price reductions.

A consumer may maintain an action for damages based on breach of an express or implied warranty, or for any unconscionable action. An *unconscionable action* is defined as an action that takes advantage of the lack of knowledge, ability, experience, or capacity of a person to a grossly unfair degree or one in which there is a gross disparity between the value received and the consideration paid.

The DTPA is a formidable law, but with the proper training and control brokers can lessen their liability.

Sherman Antitrust Act

The Sherman Antitrust Act prohibits any type of collaboration of businesses to the detriment of consumers. Section 15 of the Act states that "every contract, combination in the form of trust or otherwise, or conspiracy, in restraint of trade or commerce is declared to be illegal. Every person who shall make any contract or engage in any combination or conspiracy hereby declared to be illegal shall be deemed guilty of a felony, and, on conviction thereof, shall be punished by fine not exceeding $10,000,000 if a corporation, or, if any other person, $350,000, or by imprisonment not exceeding three years, or by both said punishments, in the discretion of the court."

Antitrust prohibits price-fixing. Price-fixing is the act of two or more competitors joining together to force consumers to pay a higher amount than they would pay if competition were unrestrained. If any two real estate brokers get together and agree to charge a certain commission, that would be price-fixing. Commissions are and will remain negotiable between the brokerage company and the client. This can happen almost unintentionally. A group of competing real estate brokers are sitting around complaining about not making enough money. One of the brokers comes up with the great idea that if everyone raised commission rates to the same amount, all brokers would make more money. If you even hear such a discussion, you must leave immediately. Defending yourself by saying it was not your idea would not save you. A price-fixing violation can be inferred from the fact of similar price conduct by members, even if no written or oral agreement is evident.

The Sherman Antitrust Act also prohibits *boycotting,* which is the collaboration of a group of businesses to avoid doing business with another business. A group of real estate brokers agreeing not to show the properties of another broker in order to force said broker out of business is an example of boycotting. Boycotting that rises to the level of a violation would also include forcing competitors to raise commission rates or refusing to do business with them.

Antitrust includes the allocation of customers as a violation. If two brokers agreed to split an area in half and not do business in the other area, that would be the allocation of customers and clearly a violation. An agreement among members of an association or group to divide customers is, in and of itself, a criminal act. The antitrust laws prohibit any understandings or agreements between competitors or members of an association that involves the division or allocation of customers.

If you are part of an association or are thinking of forming a trade group, be careful not to prohibit membership of certain people or companies to avoid competition. A basic assumption about every trade association is that its members derive an economic benefit from membership. Denial of membership to an applicant may therefore constitute a restraint of trade in that such denial of an economic benefit limits the rights of an applicant to compete. Thus, membership criteria must be carefully drafted to avoid antitrust problems.

Do Not Call, Do Not Fax, and Anti-Spam Laws

The Do Not Call, Do Not Fax, and Anti-Spam laws were recently adopted to limit the numerous telephone, fax, and e-mail spam sent to consumers. Some of these laws have been around for years with very little enforcement. Those days are gone.

THE HISTORY OF THE DO NOT CALL RULES

In 1991, Congress passed the Telephone Consumer Protection Act (TCPA). The Act was to protect the privacy of residential telephone users. It was to create a national do not call registry. A great idea, but it was not developed because of cost and technological limits. The main setbacks concerned who would maintain the registry and how. The law did define when telemarketers may call, and it required telemarketers to maintain internal no-call lists. Real estate licensees were exempt from these rules. There was very little enforcement of the laws.

In 2002, the Federal Trade Commission (FTC) amended its rules by expanding the rules to include real estate licensees. It created the first true National Do Not Call Registry.

In 2003, the Federal Communications Commission (FCC) amended its rules that required telemarketers to use the National Do Not Call Registry maintained by the FTC and gave an "established business relationship" exemption so that

- Rules apply to calls that contain a commercial solicitation (most cold calls); and
- The no-call rules do not apply to calls made when an established business relationship exists.

Under federal rules, an established business relationship exists:

1. When the caller had a transaction with the receiver within the last eighteen months; or
2. The customer has made an inquiry with the caller's firm in the last three months.

Generally, to make a prospecting call, the real estate licensee must "scrub" the number against the National Do Not Call registry and the firm's internal no call list. If the number does not appear on either list, the licensee may call.

- The real estate licensee may make calls between 9:00 a.m. and 9:00 p.m. on weekdays and Saturdays, and between 12:00 p.m. and 9:00 p.m. on Sundays.
- The caller must identify himself or herself before making the solicitation, must identify it as a solicitation call, and must disclose all material information related to the solicited service.
- The caller may not use caller-ID blocking.

Violators potentially face an $11,000 fine by the federal government for calling a number on the registry, and the state attorney general may bring a civil suit for $500 per call. The federal government does not actually want to cause real estate licensees trouble. Their main target is the massive telephone canvassing banks where several hundred people are on the telephone calling consumers. Chances are that if you accidentally call a number on the National Do Not Call Registry, you will not be fined. Make sure that as the broker you maintain the internal no call lists, and that you have correct procedures in place.

I believe that for the observant broker, this law benefits the real estate brokerage business. The law does not prohibit prospecting calls. It only prohibits the call to someone on the National Do Not Call Registry. In the real estate industry, the law has resulted in a great deal of fear and a great deal of relief: fear of being fined for calling the "wrong" person, and relief because of this fear that real estate salespeople no longer can make calls. In other words, if your salespeople "scrub" their prospecting lists and continue to call, they and you will make a great deal of money because most real estate salespeople are no longer calling.

THE HISTORY OF THE DO NOT FAX RULES

In 2003, the FCC amended its rules to require written consent from the receiver before the sender could send a fax with an advertisement in it. This law applies to any fax that contained an unsolicited commercial solicitation. The new rules eliminated any established business relationship exemption.

An "unsolicited advertisement" is defined as "any material advertising the commercial availability or quality of any property, goods or services which is transmitted to any person without that person's prior express invitation or permission."[4]

This means that real estate licensees would have to obtain written consent from anyone to whom the licensee was to send a fax that contained a commercial solicitation.

You should eliminate any fax cover sheets that contain inadvertent commercial advertisements. If a consumer verbally requests a listing sheet, a real estate professional will need to obtain the signed written consent from the recipient before sending this information via fax. The penalties could be up to $1,500 for a fax that does not comply.

Again, I don't think that this law is such a big deal. I know very few real estate brokers that prospect homeowners via fax machine. Once you have a business relationship with a client, it is easy to get them to provide you the authorization to send them a fax.

THE HISTORY OF ANTI-SPAM RULES

In December 2003, Congress passed the CAN-SPAM Act to try to limit "spam." The CAN-SPAM Act prohibits the sending of unsolicited e-mail with commercial advertisements unless the subject line is preceded with

---

[4] "New Fax Law Confirms EBR Exemption," NATIONAL ASSOCIATION OF REALTORS®, http://realtor.org.

"ADV." It requires the sender to provide the recipient with a means to un-subscribe, which must be honored within three days. This law also contains an "established business relationship" exemption. The CAN-SPAM Act supersedes any state law, places requirements on senders of spam, and imposes penalties for violations.

This law prohibits the falsification of routing information or sending information. It also prohibits any false, misleading, or deceptive information in the subject line. A fine of $10 per unlawful message or $25,000 for each day, whichever is less, can be issued.

The Do Not Call, Do Not Fax, and Anti-Spam laws are constantly changing, and it would benefit you to stay abreast of the latest changes.

The Clayton Act

The Clayton Act expanded the Sherman Antitrust Act. Section 15 of the Clayton Act states that "it shall be unlawful for any person engaged in commerce to discriminate in price between different purchasers of services and where the effect of such discrimination may be substantially to lessen competition or tend to create a monopoly in any line of commerce, or to injure, destroy, or prevent competition with any person who either grants or knowingly receives the benefit of such discrimination, or with customers of either of them." The main aspects of the Clayton Act are the prohibition of price-fixing and collaboration between brokers, both of which are also prohibited under the Sherman Antitrust Act.

Fair Housing

Fair housing is a federal law pertaining to the equal treatment of all people in the purchase or rental of real property. The first fair housing law was passed in 1866 and only protected the class of Race. Today the protected classes include Race, Color, Religion, National Origin, Gender, Handicap, and Familial Status. The broker must be aware of the fair housing guidelines and make sure the real estate company acts in accordance with those guidelines.

The Real Estate Settlement Procedures Act

The Real Estate Settlement Procedures Act (RESPA) requires consumer disclosures and specifies distinctive roles for real estate professionals and related service companies. The RESPA was first passed in 1974. One of its purposes is to help consumers become better shoppers for settlement services. Another purpose is to eliminate kickbacks and referral fees that increase unnecessarily the costs of certain settlement services. RESPA requires that borrowers receive disclosures at various times. Some disclosures make clear the costs associated with the settlement, outline lender servicing, describe escrow account practices, and portray business relationships between settlement service providers.

Section 8 of RESPA prohibits a person from giving or accepting anything of value for referrals of settlement service business related to a federally related mortgage loan. It also prohibits a person from giving or accepting any part of a charge for services that are not performed. Section 9 of RESPA prohibits home sellers from requiring home buyers to purchase title insurance from a particular company.

Generally, RESPA covers loans secured with a mortgage placed on a one- to four-family residential property. These include most purchase loans, assumptions, refinances, property improvement loans, and equity lines of credit. The HUD's (U.S. Department of Housing and Urban Development) Office of Consumer and Regulatory Affairs Interstate Land Sales/RESPA Division is responsible for enforcing RESPA.

Ethics

Ethics refers to "moral character." How do you behave when no one is around? I once saw a sign in a shop that read: "You can take anything that the Lord doesn't see you take." I like that. That is ethics. If you believe someone is always watching, you may behave in a more proper manner. My dad always said that he locked his doors to keep the honest people out, meaning that if a true criminal wanted in, you couldn't stop them. However, don't tempt the honest ones either.

The major principle of ethics comes from the Latin *primum non nocere*, meaning "first do no harm." The words "legal" and "ethical" mean different things. Legal is the lowest standard and ethical is the highest standard. Forcing real estate salespeople to be ethical doesn't work. They must realize the importance of ethics. Ethics leads to the most vital ingredient in any relationship: trust. Of all the strategies to attract consumers, nothing is as powerful or as profitable as ethics. It takes courage to follow high ethical standards, to place the interests of consumers first. In the long term, however, the rewards to consumers and salespeople are magnificent.

Here are some overall ethics brokers should incorporate in their brokerage firm:

1. Legal Law

Real estate salespeople will at all times obey the legal law and regulations applicable to real estate salespeople in their state. The real estate salesperson should keep current with any changes in the laws by taking classes and attending seminars on important topics. These regulations also apply to the rules established by their broker.

2. Moral Law

Real estate salespeople will use moral laws based on "doing the right thing" by all people with whom they do business and with whom they work. The real estate salesperson should follow the NATIONAL ASSOCIATION OF REALTORS® main ethics rule: the "Golden Rule." We are all familiar with the "Golden Rule": Do unto others as you want to be dealt with. Real estate salespeople are expected to use their character and good judgment to know what is morally right. If, in their opinion, the transaction they are involved with will lead to unacceptable results, they must excuse themselves from that transaction.

3. Staff

Real estate salespeople will treat all staff at the real estate office with respect and will expect the same from staff members toward each other. Staff will not tolerate disrespect from any salesperson. Real estate salespeople will not tolerate rudeness toward any client by any staff members.

4. Presentation

Real estate salespeople will make sure that their actions, office, and appearance represent the most profession real estate office possible. This includes professional business attire, a clean and tidy car, and an office or work area that is well maintained. Even if your salespeople are only in the office for a short period of time, you should insist on compliance.

5. Client Care

Real estate salespeople must, at all times, give priority to the interests and welfare of their clients. Numerous lawsuits have been filed and lost because the real estate salespeople were looking out for themselves and not for their clients. In the event that a real estate salesperson is incapable of servicing a client, the salesperson will refer the client to another real estate sales professional.

6. No Risk

Real estate salespeople will never create a situation where the broker-age can profit if the clients of the brokerage suffer financial loss. If the salesperson is not confident of selling the property, the salesperson should decline to accept the client. If the salesperson believes an offer for a seller is not the best for the client, the salesperson must state that belief.

7. Inspections

Real estate salespeople will make sure that all people who are inter-ested in a property have had a professional inspector inspect the prop-erty before purchase. A real estate inspector reduces the liability of all parties. If a buyer refuses to hire an inspector, the salesperson should seek the broker's advice before proceeding.

8. Qualifying of Homebuyers

Real estate salespeople will make sure that all buyers are fully qualified before being shown properties for sale. The real estate salesperson should not pre-qualify the buyers but should have a mortgage profes-sional pre-qualify them. Real estate salespeople should make showing appointments at a time to suit the buyers and not create stress for the sellers. Real estate salespeople should be sure that all property shown is secure afterwards.

9. Marketing

Real estate salespeople are required to study and have knowledge of marketing and to make sure they are always aware of the most cost-efficient and effective ways of marketing real property. The real estate salesperson should contact his or her clients and keep them up-to-date on the progress of their marketing campaign.

10. Negotiation

Real estate salespeople are required to study and have knowledge of professional negotiation. Negotiation is an important aspect of the real estate business. The salesperson should be able to successfully negotiate real estate contracts and sales.

11. Training

Real estate salespeople are required to study the real estate industry and salesmanship. In addition, real estate salespeople should at all times discover new ways to do business. Training should never be ne-glected. The real estate professional should read, go to classes and seminars, and seek knowledge from other real estate professionals.

12. Disclosures

Real estate salespeople are required to make sure that they explain all relevant points of a real estate transaction to clients before the clients make a decision to list or sell their property. Real estate salespeople must advise clients of all offers made on their properties. Disclosures must be made to buyers on the property's condition.

13. Prospecting

Real estate salespeople are to be courteous and considerate when looking for business. If a homeowner requests no contact, the real estate salesperson will respect the request. The real estate salesperson should not solicit other professional real estate salespeople's current listings.

14. Confidentiality

A real estate salesperson must keep confidential the personal information provided by a client. Disclosures must be made, but not about confidential information. Confidential information is information about a party in a transaction rather than information about the property.

15. Advice

Real estate salespeople must take care not to give investment or legal advice without advising the recipient of such advice to seek independent advice, preferably from a lawyer or a qualified investment advisor. The real estate salesperson should give advice on pricing, marketing, and negotiating.

16. Civic Duty

Real estate salespeople have a civic duty to their local area and should always be ready to help their community. Real estate salespeople are expected to be examples of good corporate citizens.

NATIONAL ASSOCIATION OF REALTORS® Code of Ethics

The NATIONAL ASSOCIATION OF REALTORS® (NAR) was founded as the National Association of Real Estate Exchanges (NAREE) on May 12, 1908, "to unite the real estate men of America for the purpose of effectively exerting a combined influence upon matters affecting real estate interests."[5] NAREE was established because at that time real estate brokers were not licensed, were writing contracts on sheets of paper, and

---

[5] "Field Guide to the History of the NATIONAL ASSOCIATION OF REALTORS®," Frederik Heller, http://realtor.org, August 2004.

would hide property defects. The code of ethics was adopted in 1913 with the "Golden Rule" as its theme. In 1916, the National Association of Real Estate Exchange's name was changed to the National Association of Real Estate Boards. The term "REALTOR®," identifying real estate agents as members of the National Real Estate Boards and subscribers to its code of ethics, was first used in 1916. NAR offers its members education, publications, and support, not to mention one of the largest Political Action Committees in the nation. Not all real estate salespeople are REALTORS®; only those that belong to NAR can use this designation. To claim to be a REALTOR® and not be a member of NAR is an ethical violation as well as a Deceptive Trade Practices Act violation. This code of ethics is a requirement for membership. The main reason the NAR has a code of ethics is to further the positive reputation of the real estate professional in the market. Deceptive and dishonest actions by one real estate salesperson are projected upon all real estate salespeople. The NAR code of ethics is intended to help make a difference by giving guidelines to performance. The NATIONAL ASSOCIATION OF REALTORS® currently has a membership of over a million individuals.

As a broker, you should be a member of the NATIONAL ASSOCIATION OF REALTORS® to support your industry. When you become a REALTOR®, all of your salespeople must also belong to the Association. In the past, NAR was the only place that a consumer could find information about available real estate. Its members had the Multiple Listing Service (MLS), which allowed any seller that had property marketed with a broker to have their property listed on the MLS. Buyers then could find out about the property using their own REALTOR®.

Today, NAR is losing control of the real estate information through dissemination of the Internet. Thousands of real estate sites are active, but NAR still has the number one site to use: REALTOR.com. NAR does provide its members meaningful service. NAR's Political Action Committees act in real estate salespeople's and broker's best interest. They support us in Congress on important issues affecting our business. NAR membership is not a requirement, but is highly recommended for those real estate companies that desire ethical and fair treatment for their customers.

Responsibility of the Real Estate Brokerage

The brokerage should have classes on the different laws and regulations for its real estate salespeople. Without that training, the real estate commission will hold the real estate broker responsible for the lack of training.

The meeting could be yearly risk-reduction seminars for the entire company. The education could be fifteen minutes at a weekly sales meeting. It doesn't matter the type of education, as long as the information is disseminated.

Conclusion

Real estate brokerage is the business of connecting buyers and sellers of real estate. It involves many laws and regulations that brokers need to be aware of, including the Real Estate Settlement Procedures Act, Agency Law, the Real Estate License Act, Contract Law, Deceptive Trade Practices Act, and the Sherman Antitrust Act.

Real estate is always changing. Most recently, the government has passed Do Not Call, Do Not Fax, and Anti-Spam laws. The real estate broker should understand how these laws affect the real estate business.

Ethics refers to "moral character" and should be the basis of all real estate business. The NATIONAL ASSOCIATION OF REALTORS® is a group of real estate professionals that furthers the profession by developing and enforcing an ethical code.

The real estate brokerage can be a profitable business, but only if the business is run in a proper manner. Never neglect your business but instead keep up with the trends and changes and monitor your business.

Chapter 1 Review Questions

1. A real estate brokerage
   A. gives the broker more flexible time.
   B. always results in more income than the real estate salespeople.
   C. is the business of real estate sales in its many forms.
   D. must be certified by the Federal Real Estate Commission before operations begin.

2. Which of the following is **not** a reason to talk about real estate?
   A. It is the "American Dream."
   B. People are interested in selling their house.
   C. It is the best short-term investment available.
   D. People are interested in vacation property.

3. Which of the following is **not** a major reason for failure in the real estate brokerage business?

A. No national affiliation

B. No training

C. No financial backing

D. No experience

4. The real estate broker/owner needs to establish an office policy pertaining to agency law.

A. The policy must be in writing.

B. The broker/owner must make sure all the salespeople associated with the company are aware of the policies.

C. The broker/owner must make sure all the salespeople associated with the company abide by those rules.

D. A broker/owner must follow all the above guidelines.

5. Misrepresentation can also involve fraud. Fraud is the intentional misleading of a person. Certain factors must be in place for fraud, including

A. the person must have a reason to rely on the information given.

B. the person committing the act must have intended to harm or deceive the other person.

C. the person committing the act must be considered an expert in the business field that the act occurred.

D. the person must incur some kind of damage or harm.

6. Salespeople who sell or lease industrial properties must know about which of the following?

A. The region's infrastructure

B. Transportation and utilities

C. Laws and regulations

D. All of the above

7. What is the one of the best reasons to become a real estate broker?

A. It is a great feeling the first time you hold your own sales meeting and all the salespeople are looking at you for leadership.

B. It is exciting to walk in front of several hundred of your peers and receive an award for a top producing real estate office.

C. It is the best way to make big dollars in the real estate industry.

D. Brokers want to see others succeed because of the broker's efforts rather than claiming all the limelight for themselves.

8. All of the following are changes in the real estate industry that have had a major effect on the way real estate business is conducted, *except*

A. regulators began limiting the role of the broker.

B. people now purchase real estate online.

C. the age of information changed the role of the broker.

D. the advent of the computer changed many things.

9. Real estate brokers deal frequently with other specialists in the real estate business, including which of the following?

A. Competing brokers

B. Engineers

C. Financial institutions

D. All of the above

10. The Sherman Antitrust Act prohibits all of the following *except*

A. price-fixing.

B. boycotting.

C. commingling.

D. allocation of customers.

11. The residential real estate brokerage business is breaking into what two main segments?

A. Mom and Pop shops and the mega-firms

B. Property Management and Commercial

C. Urban and Rural

D. New Build and Resale

12. What type of real estate office has hundreds of real estate agents and several offices?

A. The national company

B. The regional company

C. The master firm

D. The mega-firm

13. The NATIONAL ASSOCIATION OF REALTORS® found that Internet home-buyers were more likely

A. to use a real estate agent to complete the home search and close the transaction.

B. to buy a "For sale by owner".

C. to rent versus buy their new residence.

D. to demand that the agent reduce their commission.

14. Which of the following statements is false?

A. The real estate commission regulates the operation and activities of real estate brokers and their salespeople.

B. The agency laws spell out how brokers and salespeople should represent their clients and the duties they should perform.

C. Licensed real estate salespeople are required to pay fair market value for any investment property they purchase.

D. A real estate salesperson could lose his or her license for making a material misrepresentation concerning a significant property defect.

15. All of the following are truths about the Deceptive Trade Practices Act, *except*

A. it is probably the best protection available to consumers in business transactions.

B. it only applies to real estate transactions of $250,000 or more.

C. it asks two questions: Did you know? Should you have known?

D. it prohibits misrepresentation.

2 The Real Estate Broker and Owner

Characteristics of Talented Brokers and Owners

If this book addresses a single question, it is, "What makes a good and productive real estate broker?" The problem: there is no answer to that question. The same question could be asked about real estate salespeople, but we are discussing brokers, not salespeople. However, there are basic characteristics that really talented brokers have; they are

- **Emotionally stable**

  Good brokers must be able to tolerate frustration and stress. They cannot allow themselves the pleasure of getting personally involved in salespeople's disputes. Overall, they must be well adjusted and have the psychological maturity to deal with anything they are required to face.

- **Commanding**

  Good brokers are oftentimes competitive and decisive, and usually enjoy overcoming obstacles. Do not misunderstand: I am not talking mean people, I am talking strong people. Overall, they are assertive in their thinking style as well as their attitude in dealing with others.

- **Enthusiastic**

  Good brokers are usually seen as active, expressive, and energetic. They are often very optimistic and open to change. Overall, they are generally quick and alert, and tend to be uninhibited.

- **Conscientious**

  Good brokers are often dominated by a sense of duty and tend to be very exacting in character. They usually have a very high standard of excellence and an inward desire to do their best. They see the big picture and operate on a higher plane. They also have a need for order and tend to be very self-disciplined. They understand that all of their actions are being watched, and they are extremely vigilant.

- **Socially bold**

  Good brokers tend to be spontaneous risk-takers. They are usually socially aggressive and generally thick-skinned. They are good at building powerful relationships. Overall, they are responsive to others and tend to be high in emotional stamina.

- **Tough-minded**

  Good brokers are practical, logical, and to-the-point. They tend to be low in sentimental attachments and comfortable with criticism. They are usually insensitive to hardship and always remain poised.

- **Self-assured**

  Self-confidence and resiliency are common traits among good brokers. They tend to be free of guilt and have little or no need for approval. They are generally secure and are usually unaffected by prior mistakes or failures.

- **Composed**

  Good brokers are controlled and very precise in their social interactions. Overall, they are very protective of their integrity and reputation, and consequently tend to be socially aware and careful when making decisions or determining specific actions.

- **Highly energized**

  Long hours and few days off are usually a prerequisite for leadership positions, especially as your company grows. Attentiveness and maintaining focus are two of the most important traits for a broker to have.

- **Intuitive**

  Good brokers learn to listen to their intuition. Brokers have a great deal of information available to them, but that still might not be enough. Having good judgment in situations is invaluable, especially in interpersonal relationships.

- **Mature**

  To be a good broker, your personal power and recognition must be secondary to the development of your employees. In other words, maturity is based on recognizing that more can be accomplished by empowering others than by ruling others. As a matter of fact, good brokers enjoy the successes of the people they lead more than they enjoy their own successes.

- **Team-oriented**

  Good brokers today put a strong emphasis on teamwork. In any real estate office, working as a team and helping each other is a prerequisite. Real estate salespeople are independent contractors, but they also want to feel part of something bigger and more important.

- **Empathetic**

  Good brokers will have empathy, but not sympathy, for their salespeople. In other words, a broker should be able to know how others feel without crying with them. Without empathy, you can't build trust. And without trust, you will never be able to get the best effort from your salespeople.

- **Charismatic**

  People usually perceive brokers as larger than life. Charisma plays a large part in this perception. Brokers who have charisma are able to arouse strong emotions in their salespeople, staff, and clients by defining a vision that unites and captivates them. Using this vision, brokers motivate all those involved to reach toward a future goal by tying the goal to substantial personal rewards and values.

The following is an additional list of characteristics that make a quality owner/broker:

Persistent	Honest	Trustworthy
Patient	Good communicator	Opportunistic
Organized	Problem solver	Exudes integrity
Educator	Mentor	Mediator
Pleasant	Neat in appearance	Ethical
Tactful	Understanding	Motivator
Detail oriented	Great memory	Business savvy

Notice that a majority of those characteristics are traits that one either has or does not have—they can't easily be developed. If you have never been honest, I find it hard to believe that once you become a broker, you suddenly become honest. These traits are in all of us. Can you develop yours and become the best broker you can possibly be?

Questions That You Should Ask Yourself

Here are some questions to consider if you are thinking about becoming a real estate broker.

Why Do You Want to Become a Broker?

Think this one through. Do not become a real estate broker just because you think it would be fun. Write down the reasons you want to become a broker. Ask your friends if they think you would be a good broker. Would they work for you?

Do You Have the Qualities of a Real Estate Broker?

Examine the successful brokers in your area. Do you have the qualities they have? Ask others if you have what it takes in your character to do well. Look at the list above; do you have what it takes? If you don't, it doesn't mean you are a bad person, but it could mean you will be a bad broker.

What Are the "Perks" of the Position of Broker?

Perks involve the money you can make, but being a successful broker also means that mortgage and title companies want your business. They may not be able to give you valuable gifts, but they will treat you with respect, and that is a welcome perk. You get to park in the "broker's" spot up front. You get the best office in the building. You get to receive the honors for your office's production. Some may think that this is petty, but to others this is major. I knew a broker who was making $100,000 per year selling real estate. He took all his income and poured it into the brokerage company. He would draw money from the company to pay himself. Year after year he did this. I offered to buy his company and showed him that each year he made $80,000 for his efforts as a broker. That is actually a $20,000 loss per year! His response was, "But my name is on the door." Did you get that? He was willing to give up $20,000 per year just so he could be the broker and the business was his. I tell you, the perks of being a broker can be powerful.

What Are the Biggest "Trials" of the Position of Broker?

You must consider the hours you will have to work. You must consider the anguish of firing a "nice" person because you cannot carry him or her any more. You must be prepared to listen to your salespeople talking behind your back, complaining that you do not know what you're doing. You must be prepared for your salespeople blaming *you* for *their* lack of production.

You need to be prepared for the possibility of not having the capital to meet your debt obligations.

What Is It "Really" Like to Be a Broker?

Overall, what is it "really" like to be a broker? Some think that you can open an office and go and play golf, and that you will make millions because all your salespeople are working for you.

You are now not only responsible for yourself but for all the salespeople under your roof. You must be able to take care, nurture, and contribute to the lives of your real estate salespeople. Believing that your salespeople are your ticket to wealth and fame will be the fastest way out of the brokerage business. You have to spend time—and I mean a great deal of time—with each salesperson and know the salespeople themselves and their families.

You must be up at all times. A broker can never have a bad day (or at least never appear to). Your salespeople must at all times see you positive and energetic. If you as the broker wear your emotions on your sleeve for all to see, then how can you expect anything more from your salespeople?

What Is the Job Description of a Broker?

You must determine your duties to your clients. You must determine your duties to your salespeople. You must determine your duties to the community. You will have more duties than you ever did as a salesperson.

The duties to your clients include all the aspects of actually selling their property or finding them another one. It includes quality service and timely communication.

The duties to your salespeople include broker support and marketing, as well as communication, training, motivation, and responsiveness. Neglecting your duties to your salespeople is a sure way to be lonely.

The duties a broker owes to the community include support, time, and money. We want to earn money by selling real estate, but we should never neglect that we also need to give back. Helping your community and making it a better place to live directly affects your ability to sell real estate.

Do *You* Want to Get Started? When?
Now, or in the Future?

After thinking about all the previous questions, do you still want to be a broker? If so, are you ready now, or do you need to take college classes, do market research, and line up finances to be prepared for the long haul?

Are You Willing to Pay the Price to Become the Best Real Estate Broker You Can Be?

This is the "gut" check question. Some people want things in their lives and then never want to pay the price to get them. Are you that person, or do you achieve the goals you set for yourself?

Legal Requirements of Becoming a Real Estate Broker

Every state requires a real estate broker to have a real estate license. The legal requirements for becoming a real estate broker vary from state to state but generally require the candidate to have experience in the real estate industry as a real estate salesperson. Other requirements include additional education and passing the broker's exam. Generally, a college degree is not required to become a real estate broker, but some college courses in the fields of finance and management would be extremely valuable.

Brokers Need to Lead by Example

Brokers need to do the things that they require of their salespeople to maintain the credibility they need. If brokers require their salespeople to prospect for listings, then the brokers should prospect for recruits. If brokers require additional education for their salespeople, then the brokers themselves should continue their education. If brokers require their salespeople to dress properly, then they must do the same. Too many real estate salespeople believe that if they could only become brokers, their lives would be so much easier. No more problems with sellers. No more late nights babysitting a troublesome transaction. No more pressure to continually prospect. All of these issues increase, not diminish, when you take on the role of the broker. Everyone is watching you—everyone from the staff to the new salesperson will be watching your every move. Everyone from the real estate commission to your competition will be watching to see if you falter. I was once at a real estate conference and bought a REALTOR® doormat. About a month later I received the same type of doormat in the mail. Obviously, they made a mistake and sent one even though I already had one. The receptionist said, "Great! We need one for the back door!" I said, "No, box it up and send it back." Now, in the worldly scheme of things, did that doormat matter? No. But my integrity did. Imagine that later on that same receptionist felt she was cheated on her salary check. She would not trust me if she knew I took things that were not mine. Everyone is always watching.

Mentoring

Real estate brokers are expected to mentor to their salespeople, helping with their businesses and careers. Brokers also need to be mentored to improve their own businesses and careers. Mentoring is a term used to describe a teacher-student relationship. In the business world, mentoring occurs when a more experienced professional (the mentor) gives significant career assistance to a less-experienced professional (the protégé). Mentoring relationships are particularly helpful during a real estate broker's first few years as a leader.

Finding a Mentor

Finding the right mentor is not something you should leave to chance. You need to look for someone who has knowledge and business experience in areas you don't. You need to make sure the mentor you choose desires to be a mentor. A mentoring relationship requires consent by both parties. Look for what you can offer the mentor—make the relationship mutually beneficial. You can learn so much from a qualified mentor—make sure you find one.

Networking

As a broker, you should join a networking group. These groups meet usually once a month and talk about how each member could help the others by referring business. Networking groups could draw several hundred members and put you in contact with influential businesspeople. It is a great way to find your mentor. Do not miss out the power of networking.

Roundtables

Similar to networking are roundtables, informal group discussions among professionals who voluntarily serve as information and support resources for one another. Participants meet regularly and learn from each other's experiences. Over time, professional relationships develop and participants become familiar with one another's businesses. Roundtables are limited to the same select few businesspeople, so choose them carefully.

The most common roundtable discussions are online, called *newsgroups.* Newsgroups are like bulletin boards where discussions can occur and be reviewed at the participants' convenience.

Why Brokers Fail

Real estate brokers will fail in their endeavors if they approach the broker's position as they did their careers. When I owned my real estate offices, I would periodically interview each of my salespeople to see how they were doing. One of the questions I asked was, "Have you ever thought about owning or managing a real estate office?" Over 60 percent of them answered, "Yes." I found this strange, because a majority of them were not running their business efficiently. How did the feel they could train and help other real estate salespeople with their business? What happens when real estate salespeople feel they can do better than their current broker and open up their own offices? Quickly they find out they cannot do that either, and the office suffers. So the first reason a broker/owner fails is lack of planning. Here are some others:

- Lack of funds—undercapitalization
- Lack of management experience
- Lack of focus
- Lack of specialization

Let's take a look at each one of those separately. First is lack of funds, or undercapitalization, as the accountants say. A great many new real estate offices are under pressure from the moment they open because they do not have the funds to last until the money starts dropping into the till. Lack of funds is not new to the entrepreneur; as a matter of fact, it is the number one cause of small business failure. However, in real estate it is an even bigger dagger to the heart of a successful real estate business because a listing taken today may sell in six months and it may take another sixty days to get the fee. Translated, this means that a real estate company should have at least a full year's worth of money just to operate the business. This does not include any capital expenditures, such as office equipment.

Lack of management experience is the second leading indicator of success or failure in a real estate enterprise. Being a successful real estate salesperson does not translate into a being successful real estate broker/owner. A very successful real estate salesperson I knew was "promoted" to a manager's position. She knew nothing about real estate management, and soon the office failed and the doors closed. After a review, the real estate corporation she worked with decided to "promote from within." Because of that hard-and-fast rule, the company suffered and lost a real estate office and a top producer (she was so upset she left for another real estate company).

Lack of focus is evident in owners of a real estate office who tries to save money by doing everything themselves. These owners are there $23^1/_2$ hours a day, 7 days a week. They serve as managers, accountants, marketers, trainers, judges, friends, mentors, leaders, and janitors. There simply are not enough hours in a day to do everything required. With all this to do, most small broker/owners also have to sell to stay above water. They cannot concentrate on the main objective of a real estate office, and that is to make a profit.

The real estate company that fails for lack of specialization is the company that tries to be all things to all people. Such companies are not big enough to departmentalize, so they close a transaction without the expertise to continually do it responsibly. They close a residential deal here, they close a commercial deal there. They dabble in property management and investments. Because they choose not to specialize, they do everything. Finally, they eventually make a critical error, and after all the litigation, they have nothing left. Specialize in one field and become the best at it.

Those are the top five reasons brokers fail at their profession. There are many more, and I am sure more will be arise in the next few years.

Approaches to Management

There are many approaches to management; you need to choose the best fit between your goals and your salesperson's goals. You can read up on the numerous techniques, but we will only look at a select few. These techniques are listed in no particular order of importance.

- The Commander
- The Peacemaker
- The Collaborator
- The Controller

The Commander

The Commander approach to management believes it is "my way or the highway." These brokers will fire any salesperson who gets just a smidgen out of line. Their office meetings are very authoritarian. Their training style is very directive. Commanders tend to be competitive and not as sociable as any other of the types, preferring to get right to the point.

ADVANTAGES

You know what to expect. You work just as your broker expects, you get no flack. As long as the broker does not run everyone off, the office will tend to get things done and make a profit. The office expenses will be accurate. There will be no waste. Smart brokers who understand and use this style will hire assistant managers to counterbalance their actions. I observed this type of broker and assistant manager relationship firsthand. The broker would be sure everyone was selling real estate, and if not, he or she would be quick to address it. The assistant manager would be all bubbly and make everyone feel happy. Together they appealed to almost all their salespeople. When salespeople needed to get something done or a decision made, they went to the broker. When they needed a break from the hectic pace of real estate, they would turn to the assistant manager. No one was told to do so; they just knew. Either one of these managers working alone would not have been as effective as they were together.

DISADVANTAGES

Commanders tend to wear salespeople out. Most people did not get into this business to be told what to do. Funny thing, though, without being told what to do, the average real estate salesperson will do nothing. Without some type of temperance, these brokers will tend to run salespeople away.

The Peacemaker

The Peacemaker is the manager who wants to make everyone happy. This manager does not like conflict and will avoid it at all costs. Peacemakers typically hire other Peacemakers to make the culture beneficial to all involved. Peacemakers may be the most sociable of all and sometimes may need help to stay on task.

ADVANTAGES

Everybody loves the Peacemaker. The office atmosphere is calm and serene. The salespeople tend to stay with this company for many years. The office maintains its position in the market, and its clients are loyal.

DISADVANTAGES

One bad apple hired can spoil the whole bunch. If the broker hires someone who looks nice and calm and ends up being a tyrant, the broker (Peacemaker) will have a hard time with the conflict of firing the tyrant. Also, this office tends not to live up its potential, because the Peacemaker broker does not drive the organization to do better.

The Collaborator

The Collaborator wants everyone's opinion before making a decision. Collaborators differ from the Peacemakers in that they will not back down from confrontation but will want to have agreement on major decisions. These brokers will have "office committees" on any number of projects. All of the office salespeople will vote on any decision to benefit the office; everything must be agreed upon, from purchasing new computers to advertising to selecting a brand of coffee. Generally, Collaborators are sociable, enthusiastic, and visionary. Since Collaborators often neglect the details, they should hire support staff that can fill in where these brokers are weak. Similarly, brokers looking to hire staff members can look for people with complementary behavioral styles. The Commander gives orders, but the Collaborator gives direction. The Collaborator makes every effort to find a place for everyone and then guide his or her career.

ADVANTAGES

The salespeople feel that they have input on the decision-making process. This system works well for the producers who also want a voice in how the office is run.

DISADVANTAGES

No leadership. The salespeople begin to ignore the broker, because the broker leads by committee. Salespeople will begin to form alliances and vote together in blocs to get their position voted for, perhaps to the detriment of the office in general. I was once a salesperson in an office like this.

The broker made all the decisions by votes from the salespeople. We were charged a desk fee to be part of this office. The office was the largest and highest producing office in the state. Within two years, the company was bankrupt. Why? Because different salespeople want different things. I was worried about my monthly desk fee. Others were concerned about more services provided by the company. Votes went the way of services. Each service increased the desk fee until only a few could afford the costs and the company folded.

The Controller

The controller must know and control all aspects of the brokerage company. Controllers differ from Commanders in that they don't demand respect but must have their hands in all operations. A Controller is a "perfectionist" and expects others to be the same. These are detail people and they focus on objectives. Controllers are cerebral and do well at structured tasks, making them good at back-office functions, such as accounting and technology support. They may not make the strongest brokers/managers, but they could be outstanding if they learned to be more assertive and make decisions more quickly. They may not always mix well with Collaborators.

ADVANTAGES

The office is run perfectly with every single detail being performed flawlessly. Some salespeople love this system and thrive under it. However, most salespeople in general are less restrictive. This company is rarely involved in court cases because all the paperwork is filled out and filed accordingly. The office is very efficient. Controllers monitor the office supplies and distribute them only by request. They have counters on the copiers, faxes, and telephones to control those costs.

DISADVANTAGES

The Controller has a hard time making money in the real estate business because he or she is so busy with detail work that there is never time to prospect for clients. It is very difficult for Controllers to delegate because no one else could do as good a job as they can. Some Controllers are so restrictive that they read all of their salespeople's e-mail and post mail, and will listen in on conversations in the office. If they were to delegate a project, they would follow every detail and take as much time or more than if they did it themselves. Controllers are perfectionists; they believe that nothing is ever correct, and they keep working at perfection well past the point of diminishing returns.

To be well rounded and fair, the best brokers use aspects of each type. Being aware of your style will help you understand your weaknesses and your strengths.

Activities of the Broker

The broker must perform many functions and activities. The activities may vary depending upon the size of the organization. We will take a look at a majority of typical duties. The more the organization grows, the more of the duties the broker can delegate to others in the organization.

Company Direction

The broker's most important function is to determine the company's direction. Should the company pursue residential, commercial, or ranch-type properties, or maybe a combination of all types of properties? Should the company buy an office or rent space, and in what location? Should the company offer salespeople private offices and limited services, or go the more traditional route with bullpens and many more services? Should the broker sell or hire managers? These are just a few questions that should be considered.

Brokers should do research on their competition as well as on trends in and future projections for the real estate industry. To feel a certain direction is best for the company and find out later that the consumer does not agree is disastrous.

This is **not** an aspect of the brokerage business that can be delegated. You must make these decisions. You can seek help, but the decision and direction are solely yours.

Acquisitions

Another part of the business is the acquisition of other real estate companies. The broker must research and negotiate with the owners of the other companies. A majority of the work can be delegated, but at some point the broker must get involved. Acquisitions are for those companies that want to expand to other locations. If this is not in your business plan, you should not make efforts to acquire other offices, or else you need to change your plan.

Another type of acquisition is the roll-in. A *roll-in* is buying another real estate company, closing the doors of that office, and "rolling in" their current sales force into one of your existing offices as a way to buy the previous broker's salespeople. Real estate salespeople are the assets in the brokerage business and are what makes an office profitable. If two real estate companies are competing for the same client in the same area, it may be wise to buy them and roll them into your office. With the additional salespeople, the brokerage could begin to see additional economies of scale by being able to buy larger amounts of supplies at a discount.

Retention

Retention of the current salespeople in a real estate office is a key component of being a successful broker. The salespeople of a real estate office are constantly being wooed and recruited by other real estate companies, whose techniques can be very nasty. Brokers who believe that their salespeople are happy and would never leave are in line to have their offices raided. We will talk more about retention in Chapter 11.

Recruiting

Recruiting needs to be never-ending. I had a broker once tell me that he was "full up." I think that is naïve. You should always be recruiting, because nothing stays the same. If you have thirty desks and just got your thirtieth person, you are not "full up." You should always be bringing in new people and replacing the old. We will address more on this subject in Chapter 9.

Training

Overall, the most important thing that real estate salespeople believe their broker should do for them is provide training. Lack of training is the "catch-all" reason that real estate salespeople do not succeed. I have seen the best training available in the real estate business without anyone in attendance. The same salespeople who fail to attend then complain that they are not productive and leave for another real estate company because the new company offers "better" training. The broker must provide the best training possible given the costs involved. I once talked with a person from the pharmaceutical business who wanted to become a broker. My biggest concern for him was that he could not train his salespeople how best to handle this business because they had more experience than he did. He went ahead and bought a brokerage and had very little credibility with his sales force. He was smart enough to hire an in-house trainer, but I don't think he has ever had the production from that office that he could have if he had spent the time in practice in this business.

Hiring and Firing of Staff

The broker is typically responsible for hiring and firing of staff members. The hiring is easy; the firing is not. I have seen nonproductive staff members kept around simply because the broker did not have the fortitude to terminate them. These staff members become an infection, and the production of the entire team of staff drops. I bought an office once that had five staff members. We had a "get acquainted" meeting in which I fired the first two I talked with (both non-productive). The next person in line said, "Well, if you fire them then I will quit!" I said, "DONE!" I looked at the other two still left and said, "How about you two?" Both said they wanted to stay. You see, I believe if it is my office, I should have control. By letting your staff manipulate you, you lose control. I am the last person out that office door (figuratively), and I would rather lock it for good than lose control. To finish that story, the production of those two remaining skyrocketed, and they handled the workload of all five of the previous staff, saving the company thousands of dollars.

Manager/Assistant Manager Reviews

If brokers hire office managers, assistant managers, or any staff, they need to have formal yearly reviews. In addition to the yearly reviews, brokers need to make the managers and staff accountable for their work through monthly, weekly, and even daily reviews. Brokers with several offices may find that these accountability reviews take up most of their time. Whereas reviews with managers cannot be delegated, staff reviews can be delegated to the managers.

Individual Business Development (IBD) Meetings

The broker should conduct "Individual Business Development" meetings with each salesperson. This activity, also called *coaching,* can be delegated to managers if the broker hires managers. IBD meetings allow one-on-one time with the broker. This may take up a great deal of the broker's time, but do not overlook these meetings because they must be held. The number one reason a real estate salesperson leaves a company is not because of money, but because they do not like or respect their broker. If you give the salesperson one-on-one time, they will like you, or at least you can discuss difficulties before they escalate into real trouble. During the IBD meetings, the broker will analyze the salesperson's production and discuss ways to increase the production or reduce the stress and time for that salesperson. The discussions can cover anything from private obstacles to production. At the conclusion of the IBD meeting, the salesperson should walk away with several action steps to implement immediately. These IBD meetings should be held monthly, or quarterly at minimum. Waiting until the end of the year may be too late.

Day-to-Day Operations

Some brokers with little capitalization and income may have to conduct day-to-day operations. These brokers may have to handle accounting, budgeting, payroll, receivables, and taxes, as well as sell real estate and broker salespeople. The broker may have to be the receptionist, mediator, trainer, and janitor. Remember, as an entrepreneur, you have the freedom to do anything—and everything!

Review Listings and Purchase Agreements

Reviewing listings and purchase agreements is a simple but very important task. Brokers are responsible for every authorized act of their real estate salespeople. The main problem occurs when a salesperson fills in a contract with incomplete or incorrect information, obligating one of the parties to perform some detail that was not intended. This could be construed to be the "practice of law" and a violation of the state Real Estate License Act. If the broker had taken the time to review the contracts, he or she would have noticed the error and could have corrected the problem without any damage.

Being Available for Advice

Sometimes brokers just need to be available to their salespeople for advice. This is an important asset to real estate salespeople; they like to feel that their broker is available. The broker should make a concerted effort to wander around the office for a few minutes every couple of hours. You should stop in your salespeople's offices and chat for just a moment. You do no want to disrupt them, only to let them know you are there for them. I know a broker that does this every hour on the hour for ten minutes, and his salespeople "love" him.

A good broker has an "open door" policy. The broker should promote this to his or her salespeople. Then the broker must deliver. If a salesperson walks into the office, the broker must stop what he or she is doing and give 100 percent to the salesperson. Brokers are sometimes tempted to do other routine business while a salesperson is in their office. Never do this. Aside from the fact that you may miss important information, what are you telling the salesperson? Exactly, you don't care.

You should be available (or delegated) 24 hours a day, 7 days a week. That might sound like it is too much. Well, think about it, when do you want your salespeople to work? Answer: 24 hours a day, 7 days a week. If they are working, then they may need advice. I never had "office hours" because I never wanted my salespeople to think that they should not be working. If you are available at all times, you will find that you don't get the calls. It is not as much a reality as it is a comfort. Your salespeople will respect your time if you respect theirs.

Personal Education and Development

People wanting to become brokers should remember to continually better themselves though their own education. We want to train our salespeople to be the best but then neglect ourselves. There are numerous courses you can take on real estate brokerage. If you can't find one on real estate brokerage, take a business culture class, time management class, or any other course that will make you better. Think of things your salespeople need to learn, and then go out and learn those things for yourself. Once you have the knowledge, you can teach your salespeople.

Education and self-improvement can also come from reading books. With the Internet, people forget the value of a simple book. Books can help you learn about real estate, sales, and business management. Why go through your life the hard way? Learn from others' mistakes and their successes. Set a goal to read at least one business book per month. This might be a lofty goal if you have not read a book since high school. You feel your time is already taken up, when can you read? You will find time if you have the determination. Read at lunch, read while waiting, or read before bed. Take the time, take the class, read the book, and you and your salespeople will be glad you did.

We must learn to cultivate our own methods for staying abreast of developments in the real estate industry—and we must learn to ignore information we can't use. Here are a few suggestions for staying informed:

- Subscribe to industry or trade publications that focus on the real estate business. If you have a particular long-term client, you may want to read publications on his or her business.

- Read any newspapers that specifically address issues in the real estate industry.

- Visit your local library. Read books on sales, management, and real estate.

- Join a professional association, chamber of commerce, or network with other entrepreneurs in the real estate business.

- Look for information on the Internet. Watch for opportunities to interact with business or industry experts in "chat room" interviews. Several top speakers will e-mail information and motivational letters directly to you if you subscribe.

- Subscribe to Internet newsgroups that focus on the real estate industry.

- Attend real estate seminars and be actively involved in the learning process.

- Conduct informational surveys with your customers and clients. What issues are troubling them? What do they see in their future? Ask how you can help, and determine how these issues will affect your business.

- Develop a group of consultants and advisors.

- Cultivate your curiosity. Don't be afraid to try new things. The most important skill you can develop is not the ability to remember information, but the ability to seek out and find the information you need, when you need it, and then use it for the benefit of your business.

Office Meetings

The broker will have to conduct office meetings with all of his or her salespeople. Usually these meetings occur every week. During the meetings, the broker conducts a review of any new laws, regulations, or activities in the office, and any new listings the salespeople have attained. These meetings should be no longer than an hour so you can get your people back out selling. It is hard to make these meetings mandatory, but everyone should be strongly urged to attend. To increase attendance, the broker must provide some value. The meeting should never be a complaint session.

The meeting agenda is a roadmap for the meeting. It lets participants know where they're headed so they don't get off track. Most importantly, the meeting agenda gives a sense of purpose and direction to the meeting.

The typical real estate office meeting should model the following agenda:

1. Introduction to the meeting
2. Welcoming any guests, affiliates, and new salespeople
3. Announcements
4. Guest or affiliate presentations
5. Entertainment
6. Training
7. Wants and needs
8. Wrap-up

INTRODUCTION TO THE MEETING

This is where you cover the purpose of the meeting and tell all the attendees that you appreciate their presence. Allow only a minute or two.

WELCOMING ANY GUESTS, AFFILIATES, AND NEW SALESPEOPLE

This is a special time when you welcome the honored attendees. You should welcome any guests. From time to time you will have executives from your corporate office in attendance; maybe a guest speaker for the training section or simply someone's friend is in attendance. You *always* want to welcome the new salespeople to their first sales meeting. And you want to recognize any affiliates that are in attendance. Affiliates are the ancillary businesses that help you serve your clients. These affiliates include title companies, mortgage companies, and inspectors, to name a few. This should only take a couple of minutes.

ANNOUNCEMENTS

This is the time to make any needed announcements. Do not make this discussion lengthy. This is where you pose decisions to the group for their opinion. Do not allow a lot of cross talk, and speed this process up as best as possible. Keep this section to only five to ten minutes.

GUEST OR AFFILIATE PRESENTATIONS

If one of the guests or affiliates wants a moment to speak, this is where you allow it. Some brokers do not allow anyone in front of their salespeople. If this is your philosophy, eliminate this section. Do not allow anyone to present a commercial to your salespeople. Make the presenters actually provide information your salespeople can use. You should review any information that someone else is presenting to your salespeople. If you don't review it, then be ready for any surprises you may receive. You should allow no more than two presentations for no longer than five minutes each. Allow ten minutes for this section.

ENTERTAINMENT

Gotta give 'em some fun, or lose them forever. It amazed me during my career that the sillier the event, the more fun the "grown-ups" had. This section is only limited by your imagination. You should have "get involved" type action. It gets their blood flowing and makes them want to come back next week to see what you will do next.

CONTEST FOR PRIZES   You could hold contests for prizes. I have had "contract toss" for distance, business roller chair races, and "knowledge tests" on some real estate topic, to name a few. You could hold listing contests and use this time to update those contests. You could hold "spin the wheel" prize giveaway for those that had a listing or sale during the previous week. Pay attention to other businesspeople and what they are doing. Again, this is only limited by your imagination.

PRESENTATION OF AWARDS   The sales meeting is a great time to pass out monthly office awards. You should honor the top listing salesperson of the month, the top sales person per month, and the top dollar closed for the month as a minimum. I always limited these awards to production because that is what I wanted to promote. Some brokers give the "office team player" award, the "rookie of the month" award, and the "best service given" award. Be sure to cheer these awards mightily.

SURPRISE GIVEAWAY   You could surprise your salespeople by having a random drawing for a giveaway by collecting their business cards. You could put a red dot under one of the group's chairs. Whoever sits in that chair would get the surprise. These surprises don't do much to promote production, but they are great for increasing attendance to your meetings.

The time that should be allowed for entertainment is about ten minutes.

TRAINING

During this section you should offer your salespeople some valuable training. Your salespeople will indicate they don't want another training session on "Fair Housing," but if it keeps them from a violation and the intense prosecution that would follow, they will appreciate you greatly. This is your time to train. The salespeople do not determine the topics, you do. Whatever you feel is important at the current time is the training you provide. You can have guest presenters if you choose occasionally. Keep this training to fifteen minutes.

WANTS AND NEEDS

Real estate salespeople want the time to discuss their listings. I called this the "wants and needs" time. Salespeople may talk about their need to sell a listing, a price reduction, or the offer of a selling bonus. Other salespeople may describe properties their clients are seeking. Encourage cross talk and questions. If only one salesperson makes a transaction because of this promotion, you will have them as attendees to your meetings for life. Limit the time spent on wants and needs to five minutes. If you find this takes more than the time allowed, you need to encourage your attendees to shorten their talk time and put more into a handout.

WRAP-UP

Wrap up with any final comments. Briefly review important points that were covered during the meeting and thank the guests and affiliates. Then say a special thank you to all the other attendees and cordially invite them to the next office meeting. This should only take a minute or two.

The total time for an office meeting should be no more than an hour. This gives you time to cover some important points, but it is short enough not to take away from your salesperson's production.

Real Estate Office Meeting Tips

The following are some helpful tips to help you make your next office meeting successful, effective, and fun. If you make the office meetings dull and boring, you will be very lonely in a short time. Give your salespeople a reason to attend, and they will. Make the meeting fun, and they will come back.

BEFORE THE MEETING

1. Define the purpose of the meeting

Every meeting should have a purpose; otherwise, don't have one. Don't feel that you have a weekly meeting "just because." If your office can afford to hold meetings only once a month, you need to consider doing so.

2. Develop an agenda

Make sure you develop an agenda in cooperation with key participants, as discussed previously. If at all possible, put items of interest in a company newsletter. This saves a tremendous amount of meeting time. Do not allow your meetings to become a bunch of "quick hits" that the salespeople will not remember.

3. Distribute the agenda

You should also distribute with the agenda any background material, lengthy documents, or articles prior to the meeting so the salespeople will be prepared and feel involved and up-to-date. This can also limit the discussion if decisions need to be made.

4. Choose an appropriate meeting time

Set a time limit and stick to it, if possible. Remember, the salespeople have other commitments. They will be more likely to attend meetings if you make them productive, predictable, and as short as possible. Do not get in the habit of changing the time or date, because doing so will cause a great deal of confusion.

5. Arrange the room

Be sure the room is set up so that members face each other. You could put them all in a circle or semicircle. For large groups, it may be better to set the room up in U-shaped rows. These types of layouts encourage participation and are less threatening. You want your meetings to be fun, not intimidating.

6. Find the best room

You should choose a room suitable to your group's size. A small room with too many people gets stuffy and creates tension. A larger room is more comfortable and encourages individual expression. Too much space for too few people makes the meeting look unattended and unimportant.

7. Use visual aids

You should make your presentation exciting and visually stimulating. You could post a large agenda up front to which your salespeople can refer. Your presentation should use computer display projectors and a graphic slide show to add flair.

DURING THE MEETING

1. Greet each of your salespeople and make them feel welcome.

2. If possible, serve light refreshments; they are good icebreakers and make your salespeople feel special and comfortable. You could have some of your affiliates help sponsor the food. Be cognizant of those on a diet. Have someone pick up the food at five minutes before the meeting starts. This will encourage salespeople to show up to the meeting early. Always have coffee and water.

3. Start on time. This is critical. If you don't start on time, then more salespeople will show up late until they won't show up at all. If you start on time, you will demonstrate promptness. Some salespeople will insist on being late. You need to speak with these salespeople separately and discuss the need for them to show up on time.

4. End on time. To respect your salespeople's valuable time, end on time. If you have guest speakers, interrupt them if necessary to avoid additional time. You should practice your presentation to be sure the time is correct. Have additional material to cover if the meeting goes faster than anticipated. Have stopping places if the meeting looks to go over.

5. Review the agenda and set priorities for the meeting. This is simply being prepared. The worst thing a broker can do is hold an office meeting and appear unprepared. If you show up once or twice unprepared, you will run off all your salespeople from attending your meeting. It is rude to your salespeople. Spend the time necessary to make these meetings special and meaningful.

6. Stick to the agenda. Any variation will cause confusion and again you will look unprepared. If you want to add something, make a note to yourself and add it at the next meeting.

7. Encourage group discussion to get all points of view and ideas. You will have better quality decisions as well as highly motivated salespeople; they will feel that attending meetings is worth their while. Some things you could get agreement on include advertising campaigns, floor-time schedules, or arranging the next office "get-together." Keep the conversation focused on the topic. Feel free to ask for only constructive and non-repetitive comments. Tactfully end discussions when they are getting nowhere or becoming destructive or unproductive.

8. Keep minutes of the meeting for future reference in case a question or problem arises. Distribute these minutes to those who want them. Delegate this duty to your administrative assistant or anyone but you.

9. As a leader, be a role model by listening and showing interest, appreciation, and confidence in your salespeople. Celebrate their successes and help them through the challenges. This is the time to be a cheerleader.

10. Summarize any agreements reached and end the meeting on a unifying or positive note.

AFTER THE MEETING

1. Write up and distribute minutes within the next couple of days. Quick action reinforces the importance of meeting and reduces errors of memory.

2. Put unfinished business on the agenda for the next meeting.

3. Conduct a periodic evaluation of the meetings. Note any areas that can be analyzed and improved for more productive meetings.

And remember, effective meetings will keep them coming back!

Managing New Real Estate Salespeople

The broker needs to take great care when managing new salespeople. The new salesperson needs his or her hand held, but the broker cannot let that person become dependent upon the broker. Training and accountability are musts for new salespeople. More time should be spent with new salespeople than with veteran salespeople.

The biggest fear for a new real estate salesperson is lack of knowledge about how to make money. This is where the broker, assistant manager, or trainer teaches the "newbies" how to perform. It is a joy to teach them because they do not challenge you, and they are so excited to learn. Not only that, they are usually "hungry" (and I mean that literally as well as figuratively) to make some money fast.

Managing Experienced Real Estate Salespeople

Managing experienced real estate salespeople requires more talent than managing a new salesperson. A manager could get away with not knowing much with new salespeople because they don't know any better, but not with the veterans. A lot of brokers cannot retain the services of their veterans because they have nothing to offer them. The experienced salespeople do not need the broker's help or advice. They do not need the typical training offered by real estate offices. The best way to handle experienced salespeople is to put them on a schedule of "Individual Business Development" coaching meetings. During these meetings, the broker can assess the needs of these experienced salespeople and then offer the solutions necessary to fulfill those needs.

Office Philosophy

The philosophy of an office has a critical effect on the type of real estate salesperson a broker can recruit. If an office is seen as cutthroat, then that is the only type of salesperson the broker will be able to recruit. The same goes with a "non-producing" office, a "community service" office, a "100 percent" office, and so on. Ultimately the broker will determine the philosophy of the office. If a broker decides to have a "team-oriented" office where all salespeople work together as a team and then lets a cutthroat salesperson stay, the synergy of the office is ruined.

I observed a real estate office where the broker was more concerned about "partying" than business. That office was fun—but no one made any money. Eventually, the salespeople began to leave because it stopped being fun not having any income. The broker, in desperation, began recruiting experienced salespeople from other companies, to no avail. No real estate salesperson wanted to be associated with the "party" office. The office closed its doors permanently only six months after this philosophy was put in place.

Tracking

Brokers need to be aware of where their company has been, how they are doing currently, and where they look to go. The only way to do this is to monitor what is being done. The broker should track each salesperson's production. The broker should include the salesperson's number of sales, number of listings and buyer brokerage contracts, closed dollar volume, commissions earned, and average sales price. The broker should then tally all this information together to get numbers for the office in general. All this data should be accumulated into one "readable" document.

The broker can now analyze the data and take steps forward to maintain or change course as necessary. Tracking can be done with charts, graphs, and reports monitored, recorded, and finalized through off-site companies specializing in such reporting. These companies usually charge a great deal of money for their expertise. This very valuable information is also very costly, so only major real estate companies can usually afford off-site consultants. The typical real estate company must do this monitoring and reporting in-house, which may be better because the data is actually usable. Too many unusable reports are a waste of time and money. Make sure the reports are valuable and then take action in response to what the report finds. I once worked with a broker who required reports on everything. We had weekly reports, progress reports, expense reports, and listing reports, to name a few. These reports took a great deal of man-hours to produce, and once completed, were rarely helpful. The personnel that had to complete the reports were never told of their purpose, and in the end felt the time was wasted. Be sure you only produce reports you will use.

Conclusion

Once you understand and accept all your responsibilities, you must get your family's support, which is still essential. Explain to them that you will probably work evenings and weekends. Yes, you can make your own hours—and you should *not* allow clients or salespeople to control your time, because it's as valuable as theirs. But there will be many occasions when you can only talk with a salesperson in the evening, or when a problem arises that you must address right away. If you're committed to success, you'll do the work.

Chapter Two Review Questions

1. Which of the following is not a characteristic of a talented real estate broker?
   A. Persistent
   B. Workaholic
   C. Enthusiastic
   D. Opportunistic

2. What is one question you would *not* want to ask yourself if you were considering a career in real estate brokerage?
   A. Why do I *really* want to become a broker?
   B. Do I actually have the qualities of a real estate broker?
   C. Am I willing to pay the price to become the best real estate broker I can possibility be?
   D. Do I have the correct ethnicity to lead people?

3. What is *not* one of the reasons brokers typically fail in their endeavor to operate a successful real estate brokerage?

   A. Lack of enthusiasm

   B. Lack of funds

   C. Lack of management experience

   D. Lack of specialization

4. Which of the following is *not* an approach to management?

   A. The Commander

   B. The Conniver

   C. The Controller

   D. The Collaborator

5. In which approach to management does the person believe it is "my way or the highway"?

   A. The Commander

   B. The Conniver

   C. The Calmer

   D. The Collaborator

6. What is not one of the advantages of the Peacemaker approach to management?

   A. Everyone loves the Peacemaker.

   B. The office atmosphere is relaxing and serene.

   C. The office experiences a great deal of turnover in active salespeople.

   D. Their clients tend to remain loyal.

7. Which of the following is *not* one of the disadvantages of the Collaborator?

   A. No leadership.

   B. The salespeople tend to ignore the broker.

   C. The salespeople form alliances.

   D. The salespeople volunteer to take on more responsibilities.

8. What are some of the activities required of the broker?

   A. Company direction

   B. Retention of their salespeople

C. Recruiting of new salespeople and experienced salespeople

D. All of the above

9. Which of the following activities should brokers avoid?

A. Having private meetings with salespeople of the opposite sex

B. Continually improving themselves through education

C. Joining professional associations that relate to the real estate industry

D. Conducting informational surveys of your customers and clients

10. A quality real estate office meeting should cover all of the following *except*

A. review of any new laws.

B. activities in the office.

C. new listings the salespeople have attained.

D. the frustrations of the broker.

11. The office meeting

A. should be once per week.

B. should be limited to one hour.

C. should be of value.

D. all of the above.

12. An agenda for the office meeting should include

A. an introduction to the meeting.

B. guest or affiliate presentations.

C. training.

D. a properly constructed agenda should have all of these elements.

13. What is not an important factor in managing new real estate salespeople?

A. The broker should not spend as much time with new real estate salespeople as with more experienced salespeople.

B. The new real estate salespeople must be held accountable for their activities.

C. The new real estate salesperson requires a great deal of training.

D. All of these are true in managing new real estate salespeople.

3 The Real Estate Brokerage Office

There are many types of brokerages. Choosing the correct type should be a long and thought-out question. While there's no one correct answer to this all-important question, choosing a brokerage that matches your philosophies and business goals has a huge impact on your company's productivity. You need to consider several questions before selecting the type of office you want to operate. Here are just a few to consider:

1. Do you have the funds to operate a real estate office? Do you have the funds to buy the infrastructure you need to start up a real estate enterprise? Do you have reserve funds necessary to continue operations for at least six months?

2. Do you have the expertise to manage a real estate office? Be honest with this one.

3. Do you want to operate a single office, or do you want to develop into a multi-office enterprise?

4. What type of real estate do you want to concentrate on? Residential? Commercial? High-end?

5. In which geographic areas do you want to specialize?

6. What do you predict your office market share will be? And your profitibility?

7. What is the maximum number of salespeople you want in your office?

8. What are your office policies? Will you be strict or flexible?

9. Do you believe in a family atmosphere or a corporate structure? What type of reputation do you want to project?

10. What are your growth strategies for the business? Expansion? Franchise affiliation? Merger?

11. What type of training do you plan to provide?

12. Are you concerned about name recognition in the market? What will you do to address this issue?

13. Will your company offer ancillary services? Will you charge for these services?

14. Do you plan on being technology proficient or doing things the old fashioned way? How much are you willing to pay for technology?

15. Should you buy an existing real estate company, or should you form your own?

16. Should you buy or lease a location?

17. What business equipment should you purchase?

All these questions and many more must be answered before the correct decision can be made.

Office Identity

Based on these questions, you should be able to form an office identity. Your identity must be consistent throughout your organization. Lack of consistency in your message will dilute your recruiting effectiveness. Let's say you decide you want to project an office image in which the salespeople are empowered to make decisions on their own and have a great deal of autonomy, but in action you rule with an iron fist. You now are sending mixed messages to your salespeople and the real estate community.

Office Types

Selecting a type of office is one of the most important aspects of beginning a real estate brokerage office. Choosing the right office type could give you the boost to become a leader in the real estate industry. Choosing the wrong office type could ruin your business chances or at best cost you thousands of dollars. Many enter the real estate brokerage business and never think about the type of office they want and should have. There are several types to examine.

Mom and Pop Shops

The Mom and Pop shop is usually a single broker working alone or with his or her spouse. These brokers work out of their homes, so their overhead is minimal. They usually are veterans in the real estate industry and now only sell to their friends and past clients. Because of their low overhead, these shops will always be around. These Mom and Pop shops have few services and are not technologically savvy. They only survive because people love to do business with them. I wholeheartedly believe that the real estate business is a relationship business, and the Mom and Pop shops are best at relationships.

Individually they represent a very small number of sales, but when you group them all together, they can make up a huge force. That is why you are beginning to see them gather together in "associations" to have a more powerful voice and referral networks.

Niche Offices

Niche (also called boutique) offices are quite similar to the Mom and Pop shops, except that they usually have an office separate from their home. These offices will specialize. They may specialize (have a "niche") in fine homes in a specific area. They may make a "point of interest" their "niche." They may be the designated real estate company for a local business corporation. Whatever their niche, they rarely venture outside it because they cannot serve a huge community as well as they do their niche market.

Single Office with the Broker and Fewer than Five Salespeople

A single office with the broker and fewer than five salespeople is generally a start-up type real estate office. This may begin when a broker-associate of a real estate office believes he or she can do a better job and rents some office space, buys some yard signs, and starts up his or her own real estate office. On the way out the door, the broker-associate takes some friends along, angering his or her previous broker—and we wonder why this business is considered cutthroat. But I digress; this type of office is usually an independent office with no support from any other source. It is also usually underfunded, so the marketing and advertising budget is small or nonexistent. The single office firms require little capital to begin, and their limited access to capital may inhibit growth opportunities associated with investment in technology and infrastructure.

The reason this type of office can succeed is that they can specialize in one particular area or one particular type of real estate. They tend to specialize in buyer brokerage, fine homes, and estates, or the like. A smaller, independent broker is able to implement changes faster, pay commissions on the day of settlement, and keep overhead low. And the broker tends to be more of a friend, not a dictator.

Single Office with the Broker and More than Five Salespeople but Fewer than Fifty Agents

A single office with the broker and more than five salespeople but fewer than fifty agents is an agency that has grown from only a handful of people to a mid-sized real estate office. The office will begin to specialize in the services offered to their salespeople. They will first seek a real estate trainer to help the salespeople make more money. Then they hire a recruiter to go out and build the office. Accounting functions will become more centralized, and the broker will begin to concentrate on the direction of the company instead of day-to-day operations. The broker/owner will continue this process until the office grows into the next type.

Single Office with the Broker and More than Fifty Agents

A single office with the broker and more than fifty agents is a large office and usually has several people managing the office. The space occupied must accommodate the large number of salespeople. This type of office can balloon to have more than 1,000 real estate salespeople under one roof. Because of the number of real estate salespeople, you will generally find these offices in large metropolitan areas. The services offered to their salespeople are very specialized, with numerous support staff. These large market single firms are more likely to be franchised firms and use this affiliation to offer larger firm services.

The advantage of a single firm is that the company can negotiate for floor space for only one office instead of negotiating for multiple offices in remote locations. Having all operations under one roof is a huge cost savings. All the services to the community and to the sales force are located in one place. The disadvantage is that they may be a considerable distance from some of the communities they serve.

Two to Five Offices Owned by One Broker and Fewer than 100 Salespeople

Two to five offices owned by one broker and fewer than 100 salespeople practices the theory that it is better to have several small to mid-sized offices in several areas than one centrally located large office. Both have their advantages and disadvantages. The large, centralized office has many economies of scale and can buy and move supplies around with ease. The multi-office setup can service the community in the community.

The services offered to the salespeople are usually offered at the local offices. Each office works independently with the company providing marketing and support. The two- to five-office system can still be managed by one broker/owner with office managers in each office handling the day-to-day operations.

More than Five Offices and More than 100 Salespeople

Once a real estate company achieves the status of having more than five offices and more than 100 salespeople, it has usually formed a corporation. These companies control major segments of the sales process. Most have huge advertising budgets, expensive marketing materials, and may even venture into television. Almost all real estate offices are constantly hiring real estate salespeople, but in these types of offices hiring becomes their lifeblood. Without a steady stream of new real estate salespeople, the company cannot afford the structure they have put in place. The top 250 firms (over 30,000 real estate firms) represented 24 percent of all real estate salespeople and one in six home sales. This number represents the impact the mega-firms have on the real estate industry.

Some believe a bigger office offers more opportunity once it's established. These salespeople do not want to be the "big fish" in the small pond; they would rather be a little fish and still have room to thrive and achieve.

To grow and prosper, these vertically expanded firms have broadened their operations and product lines to include ancillary services. *Ancillary services* are real estate–related businesses that turn into profit centers for the brokerage business. These services will be discussed later.

Marketing Companies

A real estate marketing company is a non-traditional real estate company that does not represent a party to the transaction but rather helps the seller market their property. The marketing company offers services in a smorgasbord-type package. Each service can be paid for separately or in bundles at a discount. These services are paid for up-front, and the seller pays only a commission to the selling salesperson who finds a buyer. These marketing companies appeal to the price-conscious consumer and do-it-yourself home sellers who are willing to conduct some aspects of the real estate transaction themselves. Customers of marketing companies are likely to be drawn from the For Sale By Owner (FSBO) clientele, who represent less than 20 percent of transactions in any given year. New construction (builders) is another source of potential clientele for the marketing company.

The marketing companies rarely provide representation for a client but rather provide the marketing that is difficult for individual sellers. Some of the services could include:

Print advertising	Yard signs	Open houses
Office tours	Internet exposure	Contract forms
Buyer qualification	Mortgage support	Title support
Key boxes	Access to MLS	Color graphics
Sign info boxes	Broker luncheons	Home warranties
Property staging	Property showing	Seller's net sheets
Real estate advice	Contract negotiations	Inspections
Price determinations	Appraisals	Closing details

Typically the marketing company will group these services into packages and offer their client a discount if they order a package. If they chose "access to MLS," the client would have to insure that the selling salesperson who brought the buyer would be compensated separately. The "marketing" concept is growing in status, but will be mostly concentrated in a few sellers that have the time and patience to sell their own home.

Independent Offices

Independent offices are those real estate brokerages owned by a person or entity not associated with a national franchise. These companies survive and thrive because they can act and react on a moment's notice. They tend to serve niche markets and specialize in their marketing. Their size is typically small, but some dominate multi-state regions. The mentality of these companies is that of a family and the corporate structure: very flat, with the owner making the decisions. Generally, the owner knows each and every one of the salespeople and knows their families as well. The independent office is the easiest and least expensive real estate operation to start up, and as such is the most frequently used type. Independent offices can survive in the future, but they must remain on the cutting edge and be open to the changes their clients demand.

National Franchise Offices

The national franchise office is part of a group of brokers that have national ties with a larger company. The national franchiser usually does not own individual offices but rather offers services and systems to the local franchisee. The advantages of this type of company include proven brokerage systems and an advertising budget that gets into the tens of millions of dollars.

Most actual real estate offices have very little contact with their corporate franchise. Instead, they operate day-to-day operations just the same as independent offices. The advantages include marketing on an international level, real estate systems that have proven track records, and the support of a team of real estate professionals that only big money could buy. The disadvantage of the franchise is that there are certain franchise rules the franchisee must abide by. Most of the rules are determined to be the best for all franchisees, but occasionally they limit the quick response that this business demands. Second, not all these services are provided for free. The cost to the franchisee could be staggering.

International Franchises

The national franchise and the international franchise operate in virtually the same way, except that the international franchise has real estate offices in foreign countries. That being said, international operations bring countless new challenges. The laws, regulations, and customs will vary drastically and pose critical problems and opportunities. The "big boys" are the only ones to tackle this type of real estate company. I know of no independent international operation.

Neighborhood Offices

A neighborhood office is usually a smaller office with sights set on being the experts in a localized area. These offices specialize in knowing the area, people, and events in that specific neighborhood. The neighborhood office is almost always an independent office with no ties to a national franchise.

Unlike a "niche" office, the only thing this office specializes in is location. They are located in a neighborhood and that is their market. Their marketing efforts are solely targeted at their neighborhood. Most of their business comes by referrals and "word-of-mouth," so a huge advertising budget is unnecessary. Any listings or sales outside their market come up only by chance. These offices are very visible, always present in the area. They participate in and often lead neighborhood activities and events.

Community Offices

Community offices serve a wider area than the neighborhood offices, often encompassing an entire community. These offices take pride in being a centerpiece of the community. Several members of the office usually have prominent places in the local government or on school boards. The salespeople are active in charity events, sporting events, and school activities. Very little advertising outside the community ever takes place because it is not necessary for this type of office.

Community offices generally start off as neighborhood offices and expand their reach until they have encompassed the entire community. These offices work hard to have the respect of the community they serve.

City Offices

City offices are located within a city and concentrate their efforts on the entire city. In many cases, this type of operation will have multiple offices to cover the entire city. The marketing is not as fixed on communities as it is on exposure throughout the entire city. You will see less and less of marketing to events and activities and more and more a "shotgun" approach, appealing to the masses. Local marketing is left up to the salespeople.

These companies receive a great deal of their business from the media, and their salespeople usually work with clients they are meeting for the first time. This needs to be explained to their salespeople because it is tempting to "sell 'em and leave 'em," meaning simply that the salesperson makes a sale and never contacts the client again. If a city office is ever to succeed, it must make a concentrated effort to build referral business.

Regional Offices

Regional offices focus on an entire region. A real estate brokerage company in California may take the region of southern California as its market area. A broker in Texas may take the north Texas region. A company near a state's border may select a tri-state area as its market area. Each of these choices brings with it any number of problems and scenarios. The coverage can almost always only be obtained by the use of multiple offices. Marketing in this type of real estate company is twofold. First, such companies must market each separate office locally. Second, they must market the company as a total entity to their region.

Multi-State Offices

As mentioned above, a real estate company could consider its market in multiple states. The company must have licenses in each state it is to serve. Generally, where the transaction actually occurs is the state of record. The coordination of this type of operation is complex. The "home" state salespeople may feel that they are superior to all other salespeople. The events that occur must include all members, and no matter what, some will feel left out. If operations are not monitored carefully, there might be a mutiny.

If you observe carefully, you will notice that the national franchises started out as a single office. They grew in stature and wealth. They then expanded markets and bought or developed surrounding offices. That expansion continued even into neighboring states. And finally, they formed a franchise and sold the rights to the organization across the globe. So if you see a multi-state operation, you may be looking at the next international franchise.

Sole Proprietorships

Sole proprietorships are single-owner operations. Sole proprietorships are smaller companies, because once the liabilities of a larger operation begin to take shape, the owner(s) will want to protect themselves from those liabilities. A sole proprietorship is the easiest form of operation a real estate company could choose. Once the sole proprietor has a real estate broker's license, all the owner normally is required to do is complete some paperwork, pay a small fee, and begin selling real estate. Be sure to check state and local small business regulations as well as the state real estate commission for the exact procedures.

Sole proprietorships are the easiest to operate and sell. The accounting necessary is simple and the overhead (without the corporate structure) is minimal. Sole proprietorships are the backbone of the real estate industry and are where most big real estate corporations got their starts.

Partnerships

Partnerships are the forming of a company by two or more individuals or entities. These are usually two real estate associate brokers who believe they can do a better job at real estate brokerage than where they are currently associated. They talk themselves into opening their own business but want to do it as partners. "Split all the costs and profits!" There are several types of partnerships that could be formed to operate a real estate company. Tenancy in common is the typical way a partnership is drawn up.

An attorney (because of the intricacies of real estate partnerships) should draw up all types of partnerships. We will examine each separately:

JOINT TENANTS WITH RIGHTS OF SURVIVORSHIP

With *joint tenants with rights of survivorship,* there is unity of ownership of the real estate company. The ownership is vested in a group of individuals. Any single individual cannot claim any separate ownership of the real estate business. The group can collectively dispose of the joint real estate business, but only with the entire group's consent. An individual can act on behalf of the group and bind the group to an agreement. Each member has an "undivided" interest in the real estate business. An *undivided interest* means that a division of the business cannot be separated from the rest. Each tenant has rights to the entirety.

The central character of joint tenancy is the right of survivorship. Until the group is reduced to one person, ownership remains in the group. The tenants have no separate ownership of the real estate business and cannot leave any rights in their will. If one of the members dies, the group gains the interest of the deceased. The ownership is still vested in the group. If all of the members die, the last remaining member will own the business in severalty, the rights of all others having been severed away.

I opened a real estate office with a real estate salesperson who had been loyal to me for years. She was talented and trustworthy. Her husband, however, was not, and furthermore, he was not in the real estate industry and knew nothing about it. The salesperson and I formed a joint tenancy because if she died, I did not want her husband to be my partner. I would have done all the work, and he would have taken half of the profits. The problem was, my family was exposed if I died. The company paid for "key man" insurance in case of either partner's death. The remaining spouse would have received several hundred thousand dollars from the insurance—a considerable amount more than the real estate brokerage was worth.

TENANCY IN COMMON

Tenancy in common is a way for two or more people to own a real estate business together. Each can leave his or her interest upon death to the beneficiaries of their choosing. Each tenant has a separate share of the business and those shares do not need to be equal. Each co-owner may deal with his or her share as he or she pleases. This type of partnership is noted for the ease of transferability of ownership. Anyone that is invited can join and leave any time they want. The direction of the company is by those that own the most of the tenancy. As mentioned above, this is the most common form of partnership.

GENERAL PARTNERSHIPS

A *general partnership* is an association of two or more individuals conducting a real estate business. The partnership agreement has very little formality. For the most part, the partners own the business assets together and are personally liable for business debts. In terms of asset protection, general partnerships can be even worse than sole proprietorships. Anything that one partner does will affect all of the partners. Thus, each general partner's exposure to risk is increased by a factor equal to the number of general partners in the business.

Most real estate partnerships are informally operated under a general partnership. A group of five real estate brokers get together and decide to form a general partnership. All five now have decision-making ability for the real estate company. Can you see how this may become tense? The real estate industry is an independent industry. Partnerships rarely work with real estate salespeople and far less with real estate brokerages.

LIMITED PARTNERSHIPS

In a limited partnership, one or more *general* partners manage the business, whereas *limited* partners contribute capital and share in the profits but take no part in running the business. General partners remain personally liable for the partnership debts, whereas limited partners incur no liability with respect to partnership obligations beyond their capital contributions. The purpose of this form of business is to encourage investors to invest without risking more than the capital they have contributed.

Limited partnerships are infrequently used in the real estate business because almost all brokers want to run the show. What real estate broker wants to pour their money into a real estate business and then have no say in its operation?

JOINT VENTURES

Joint ventures are a special type of partnership that only exists as long as the venture lasts. Once the venture is completed, the partnership is dissolved. Quite frequently a builder will form a joint venture to get the capital to build a subdivision of houses. The builder will gather some wealthy investors together and form the joint venture. Once the subdivision is built out and the investors are paid, the venture is dissolved.

Corporations

A *corporation* is a type of operation that is designed to protect the owner/operators from the possible liabilities that occur in the real estate business. Corporations tend to be larger real estate companies that have many assets and liabilities. Corporations that are formed simply to avoid taking responsibility for their actions will be dissolved, and the liability will then fall on those responsible. I say that because I know a lot of real estate brokers/owners that form corporations with only one person (the broker/owner) as the sole stockholder. These corporations have a good chance of losing their corporate shield, and the owner would be liable.

Building Types

There are many building types within which a broker can choose to operate a real estate brokerage. Some are more practical and some more exciting. Some are more expensive, and some are less so. The choices are many, and the decision is critical.

Stand-Alone

A stand-alone building is not attached to any other building. It is usually a building containing one business rather than a row of stores or businesses with a common roof and sidewalls. This is the typical real estate office. You see them near residential neighborhoods. Some are very fancy white stone palaces with marble entry and massive double stained glass entry doors. Some are metal buildings with brick or wood front elevations. Some are converted residential houses that have been re-zoned for commercial. The public can easily recognize your operation with this type of building. The disadvantages usually include higher utilities and maintenance.

House

As previously mentioned, operating a real estate business out of a house is a popular idea. Buyers want to buy a house, so what is better than settling that transaction in the comfort of a home? The bedrooms are converted into salespeople's offices, and the living room serves as a conference room. The kitchen and bathrooms stay the same. The renovation to convert a house to a real estate office is remarkably simple.

The downside to having a house as a real estate office is that even though older homes are the best for looks, they do not make the best real estate offices. The house is usually chopped up so that there is no open work area. The best and most effective real estate offices have huge bullpens where a majority of salespeople operate. Never underestimate the synergy that comes from a bullpen. Other disadvantages include the fact that the overall floor plan will not be fit for a real estate office without major construction expense.

Brick-and-Mortar

A brick-and-mortar type of building is the standard commercial building. The costs savings are great, but the uniqueness is limited. The term *brick-and-mortar* refers to the construction method rather than to an actual building. These buildings can be constructed in any shape or size, but the more differentiated you intend to make your building, the greater the cost you will incur.

Brick-and-mortar buildings are very strong and sturdy. They can take the weather and will still look good. Expanding a brick-and-mortar building tends to be more difficult than expanding a wood-constructed building.

Strip Center

A *strip center* is a business center with outside entrances to each tenant and its clients. Frequently, a real estate office will set up in a strip center to locate close to the market in which they specialize. The business center is not a shopping center; a business center attracts business, and a shopping center attracts shopping. Brokers could write their bankruptcy papers by not knowing the difference.

The office space can range from a few hundred square feet to several thousand square feet. The leases, rights, and obligations must be spelled out in writing and reviewed by an attorney. This is a long-term decision and should never be taken lightly.

Office Building

An office building is a less frequently used real estate office because most office buildings are located in commercial areas that are not convenient to residential real estate. On the other hand, office buildings are ideal for commercial real estate brokerage companies. If a residential real estate brokerage is large enough to have a business headquarters separate from an actual real estate office, then the headquarters could be located in an office building.

Buying versus Leasing

When opening a real estate office, should the broker/owner go to the expense of buying a building, or should he or she simply rent a space and operate their business from there? This is an important question and needs analysis before operations begin.

Buying

The decision to buy a building to operate a real estate company is one that should not be taken lightly. Some brokers begin a real estate company *because* they just bought a business building as an investment and no other business is eager to move into the space. That is the wrong reason to begin a real estate company. Other brokers transfer their current (profitable) real estate company from one location to the new building they have bought *because* they need the building rented. Again, not smart. You should only buy a building to use for a real estate company if it makes logical economic sense. Some logical reasons are discussed in the following sections.

RENT REPLACEMENT

Rent replacement is transferring from paying rent to paying principal. Suppose the real estate office is currently paying $850 per month in renting a small office space. If the company could find a place to buy where their monthly payments would total $1,000 per month, the bank would see that as an increase of only $150 because the $850 would be rent replacement.

AREA RECOGNITION

Area recognition is higher if you buy versus rent. Everyone knows where the "Acme Real Estate" company is located because it is visible, and the best way to become visible is to purchase a building. Taxing authorities know the name of the real estate company. The community respects business owners with permanent stakes in the community more than "passersby" who are just renting. You can also have the signage that you want without restrictions by a landlord.

COST SAVINGS

Once a real estate company begins operations in a facility that is owned, certain cost savings can begin. The owner can better negotiate utilities, maintenance, landscaping, and any other services that are required for a building. A landlord may not be interested in cutting the best deal on those services because the tenants have to pay them anyway. Any interest that is paid is a tax savings, whereas none of a rent payment would be. As with any tax advice, please consult your accountant to be sure to take advantage of any tax savings that is due to you.

LONG-TERM INVESTMENT

Before making the decision to buy a building for a real estate office, make sure the decision is based on logic and not emotion. To own a building on the "Main Street" of your town is cool, but if it bankrupts you, it is not a wise decision. Buying a building to house your real estate brokerage is a decision whose effects could last sixty years or longer, so be sure you take that into consideration. Over the long term, buying should be the better investment.

Leasing

Before leasing a space, you must analyze several factors, discussed in the sections that follow.

ACTUAL RENT

The actual rent you pay to operate a real estate brokerage company is an extremely important decision; however, it may not be the most important factor in choosing a site. For example, the cheapest rent in town is also probably the most dangerous part of town and not a good place to meet potential clients. Actual rent is based on supply and demand. If the area you are looking to put a real estate office is in high demand, expect to pay a greater monthly rent. The good thing about placing a real estate office is that you do not need the highest traffic areas. People will seek you out provided they know where you are located. I have seen some of the best real estate offices in high-traffic shopping areas but off to one end. The shoppers create the traffic. These are not prospective clients, but when these same people decide to buy or sell real estate, they know where that real estate company is because they have driven by it dozens of times. Second, because the company is not located in the heart of the shopping center, the rental rate is high but not terribly excessive.

How much is the rent rate? Is it comparable to the area? Is the area increasing in stature or in a declining state? Where is the rental space located? Will the location draw drive-by traffic? All of these factors affect the amount of rent that should be paid.

TERM OF RENT

The term of rent is the length of time the rental agreement is in effect. Usually the term of rent is in accordance with the needs of the parties. A landlord may want a long-term lease to give security that the property will have a tenant for a long period of time. A landlord may want a short-term lease if he or she feels rental rates for the area will be escalating. The tenant may want to have a long-term lease to be sure to lock in the current rental rate and to be able to establish the company in that spot. The tenant may want a short-term lease if he or she expects to move in a short period of time. All of these factors must be negotiated in the lease.

A real estate broker should not operate with a long-term lease unless he or she plans to be in the location for over six months. Operating under a "handshake" agreement may expose the broker to major trouble. Suppose that a broker wants to open up a real estate company and knows a friend with a rental spot that would be perfect. They consummate the transaction with a handshake. The real estate company spends thousands of dollars in marketing to let the public know they are in business and where they are located. A year later, the two "friends" get into a dispute, and the owner of the location tells the other to vacate in thirty days. The broker has no recourse because a long-term agreement had not been signed. Do not allow this to happen to you; be sure that once you have a place, you have a long-term agreement of at least five years with options to renew at the end of the lease.

TIMING OF PAYMENT

When is the monthly rental payment due? This can have a major effect on how easily the payment can be made. Real estate transactions tend to close at the end of a month, so if the rental payment is also at the end of the month, it may be hard to pay if the closings are delayed. The ideal payment date would be around the fifth of the month. Owners also tend to want the payment at some time other than the first of the month because it looks bad if two or three tenants are moving at one time. You should be able to negotiate the timing of the rent payment to meet your schedule.

PENALTIES

Will there be any penalties for late payments? If so, how much? Will there be any penalties for additional salespeople, additional parking spaces? Will there be any penalties for working after normal working hours?

Be careful to understand all of the potential penalties and whether they could be a burden to you. Some landlords create "penalties" to create an additional income stream. They bury the penalties deep in the contracts knowing you are excited and will agree to almost anything. Then you move in and start incurring penalties every month that you never dreamed would occur. You have signed a long-term contract and are bound by the contract. The best protection is to have an attorney examine the contract and detail any penalties you may incur.

ASSIGNMENT

Assignment of a contract is the changing of principals to the contract. The new principal has all the same rights and obligations as the previous principal. If you can assign a contract you have the right to find another tenant and assign the lease agreement to the new tenant without recourse from the landlord. The new tenant now rents the space from the landlord under the same lease agreement you established in the beginning.

Can the rental agreement be assigned to another person? If you have plans to sell your business, you maybe want to have this consideration written into the lease. If you are undercapitalized, you may want this right just in case the real estate business does not make the money you anticipate and you need out of the lease. We all hope this is not the case, but good brokers always think of the best-case scenarios and strive to achieve them, and they think of the worst-case scenarios and determine how to avoid them.

COMMON AREAS

Are there common areas associated with the lease? This can be beneficial or negative. The benefits would be such things as a common break area, restrooms, and even secretarial staff. If the space provides these services to all the tenants, the cost is divided and as such is less to each individual. The broker/owner will not pay totally for the space used. The negative is the payment for things not important to the operation of the business. I know of one broker who was paying several hundred dollars per month for a huge entryway complete with flowers, trees, and a waterfall, none of which was necessary to complete real estate sales.

TOTAL SPACE

What is the total space offered and what is the total space needed? The biggest waste possible in a lease is paying for unused space. Negotiate in the lease the possibility to expand your space, but do not pay for it when it is not needed. I have been in small real estate offices where everyone seemed to be getting things done and huge real estate offices that seemed dead. Both offices had the same number of salespeople. The only difference was the size of the office. The first office had the perfect size; it was big enough to get things done and yet small enough to seem active. The second office was way too big for the number of salespeople they were carrying, and as such it looked empty. I understand the thinking of the second broker. What if I get more salespeople and then I cannot expand? The problem is that it is extremely difficult to recruit to an office that appears to be dead. It is better to start with a smaller office size and negotiate for more space in the lease or determine a separate location all together.

SIGNAGE

What, if any, type of signage is permitted on the exterior of the building? Does the lease provide access to the main sign on the street front? Can you place signs in the window or on your front door? These are all important questions. A great location is of little value if no one knows you are there. Lighted signs are best because they can be seen at night and work as a silent salesperson 24 hours a day. The problem with lighted signs is that they are very expensive, and a start-up brokerage may find them out of financial reach. The more signage you have (to a point), the more clients you will attract.

Some brokers place color graphics of their listings in their front windows for passersby. This can be a great marketing tool in certain "walk-by" type locations, but make sure the window display is professional looking and the information displayed is current.

OPERATIONAL HOURS

Some leases will limit the operational hours of the tenants. Real estate is a 24-hour, 7-day-a-week business. If the landlord will only allow access Monday to Friday from 8:00 a.m. to 5:00 p.m., it may not be the lease for you.

My real estate office never closed. If a salesperson wanted to unlock the doors for a client, then so be it. If the salesperson wanted to open up on Christmas Day, that was his or her choice. I wasn't there, and neither was the staff, but the office was never "closed." If my office were located at a place that limited the operational hours, I would have to have hours I was closed.

The counter to that argument is control. Never "closing" my office meant that salespeople could go to the office, and I had no idea what they were doing. I hoped and believed that it was business, but I know other things I would not approve were occurring. I walked into the office one evening way past normal business because the lights were on and I noticed a low-producing salesperson was inside making copies. When I say she was making copies, I mean hundreds and hundreds of them. When I approached her, she looked like she had been caught red-handed, and she had been. She was copying booklets for her church. Each booklet had hundreds of pages, and there were hundreds of booklets. I was livid. She retorted that it was for a good cause: her church. I fired her. I am not sure her church would approve of her "stealing" my paper and ink. This would never occur during the day when someone else would be around.

The bottom line is that you must consider the restrictions you will have within set business hours. You then need to determine if you can operate a successful real estate enterprise within those limitations.

FINISH OUT

Most spaces will need to be designed and remodeled (*finished out*) for you as a new tenant. Bullpens will need to be set up; a reception area with a desk and any special accommodations your particular office will need should be negotiated. Telephone systems must be installed. These things are easier and much less disruptive if completed before you begin moving your business furniture and equipment into the space. Whether your brokerage firm will pay for all, part, or none the finish out is part of the negotiations in the lease. The longer the lease term, the more finish out the landlord will be willing to complete.

The finish out for start-up or smaller real estate operations is rather ordinary and not expensive. The larger the office operations, the more complex and intense the finish out can be. Large offices have been known to buy the services of an interior designer specializing in office space management and functionality. Yes, that is best, and yes, that is expensive.

PARKING

Do not forget to negotiate adequate parking in your lease. The brokerage company will need parking for salespeople, staff, and clients. Too little parking can result in a drastic drop in sales. You can do estimates, or you can hire a space planner to design the parking needs you will have over the next ten years.

You need to consider where the parking is located. Is it across the street or in a separate area? Is there parking in front of the building, or is all the parking in back? This may not seem like a big deal, but I have seen real estate brokerages struggle because they had limited parking up front so their salespeople had to park in back, and from the street the office always looked closed.

You will need to determine the condition of the parking. Are there holes and cracks in the parking lot? Are the painted lines visible? It is best to have these things addressed and repaired before you sign an agreement because they may be difficult to remedy after the fact.

Mergers and Acquisitions

One of the best ways to get started or expand in the real estate brokerage business is to merge with another real estate company or simply to buy them out. The start-up headaches are avoided, as are most of the start-up costs. Buy today and operate today.

When buying a real estate office, do not make the mistake of paying too much for it. Real estate offices are basically valued on their production. Production is based on real estate salespeople, and real estate salespeople can leave you at any time. I have seen brokers who want a fortune for their office even though they actually lost money the previous year. They base their value on some hidden future worth or on their so-called "good will," neither of which makes you money today. Here are a few questions you want answered before you consider buying another real estate company.

Why Do They Want to Sell?

Finding this out is as important as almost all the other information combined. If I can truly find out their motivation for selling, I can structure a very beneficial agreement. The first office I bought was in the great state of Texas for $50,000 less than the owner had paid for it, and he financed the entire amount for me with nothing down. He was more than willing to negotiate. He was in bad health and had a new home waiting for him and his wife in Colorado, where they always wanted to live. I did not take advantage of him, but I did get a favorable deal. I also negotiated with a different owner who wanted to sell but had no real urgency. She wanted $600,000 cash, and it was worth around $80,000 at the most. See the difference?

It is not that easy to find out the real reason the broker wants to sell. Don't believe the first thing you hear. Do some research. It is best to talk with some of the real estate salespeople in the office you want to buy. Ask one of the salespeople to lunch. Ask them about current operations and the things they feel ought to change. You can find out some helpful, truthful information.

What Are You Actually Buying?

As mentioned before, you want to be sure of what you are buying. Look at the accounting books and analyze every detail. It might be best to hire a "mergers and acquisitions" accountant to help analyze that data to determine if it is a sound investment. I was reviewing the records of a potential buyout because the business was showing a profit of over $150,000. Not bad for a real estate company. After closer scrutiny, I noticed that there were no salaries being paid even though there were seven people working there (not including salespeople). The seller explained that those were his relatives, and that they stayed at his home and he paid them directly. This immediately raised two **major** problems.

1. There could be negative tax consequences from that arrangement. Be careful of buying someone else's liabilities. If the Internal Revenue Service allocates unpaid taxes and penalties for "unpaid" employees, there could be a huge loss.

2. The business was not at a profit but was actually a loss. If you take the $150,000 and divide it by seven (the number of "unpaid" employees), you will find that each employee was paid a little over $20,000 per year. It would be difficult to hire any talent for $20,000 per year, and you can expect that the "relatives" will not continue to work for free.

Without a detailed review of the owner's records, the employment fiasco would have been undiscovered. I did not buy the business and am thankful

I never did. Be sure to inventory every item involved in the purchase. Do not leave anything out or take anything verbally. If the owner tells you that you can have everything, great, but get it in writing.

Another discussion that needs to be held is over commissions. Will the owner want the commissions on the current pendings? Listings? What about the current liabilities? Dues? Deposits? Leases? Every cost or income must be evaluated and agreed upon.

Is the Company Managed Properly?

This is a key question, because if it is being managed properly, then what is the advantage to you to buy it? If it is not managed properly, you may be able to make adjustments to the current cost structure or revenue flow and put yourself into profit in a short period of time.

Once these three main questions are answered, you should have a better estimation of whether you want to move forward with the purchase or move on to a better project.

Valuation of a Real Estate Company

Valuation of a real estate company is completely different from evaluating a residential real estate house. The complexities and uniqueness virtually eliminate the normal avenues available for comparison. One office is totally different from another real estate company just down the street. Office space, inventory, and good will cannot be compared adequately. However, the basis of all evaluation—the definition used in our fundamental real estate courses—still applies:

<u>*VALUATION:*</u> *Valuation is what a typically motivated buyer would be willing to pay a typically motivated seller in open market conditions with all parties operating in their own best interest and all pertinent information known.*

This definition provides the foundation for rational evaluation of the real estate office. The key point on valuation is that very often real estate is *not* included in the sale. The only thing the purchaser is buying is the business itself, not the building.

Office Layout

The layout of the office is of utmost importance. If the office doesn't flow, the day-to-day operations suffer. I have seen real estate companies that had office machines located all over the building, or where the break room is also the conference room and the bathroom is adjacent to the front desk. Some things can't be changed, but those that can be changed should be.

Reception Area

The reception area should be comfortable and inviting. The colors should be neutral and warm. Reception should be separated from the workings of the office to reduce the noise. A video screen should show a buyer happily enjoying the purchase process. The receptionist's desk should be large enough to hide all the papers, files, and equipment but should not look like a fortress.

The reception area is the first impression a potential new client or real estate recruit will see about your office. If the reception area is clean and bright, so will their thoughts be about you. If the reception area is neglected, can they expect the shabby treatment? Spend some time and money on the design and layout of the reception area.

Conference Rooms

Conference rooms should be provided in each office. I state this specifically because some brokers/owners believe their real estate salespeople can take clients to their personal desks. That policy is less than professional. If you do not have a conference room, wall in the space to provide one. The conference room should have a table big enough for at least four people. If the space permits the luxury of two conference rooms, one should be large enough to hold eight people. The conference room should be equipped with a telephone and a computer system with access to the Internet.

The conference room should receive the same reverence that the reception area does. Don't just throw old chairs and a kitchen table from your garage in there; take the time to do it right.

Bathrooms

Yes, you should have bathrooms. In fact, two are better than one. Clearly mark the difference. They should be nicely decorated and adequately supplied. Be quick to clean them even if you have to do it yourself. And have some air freshener handy.

The bathrooms should be located between the public and the sales areas so that both have access to them. The bathrooms should not be located so that a guest would have to walk through the salespeople's work area to get to them. You may have to redesign the layout of the entire office if necessary or consider another space—it is that important. If real estate companies are large enough, they tend to have separate bathrooms for clients and for salespeople.

Bullpen

A bullpen is an open area with several desks or work areas close together and half walls separating the spaces. Agents tend not to like the bullpen because (they say) they work better without the distractions. I have found that reality is quite different. I have owned several offices and the ones with open bullpens always out-produced the offices with cut-up private offices. This has to do with the mentality of the salesperson. If left alone, the typical salesperson will find anything to do *except* prospect for business. This is referred to as "nesting." Just like a bird in a nest, real estate salespeople can be so happy at their desks that they never venture outside their area. Needless to say, they also never make any money either. In a bullpen, work is contagious, and one person working breeds activity for all the people around. Also, feedback is immediate. If a rookie salesperson needs help, it is usually right around the corner. If an office has both a bullpen and private offices, the bullpens are usually reserved for the new or lower producing salespeople.

Semiprivate Offices

Semiprivate offices are larger offices that have two or more desks and salespeople at each desk. Most of the time these offices seem private because rarely are all of the salespeople in the office at one time. These offices are a hybrid between the bullpen and private offices. Sometimes a broker uses these as a type of promotion out of the bullpen.

Brokers are always concerned with the number of salespeople they can house in their offices. Some have analysis done that compares the square feet of the building to the dollar profit earned. With that data, they determine that they need twenty-two real estate salespeople per office. Needless to say, the salespeople don't agree. Overcrowding a single office demoralizes the salespeople.

Private Offices

Private offices are usually reserved for the top producing salespeople, the brokers, and the managers. The total office space needs to be mid-sized or larger because of the space these private offices use. Frequently, a broker will charge a fee to the salespeople who occupy the private offices. Private offices might be prestigious, but they can also take away from office synergies because the salespeople don't have an opportunity to interact.

Private offices can create motivation for those real estate salespeople who don't have one yet, and constant motivation for those who have one not to lose it. For example, if the broker awards the three private offices to the top three producers of the office, then those who don't have an office may work harder to get one. The top producers may work harder to keep their offices. Be careful, though, to award the offices for yearly production, because any less will mean a lot of people moving around all year, which will distract from sales.

Some people reading this will think that would be horrible for a salesperson to have to move out of a private office back to the bullpen. It might be so bad that they leave your office. This is a business that rewards productivity, not longevity. If you have a private office, you should have to earn it every year.

Computer Room

The computer room is ordinarily located toward the back of the real estate office to separate it from the general public. Real estate salespeople spend a great deal of time on the computer, and it is somewhat inappropriate to have people watching that work. Almost any office needs to have at least two computers of some power and speed for multiple salespeople to operate. Smaller offices may convert a desk at the edge of the bullpen and designate it as a computer work area. Larger offices may have two separate computer rooms, each complete with the latest in computer technology.

Equipment Room

The equipment room houses the office equipment to help run a real estate office. This equipment includes the facsimile machine, copiers, and central printers. The equipment room needs adequate space to accommodate several people in the room operating different office machines. This room should be closed and locked to protect the machines after hours. It should be located in the back of the office near the bullpen. In larger offices there may be more than one equipment room. In smaller offices this room is frequently combined with the computer room and the forms room.

Forms Room

A forms room is a room where the real estate salesperson can go to get all blank contracts and forms necessary to conduct real estate business. The broker should assign some staff member to check this room periodically to be sure there is an ample supply of blank forms. This room should be adjacent to the equipment room so the copier is handy. These days, the equipment room is becoming less and less important because most of the forms are now on the Internet and contracts are seldom filled in by hand. A majority of real estate offices have a forms rack on the wall of the equipment room.

Storage

Storage is mandatory in a real estate office. Real estate salespeople are pack rats. They save everything, and if there is no storage, things end up on the floor next to their desks. I am not saying you should provide storage for real estate salespeople, but if you don't have something, you will soon have a mess. I bought a real estate office once that had so many files stored in the attic that it was weighing the structure down. I started going through the files and found out that they were fifteen to twenty years old. I placed all of them outside to be hauled off. The salespeople went nuts. They told me I needed to keep them because who knows when they will need them. As my daughter says, *whatever*. If they haven't looked at them in a decade, I don't think the information is relevant. So I told them they could take any files they wanted home with them. None were taken. Notice: they wanted me to store them, but they didn't want to take them home.

There are two types of things that need to be stored: items that are infrequently needed and past client files. The item storage should be in the office. The client file storage could be in a separate location because a file three years old is never looked at but must be kept in case of a dispute. There are companies that will store these files relatively cheaply, which would free up space in your office.

Operational Offices

The administrative staff uses the operational office to perform their duties. In smaller offices, the broker might provide all these services. In the larger companies, this office (or offices) might house accounting, finance, marketing, administrative, and or processing. Some real estate operations are so large that the operational offices are in a separate building altogether.

The operational office should have some office equipment to make the administrative staff more efficient. Equipment needed might include a fax machine, computers, and a small desk copier. These machines are for administrative use and not for the salespeople. Because the administrative staff has confidential information and valuable equipment, these rooms should be larger and have a locking system to prevent access.

Broker's Office

The broker's office is typically located near the front of the real estate building. At some locations, the broker's office is finely decorated to demonstrate opulence. Some brokers choose a more conservative look. Whatever office is chosen, the broker's door should always be open to the salespeople. Even further, the broker should not get comfortable in his or her "nest." Every hour or so, the broker should get up and make a tour through the office, checking with their salespeople to see if they need any help.

Library

A real estate library is a test of the broker's seriousness. If I were considering joining a real estate broker, the first question I would ask to see is the library. If the broker did not have a library, I might not join, because they do not demonstrate their interest in this business. I developed a library from the first day in my career. I now personally have hundreds of books that I have read and can refer to for information. Some offices have an entire room set aside for their library. Some offices have a wall in the broker's office.

Break Room

The break room can be a simple area with a table and two chairs outside under an awning. It can be as complex as a large cafeteria type room with several tables and all the appliances to cook a feast. Most have a table or two with a refrigerator and a microwave. Some have vending machines that can be a revenue source if a broker so chooses. Without this area, the salespeople will eat at their desks, creating the opportunity to see all kinds of leftover sights and smells that should not be in a work area. A break area also allows the salespeople and staff to enjoy some time together without the pressures of work.

Office Equipment

Office equipment should help the real estate office become more efficient. The wrong equipment is a waste of money and office space. I have seen brokers order the largest and most expensive copier money can buy, only to have no one understand how to use it.

One consideration is whether to lease the office equipment or to purchase. Some factors to consider are cost and repairs. To lease the equipment is a lower up-front cost but over the years a great deal more expensive. Some have available maintenance contracts that provide any necessary repairs and maintenance; if the equipment breaks down, it will be repaired or replaced at no cost to you. Some leases even provide printer cartridges with limits on the copies made.

Computers seem to change daily. The best computer today will seem a dinosaur in a few months. Leasing provides the ability to upgrade with a lot less capital expense. Be careful with leases, though, because the contract is binding, and if you find yourself short of funds, the leases still need to be paid.

Signage

A real estate office should have some sort of outside signage. The signage allows the general public to know you are around and what service you provide. The outside sign should be elevated on a pole or rooftop. The best and most expensive signs are lighted. The sign should be simple and visible from both directions. Do not have a lot of information on the sign, because it will be too busy. When you drive by, pay close attention to be sure no tree branches block the view of the sign. Once the sign begins to wear and fade in color, you need to replace it, no matter what the cost. The only thing worse than no sign is a sign in disrepair, indicating that you are not successful, or that you simply don't care.

The front door should have signage to indicate your company and the business hours. This can be lettering or a professional separate sign.

Facsimile Machines

Facsimile machines, or fax machines, are a necessity for a real estate office. These should be as fast as the broker can afford. They should be plain paper and adaptable to legal size. In a real estate office, a great deal of business is transacted using the fax machine. Contracts, notifications, and other valuable pieces of information are constantly faxed throughout a normal workday. Some real estate offices recognize the importance of a fax machine and have more than one at the office. With today's technology, computers and copiers can serve as fax machines, eliminating the need for space for the fax machine and saving the capital cost.

Personal Computers

Personal computers should be provided to the real estate salespeople. Not a computer per salesperson, but a few for all to use. There should be computers located in the computer room and the conference rooms. The computers should have a passcode to eliminate any trespassers. The computers should have a way to track which web sites the operators are viewing and should restrict what information can be downloaded.

Computer networks are very common in today's real estate company. The networks allow several individuals to work on the same project throughout the network. Software is very expensive, and a network allows multiple individuals to access the programs. With a normal computer system, you would have to buy software for every computer terminal, and the information would be more difficult to share.

High-Speed Internet

The real estate office should provide high-speed Internet service to their salespeople. Dial-up Internet access ties up telephone lines. Real estate salespeople use the computer to search the Internet or the Multiple Listing Service. They search listings to determine properties their clients may want to view and to help sellers determine the best possible price for their property. Without high-speed Internet, these searches would take forever.

Printers

Printers are used to print out information and pictures from the computer. The printers have a wide range of functions and quality. Some can print brochures that look as professional as anything on the market. Most real estate companies cannot afford the cost of such machines and have instead the standard black and white or color printers off the shelf, which is sufficient for most of the work a real estate salesperson needs. All other printing needs can be taken to the professional printers.

Some real estate companies spend money on one really good printer and network all computers in an office to that printer. The only problem with that is that when someone has a big project, it could back up the print jobs.

Copier

A generic copier makes reproductions of what is placed on the "glass" to be copied. Some have collators, sorters, staplers, enlargements, and multi-sided and multi-sized functions. All those things are great, but the broker/owner should do a "needs analysis" to determine what is really necessary. A copier salesperson is paid to get you to buy all the "add-ons," but don't buy them if you don't need them.

A typical real estate office should have one main copier for all the heavy workloads and a couple of smaller units for convenience. The main copier should collate and staple mass quantities of paper. There are forms and contracts that would require copies so the main copier needs to handle that production. It should have the capability to print in color for marketing pieces.

A copier can be linked to several computer terminals. This allows access to a top-of-the-line copier from the salesperson's desk so that he or she can print color documents directly to the main copier, eliminating the need for color printers at every desk.

Telephone Systems

One of the largest expenses of a start-up real estate company is the investment in a telephone system. The number and volume of calls, the number of telephones needed, and the number of lines all add to the cost of a system. Beware of spending the most money for the latest technological innovations, because they could be way beyond your needs or understanding. I learned of a broker who spent a fortune on that type of system, only to find out his people could not understand how to use it.

Desks

It is somewhat surprising the emphasis real estate salespeople place on their desks. It should be a place to work, but some feel it is a status symbol. The larger the desk, the more "productive" the real estate salesperson feels. This is counterproductive to the goals of the broker/owner because the larger the desks, the fewer salespeople an office can hold. Having more real estate salespeople does not correlate to the profitability of the office, but it usually doesn't hurt.

Some offices have desks that are shared among several real estate salespeople. If a salesperson needs a desk, he or she goes to one of the community desks and works. Once the salesperson is finished, he or she takes the paperwork too. These community desks are perfect for larger offices. Salespeople must produce to get desks of their own.

Chairs

Chairs are another of those "mine" items the real estate salespeople in an office claim. They will fight over the best chairs in an office. If someone leaves the company and leaves behind a special chair, one of the remaining salespeople will quickly take it. The chairs should have rollers to move around and should be comfortable, but they do not need to be the top of the line or ergonomically constructed. It does look more professional if they all match.

File Cabinets

File cabinets are an evil necessity—evil because they are typically ugly and always in the way, and necessary because they are absolutely required in a professional real estate office. Files should be kept on all employment contracts (listings and buyer-broker), current pending sales, and past sales. Files should be kept for at least ten years. Some attorneys claim you only have to keep files for three years. Others say you must keep them for a minimum of seven years. I feel safe if I keep them for ten years; better to be safe than sorry, especially when it comes to documentation.

Art

Art should be displayed throughout a real estate office, but at the very least in the main reception area and conference rooms. The art should be tasteful and conservative. It can be in the form of paintings, vases, tapestries, and floral arrangements. If you have display cases for awards the office has received, be sure the display is attractive and up-to-date. All of the art should be maintained and cleaned. The art does not have to be extremely expensive but it should definitely not be cheap. If you go cheap, don't bother—it will send a very bad message.

Library

As mentioned earlier, a library (at least several shelves in the broker's office) is a must in a real estate office. How else can you prove your commitment to the real estate business? How else can you expose your salespeople to better sales?

Office Supplies

To operate an office, you will need office supplies like staples, paper clips, and writing instruments. You will also need space to store all that is needed and some type of inventory tracking to be sure you don't run out of needed supplies. There is no worse beating than having to run to an office supply to pick up *one* item (even a very important item) because you have run out. You do not want to inventory too many supplies for two reasons. First, it takes up too much valuable space. Which would you rather have: a room full of paper clips or a room full of productive salespeople? The second major reason is to keep your honest salespeople honest. If you have a limited amount of supplies versus a room full of them, the salespeople will be less likely to take the supplies home.

Landscaping

Landscaping is one of those capital expense items that are most often forgotten. However, if the property you are buying or leasing has neglected the landscaping, you may have to compensate. Landscaping may be the first impression a potential client will receive. If your landscaping is impressive, you are impressive. If that impression is dead, so are you.

Make regular strolls around your property and bring a checklist that allows you to make notes on additions or subtractions you should make to your exterior landscaping. It is easily overlooked and neglected.

Conclusion

In choosing a real estate office, you must make countless decisions. The best advice I can give is to take your time. We make the decision to become the broker of our own offices, and then without hesitation we spend our money and open our doors. Upon reflection, I can advise you to spend more time laying out your business decisions before you make that leap.

Chapter Three Review Questions

1. In choosing the type of real estate office a broker should operate, what is *not* an important question to be asked?
   A. In what geographic areas do you want to specialize?
   B. To what particular group or race do you want to provide service?
   C. Do you believe in a family atmosphere or a corporate structure?
   D. What are your growth strategies for the business?

2. What type of office is a single broker working out of his or her home?
   A. Mom and Pop shops
   B. Single entity operations
   C. Sole proprietorships
   D. Dime operations

3. In what type of office have owners formed a specific "niche" that they solely operate?
   A. Offices that target only "high-end" property sales
   B. Community offices
   C. Boutique offices
   D. Offices located inside "strip" malls

4. What type of office has huge advertising budgets, broadened operations, and specialized agent services?
   A. Mom and Pop shops
   B. Marketing companies
   C. Franchises
   D. Mega-firms

5. The community office has all the following traits, *except*
- A. huge advertising budgets.
- B. members active in the local government or on school boards.
- C. participation in local charity events.
- D. respect of the area they serve.

6. All the following are benefits of a "sole proprietorship," *except*
- A. easy form of business.
- B. easy to operate.
- C. easy to sell.
- D. easy to avoid personal liability.

7. What type of tenancy provides that each partner cannot leave his or her interest in the venture to his or her heirs upon death?
- A. Joint tenancy with rights of survivorship
- B. Tenancy in common
- C. General tenancy
- D. Limited tenancy

8. What type of partnership allows an investor to assume only the liability of their investment?
- A. General partnership
- B. Joint venture
- C. Limited partnership
- D. No "legal" partnership allows this.

9. What is the building type of most residential real estate offices?
- A. Converted residential house
- B. Strip center
- C. Business plaza
- D. Stand-alone

10. Which of the following is not a valid reason to buy a building to house a real estate brokerage office?
- A. To help out a friend
- B. Rent replacement
- C. Area recognition
- D. Cost savings

11. All of the following are advantages to a tenant of a long-term rent agreement, *except*
A. flexibility to move.
B. avoidance of rent adjustments.
C. possibility of finish out paid by landlord.
D. assurance of location.

12. Which of the following is important in negotiating a lease?
A. Parking
B. Signage
C. Operational hours
D. All are of the above

13. The reception area should *not*
A. be located next to the bathrooms.
B. be painted with neutral and warm colors.
C. have a video screen to entertain guests.
D. be comfortable and inviting.

14. Private offices never
A. create motivation for those that want one.
B. create motivation for those that have one to keep it.
C. should be given based on productivity.
D. should be given based on time with the company.

15. Larger real estate offices may have all of the following separate rooms, *except*
A. computer room.
B. forms room.
C. equipment room.
D. incarceration room.

16. A real estate office should have a library for all the following reasons, *except*
A. it proves the broker is serious about the real estate business.
B. it allows salespeople a resource for self-paced training.
C. it provides a spot to store things.
D. it provides an in-house research center.

17. Which of the following business equipment is least important for the functionality of a real estate office?

A. Facsimile machine

B. Cappuccino machine

C. Copier

D. Telephone system

18. For the profitability of a real estate office, desks

A. are seen by some as a status symbol.

B. could be shared among several real estate salespeople.

C. should be given based on production.

D. all of the above.

4 Real Estate Brokerage Operations

The operations of a real estate brokerage include many different facets of business. All of the brokerage operations need to be analyzed to determine if they are being performed effectively and efficiently. The overall operations need to be compared to the mission and vision statements to be sure all operations are in line with the overall company goals.

Operations of a Real Estate Brokerage

A broker who is new to the business of real estate brokerage may begin to think that his or her activities are all over the place: running here and there, never having the time to breathe, let alone time to take lunch. This chapter breaks down the brokerage activities and explains the broker's role in the operations. The operations of a real estate brokerage include but are not limited to the following:

1. Day-to-day operations
2. Salespeople operations
3. Monthly operations
4. Yearly operations

Day-to-Day Operations

The day-to-day operations are things that have to be completed by the manager or assigned to another competent person. These things must be completed each and every day. Neglecting the accomplishment of day-to-day operations spells doom for many a brokerage.

The following are some items the broker needs to be monitoring on a day-to-day basis to avoid problems at a later date. Burying your head in the sand will not make these tasks disappear.

EXPENSES

Expenses are defined as the cost of doing business. Expenses are necessary, but if monitored, they can be reduced. Every penny saved in expenses is a penny added to the bottom line. Companies that are scraping by tend to not spend as much money as needed to make a profit. Companies that are making a lot of money tend to waste it. Be careful of both.

UTILITIES

Utilities are necessary for every real estate office, and include electric, water, garbage, telephone, and gas (natural and/or propane). Real estate brokers, owners, and/or managers should monitor all of these expenses to be sure they can save as much money as possible. The broker needs to look at expense trends with utilities to detect any drastic fluctuations in cost. These fluctuations could be a sign of problems. If the average gas bill is $120 per month and in a specific month it escalates to over $200, it may mean there is a leak in the gas lines somewhere and the gas company needs to be alerted. In an office owned by a friend of mine, the water bill was much greater than it should have been. The water company determined that the usage was occurring early in the morning. The broker spied on his office and found that the person next door was tapping the water spigot and watering his yard with the broker's water. Needless to say, that usage was stopped, but it would never have been taken care of had the broker not been so thorough.

All thermostats should be programmable and only by secure access. Telephone service, including long distance, should be investigated to find the best prices and deals. The telephones should have access codes for long distance to prevent misuse. Maybe the company in the office next door could share in the garbage collection and cost.

OFFICE CLEANING

Should the owner have to clean the office or have it cleaned professionally? You should not expect the salespeople to clean the office. At best they will pick up after themselves, and I wouldn't count on that. The owner may save some money by cleaning the office, but is that the best use of his or her time? If a cleaning service is hired, be sure the company is bonded and has references. You are entrusting the cleaning service with access to your office after hours. When negotiating with a cleaning company, be sure you have your wants and needs predetermined. Some questions you should ask yourself include:

1. Do you want to save a little money and let one of your salespeople's children clean the office, or should you pay a great deal more and have professionals do the job?

2. Does the office need to be cleaned every day?

3. Could the office trash be picked up once a week and a thorough cleaning be done only once per month?

4. Should the cleaning company clean the salespeople's desks?

5. Do the windows need cleaning and if so, how often?

6. Should the cleaning company stock bathroom supplies?

7. Should the cleaning company have its own cleaning equipment, or should you provide it in return for a discount?

All of these questions should be answered before you pick a cleaning company, or all of your efforts could be a waste.

LANDSCAPING

Landscaping ranges from planting a new bush to putting flowers in a pot to mowing and trimming the lawn. As with office cleaning, make sure you trust the company you hire.

When negotiating with a landscaping company, be sure you have your wants and needs predetermined. Some questions you should ask yourself include:

1. Do you want to save a little money and let one of your salespeople's children mow the grass, or should you pay more and have professionals do the job?

2. Does the property need to be maintained weekly, or is once per month adequate?

3. Do the trimmings need to be picked up?

4. Should the landscaping company have their own equipment, or should you provide it in return for a discount?

All of these questions should be answered before you pick a landscaping company.

MAINTENANCE

Office maintenance is the repair and remodeling that occurs in all offices. A window gets broken. The carpet gets worn. All of these things occur in offices all the time. Larger, multi-office companies usually have their own maintenance person or persons. Smaller companies without their own maintenance crew must hire from the outside. As with all that are hired to perform service for your company, the workers need to have credentials and be bonded.

Salespeople Operations

The broker should be keenly aware of the salespeople's actions. A broker's number one job is to take care of the salespeople. If a broker correctly understands the business, he or she will understand that the salesperson is the only asset. The copy machine is a necessity for a brokerage firm, but it will not make the broker a dime—it is clearly an expense. A broker needs to be spending a great deal of time observing the salespeople. A broker who is alert should watch for both burnout and slumps.

> ## *BURNOUT*
>
> *When a person concentrates on one aspect of his or her life and loses perspective and balance. After a period of time, the person will disengage from all activity and will go into seclusion, either physically or mentally. Once this occurs, no amount of motivation can shake the person out of it; only time will help. During the time of burnout, the person resembles someone with severe depression. Many brilliant real estate careers have been ruined because of burnout. The problem is that a person heading for burnout generally will not recognize it until it is too late.*

SLUMP

A slump occurs when a salesperson no longer has the motivation to do what is necessary to accomplish his or her goals. The slump is triggered by lack of success for actions taken. The salesperson is doing what he or she needs to do to be successful and yet is not receiving the expected rewards. This lack of success leads to the reduction in action, which leads to less and less chance of success until the salesperson no longer does anything.

Salespeople will go through both burnout and slumps. The successful broker will pay close attention to both of these situations. If the broker detects a salesperson who is heading for burnout, the broker must require the salesperson take time off away from real estate. This sounds counter to what a broker would want, but not doing so would be like killing the "Goose that lays the Golden Egg." Do you want to make a lot of money from a salesperson and then lose that person forever, or make steady income from a salesperson long term? Preventing burnout is best for both parties. I have had to take cell phones from salespeople and demand that I don't see them for three days. It might drive the salespeople "nuts" to be away from the business for that long but it is for the best. I have seen the surprise of salespeople when they come back and realize that their business is still there. Now they are reenergized to do even better with the knowledge they can take time for themselves. You can arrange for two real estate people to watch each other's business when they each take time off.

Burnout almost cost me my career. I was new in real estate and I had a family to support. I wanted to be a success so much that I devoted all my time to real estate. I had no balance. I did not spend time with my family. I did not go out. I did not spend time winding down. All I did was work on real estate matters. Because all of my time was spent on real estate and generating real estate income, I became a real estate success quickly. The problem was, my broker never spotted the "train wreck" that I was steaming toward. She was excited about my production. Within my first year, I became the top producer of the office and in the top ten of the entire real estate community. Then one day I couldn't do it any longer. I remember sitting in my office staring at the walls in a numb trance. I could not go home, and I could not conduct my real estate business. The problem with this is that I did not recognize my predicament. If I had had guidance, I could have taken a vacation and recharged and got back to business. Instead, this "funk" lasted almost eight months. My production fell to nil, and I lost all the contacts I had made previously. Once I realized what had happened (with help from a mentor, not my broker), I got back on track. I was so disillusioned by my broker that I went with a competitor and became their top producer—with time for family and myself. Notice the broker made a great deal of money from me quickly, but lost the long-term income I could have made for her. I would estimate that my burnout cost her over a half a million dollars of income!

A salesperson will also experience slumps in the real estate business. When brokers realize that salespeople are in a slump, their job is to encourage and motivate the salespeople to continue their activity until they see the success they want. Brokers first need to analyze their business plans to see if they are in line with their activity. New salespeople who want to make a million dollars their first year will experience a slump within the first three months when they haven't made a dime. Brokers need to work with those salespeople to help them make their goals and plans more realistic. Salespeople need to be encouraged that they can make a million dollars in their career, but maybe not their first year. Brokers need to reward the "slumpers" for the actions they have taken, rather than for the results of their actions. In my brokerages, I gave very few production awards; I gave action awards instead.

WAYS TO REWARD SALESPEOPLE

Most brokers give trophies and plaques for top producer, top lister, and top commissions earned. I gave awards for some of the following achievements.

MET PERSONAL GOALS   This is one of my favorite awards to give because not all people are on the same level. A person who has been in the business for years and has established numerous contacts may easily win the "Top Producer" award. It doesn't mean much to them because they would have produced that much anyway. The "Top Producer" award does not motivate new salespeople who realize they cannot compete with the veterans. The "Met Personal Goals" award rewards the achievement of personal goals that are not competitive with each other. Each person has a legitimate way to win.

NEW CONTACTS   Set a goal for each salesperson to call ten new contacts per week for twelve weeks. Anyone achieving that contact goal will win the award. The contacts can be geared to what you want. If you want your salespeople to contact more "For Sale By Owners," then make the award based on contacting FSBOs. The awards can be small trophies, gifts, or cash prizes. Again, all of your salespeople can participate and all have a legitimate way to win.

SMALL THINGS   Your job as a broker is to notice the small things salespeople are doing to accomplish their production goals. If you see them wearing their nametags in public, announce that at the next sales meeting and give them a small award. If you notice them calling homeowners that had their house listed with a real estate company but now that agreement has expired, reward them. Some brokers walk around with lottery scratch-off tickets or actual cash to give to those who are doing the small things to build their business. Be careful here; only reward those things you want repeated. Do not reward someone for making the coffee instead of prospecting.

RECRUITING OPERATIONS

Recruiting is such an important operation we have set aside an entire chapter to discuss that topic. See Chapter 9.

MARKETING OPERATIONS

Like recruiting, marketing operations is such an important operation we have set aside an entire chapter to discuss that topic. See Chapter 5.

Monthly Operations

Monthly operations must be performed each and every month. These operations should be set up on a schedule so you do not forget about them while you are conducting day-to-day operations.

ACCOUNTING

Accounting must be a daily task for the staff, but brokers should analyze the results at least monthly. Accounting should provide monthly reports, charts, and graphs showing how the real estate brokerage is doing financially. Accounting should provide at least the following reports:

- Income/expense report
- Break-even report
- Accounts payable/receivable
- Balance sheet
- Salesperson production report

Each of these reports will be discussed at a later time. We will look at how a broker reviews some of the monthly operations in the next section.

MEETINGS

Brokers need to have certain meetings in any given month. They should meet with all of their managers, staff, and salespeople on a monthly basis. The broker should have scheduled "sales meetings" in which he or she updates the salespeople on the activities of the office. The details of the sales meeting are discussed in a later chapter. Depending on your office needs, you may feel that weekly meetings are more appropriate.

If you have managers, you should meet with them monthly to be sure you are on the same track and that they are meeting their specific goals. You may want to hold weekly conference calls to be sure that you don't wait for an entire month to discuss important topics with them.

You should meet with each of your salespeople each and every month. You may be able to delegate these meetings either to either managers or to assistant managers, but it is *your* duty to arrange this. These meetings can be informal, such as stopping by the salesperson's office and simply chatting. You just want to make contact with them in person. One major reason salespeople leave an office is because they don't feel their broker is around and/or they have no relationship with their broker. By requiring yourself to meet each salesperson once a month, you can head off such problems.

Yearly Operations

Yearly operations may be the most important for long-term viability, but they don't necessarily have to be revisited on a daily basis.

COMPANY DIRECTION

The broker needs to be continually aware of the company direction. However, the broker needs to sit down at least once a year with the key players of the brokerage firm and discuss the company direction and any changes the market requires. The key players could be any staff members, respected salespeople, managers, or outside counselors, accountants, bankers, and businesspeople. Preferably, the meeting will not be held at the real estate office. If this is not possible, be sure to hold all calls and interruptions. This meeting only occurs once a year, so take it seriously.

This meeting should address the current status of the real estate business. All the accounting reports should be readily available. The meeting should discuss any new directions in order to keep ahead of the market trends. The meeting should include business planning to give guidance to day-to-day operations. This will be a lengthy meeting. so plan accordingly.

VACATION

This is one thing that the broker never thinks about. Remember burnout? Brokers can easily fall into that trap as well; the problem is that no one is around to help them recognize it. A saving grace can be taking at least one two-week vacation per year during which you have no contact with your office. Arrange for your duties to be taken care of by your staff or by a salesperson in manager's training. Do not neglect yourself.

Conclusion

The professional real estate broker should take into consideration all of the factors above in setting up operations as a real estate brokerage. Each one can be a cost savings or an expense—it all depends upon the diligence of the broker.

Chapter Four Review Questions

1. What is defined as a cost of doing business?
   A. Taxes
   B. Work
   C. An expense
   D. Profit analysis

2. Which of the following is not considered a utility expense?

A. Water

B. Telephone

C. Garbage

D. Advertising

3. When choosing an office cleaning company, the following are all questions to consider, *except*

A. do you require professionals to do the job?

B. does the office need to be cleaned every day?

C. should the cleaning company stock bathroom supplies?

D. is the cleaning company within five miles of your office?

4. When choosing a landscaping company, the following are all questions to consider, *except*

A. do you require professionals to do the job?

B. does the property need to be landscaped weekly, or is once per month adequate?

C. should the landscaping company have its own equipment, or should you provide it in return for a discount?

D. is the landscaping company within five miles of your office?

Real Estate Brokerage Marketing

Marketing in the real estate brokerage business is the single most expensive effort that is undertaken. Much of the marketing a real estate company provides is wasted and should not have been tried. This section will help alleviate those mistakes.

Services Offered to the General Public

The services offered to the public need to be carefully analyzed to determine if they meet the company's mission, vision, and culture statements. Choosing the wrong services to offer will cause confusion and frustration, which leads to failure. These services need to be viewed in terms of how they affect the public and the bottom line.

Residential

Most real estate companies are residential in nature. The larger the city, the more specialized the office will become. In metropolitan areas, real estate offices will tend to concentrate on a narrow range of clients, such as a particular community. In a more rural area, the real estate office may have to perform such diverse duties as residential, commercial, and farm and ranch.

Residential real estate companies handle the sale of homes for their clients. They also handle the purchase of homes by their clients. Residential real estate salespeople must be better at relationships than their commercial counterparts. Brokers of residential real estate company must be aware of the relationship aspect of this industry and coach their salespeople into greater success.

Commercial

Those offices that specialize in commercial brokerage will need to choose their niche. Commercial includes small retail, big box, office, industrial, business brokerage, and high-rise, to name a few. Brokers will concentrate their efforts on one or only a few of those types of commercial brokerage.

Commercial brokers deal with clients in a more business-like manner than do their residential counterparts. Commercial brokers rarely work weekends or after normal business hours. The commercial broker deals with little emotion and mostly facts: Does the purchase make economic sense?

Property Management

Property management occurs when a property owner who is renting property no longer wants the duties associated with being an active landlord. The duties a property manager performs on behalf of an owner include:

- Leasing
- Contract negotiation
- Rent collection
- Reporting
- Marketing

The property manager and the owner typically have a general agency relationship that allows the property manager the right to bind the owner to lease agreements with tenants.

Farm and Ranch

Farm and ranch type properties are the large-acreage ranches located away from any major city. There are many unique challenges to marketing and selling these properties. Some buyers will negotiate a crop that is in the field. Some buyers will want all the livestock that is present. How much is cross-fencing with cable and pipe construction? Is the property a working ranch or a show place? Could the property be leased as hunting land or farmland? A farm and ranch broker may have to market worldwide to find just the right buyer for a particular ranch.

Fine Homes and Estates

Upper-end properties are referred to as "fine homes and estates." Like the farm and ranch type properties, the ultra-high priced homes are unique in that there are few eligible buyers for them. The interest in a multi-million dollar luxury estate may be high, but an actual qualified buyer may be rare.

To adequately market a fine home, the broker may require the seller to pay an up-front marketing fee. If not, the real estate company may well invest thousands of dollars before seeing any income from these types of properties.

Vacation

A true specialty in the real estate sales business is the marketing and sales of vacation properties. Usually thought of as resort type properties, they can actually be found around any lake or recreation area. Buyers for these types of properties must be able to afford their current residence while also affording the payments on their vacation home.

Some vacation properties of are the *time-share* variety. A time-share has multiple owners, each having one or two weeks per year that is theirs. The rest of the year the property belongs to each of the other owners. The reason time-share properties work is that most resorts are for the vacationer who has a week or two away from work and wants to spend it relaxing and enjoying some time off.

Areas Served

The broker/owner will need to spend a great deal of time deciding what areas to serve. Picking too broad of an area will dilute the marketing efforts, and choosing an area too small will diminish the total number of possible sales.

The area can be chosen because of location, such as proximity to the brokerage office; because of its proximity to a business; because of sales projections, as when trends indicate increase growth for that area over next decade; or based on a natural amenity, such as a nearby lake or other natural attraction. All of these decisions will determine how the marketing dollar will be spent.

Hard-Dollar Costs to the Brokerage Firm

The following services are *hard-dollar* costs and are provided to serve the client. These services will also help the salespeople, but they should be viewed separately. The broker/owner also must determine if the company will pay for each service, or whether the salesperson must pay.

Hard-dollar costs are those that actually take money from the active bank accounts of the company. One cost not included in this measurement would be the time involved to see a project through to its completion. It is very difficult for brokers to determine the cost to charge their customers if they have no idea how much it costs to provide the service.

Marketing

Marketing is the overall concept of offering a property for sale to the general public. Good marketing reaches more people than if no marketing occurred. The brokerage firm wants to market the office and their inventory of properties. The more people that know about a real estate office, the better chance that broker will have to recruit new salespeople. The more people that know a property is available, the better chance it has to sell for the most money in the fastest time. Marketing does not sell an overpriced property, but it will help sell the properties that are priced correctly. Advertising is only one aspect of marketing, but probably the most recognizable.

> *"Advertising is the fine art of convincing people that debt is better than frustration."*[1]

Each real estate company will market its listing inventory in the way it feels is the best for its clients given the resources the company can apply. Real estate companies can market a property many different ways, but newspaper advertising is the most widely known. Most companies place listings on a rotating basis depending on the number of listings in their inventory and the advertising space available. A rotating basis simply means that if the real estate company has slots for advertising ten properties each week and is carrying 100 properties, each property will be in the advertisement every ten weeks.

---

[1] "Advertising Humor & Quotes," Tom Antion & Associates, http://www.antion.com/humor/speakerhumor/advertising.htm.

Company Marketing Strategies

A marketing strategy is a brokerage firm's overall marketing direction. It should guide the broker in the decision-making process for spending money and spending time. The marketing strategy should include projections for what you want to accomplish by marketing. It should detail the philosophies and concepts you will employ. It should be mostly in text format with very little in numbers and finite dates. Those items will be in the company's marketing plan.

McDonald's dominates the fast-food market. It discovered that the most vocal group when it comes to choosing where to eat is usually the children. McDonald's strategy was to specialize in what the decision maker wants most, and in the case of children, it's a hamburger, French fries, and soda.

McDonald's targets the advertising to children, and it works. As the broker, you need to determine who the decision makers are for your service and then give them what they want, and you will be a success.

Your marketing strategy is the reason behind marketing for your company. What are you trying to accomplish? What are your short-term goals? What are your long-term goals? The marketing strategy is not specific but written in general terms. You can have multiple marketing strategies, but it is not recommended. Multiple marketing strategies divide your loyalties and double your expenses. Limit yourself to one main area of marketing, and then sell to anyone. Remember, just because you did not market to a person does not mean you cannot help them.

The marketing strategy is used to monitor all your marketing ideas. Before you spend a cent on marketing you must ask yourself, "Is this in alignment with my marketing strategy?" Your marketing strategy can be as simple as: "My main focus for marketing is First-Time Home Buyers in the Garland area between $60,000 and $120,000." So you would refuse to pay for advertising in "Elite Homes" magazine that offers properties of $500,000 or more.

Company Marketing Plan

The company marketing plan should put forth in an orderly manner the company marketing strategy that has already been developed. It should have each step detailed with exacting standards. Each step should have a beginning date and an end date. Each step should be analyzed to determine its purpose and whether it aligns itself with the marketing strategy. The costs of each step need to be analyzed to determine the best approach. All contact people should be addressed. If you, as the broker, are directly involved in any step, your time needs to be analyzed. Finally, the entire marketing plan needs to be compared to your competition and what they are doing. A complete stranger should be able to pick up your marketing plan and understand all aspects of it.

All types of promotion, marketing, and advertising should be included in the company marketing plan. All planned promotional events, direct mail campaigns, or advertising in your local newspaper needs to be included. If you do advertise, you will need to separate name recognition advertising from prospect generating advertising.

Name Recognition vs. Prospect Generating

Name recognition advertising gets people to know your name and what you do. It is used to create a name that the public will know and will want to do business with. It is not done to make the prospect call you on the telephone; that is prospect generating advertising. These two are often mistaken. If billboard ads say, "Call me at 817-555-1212," we think that is prospect generating advertising. It is not, even though you might get a call. Your pretty face plastered on a billboard is just to get people to know your face, name, and what you do. Name recognition advertising is critical to making your job easier, but it is expensive and takes a long time to work. Most national real estate companies spend millions per year on name recognition advertising. Examples of name recognition advertising include, but are not limited to, television advertising, radio advertising, bus stop benches, airplane trailer banners, personal brochures, shopping cart cards, name badges, career apparel, and car signs. This type of advertising is very expensive because of the media and frequency that must be used. Companies like McDonald's, IBM, Home Depot, and General Motors also spend millions so you recognize their names. You can even visualize their logos without seeing each one, can't you?

Prospect generating advertising makes the telephone ring. Ads showing houses for sale in the newspaper make the phone ring. If you are on a limited budget, you should concentrate on prospect generating advertising to get the most for your money and let your competition worry about name recognition advertising. Examples of prospect generating advertising include telephone directories, direct mail, yard "for sale" signs, and business cards, to name a few. Determining which type of advertising is right for you will be part of your company's marketing strategy.

Every dollar spent in this medium is meant to generate business. A picture of a house is advertised to get a potential buyer interested enough to pick up the telephone and call the real estate company. Real estate salespeople spend most of their marketing budget in this area.

Marketing Budget

The marketing budget spells out the money to be spent in the marketing plan. The plan should budget the money for marketing for an entire year. The marketing budget needs to be an act of self-discipline. If the money isn't there, don't spend it! The budget should analyze the money in the bank and the anticipated income for the year. If a *great* marketing idea is presented but it will wreck your budget, you cannot do it until you have the money in the budget. Too many good brokers have gone down because they banked on a marketing campaign and then the marketing did not work and there was no more money to do anything different. Ten percent of all you earn in your real estate brokerage should be put back into the budget.

Marketing Campaign

A marketing campaign is the marketing of individual properties in alignment with the marketing strategy, marketing plan, and marketing budget. Campaigns are ongoing and continuous. You should have several operating at one time. One marketing campaign might be to get the listing on 2345 Montgomery Street sold. You can also have a marketing campaign to recruit three new salespeople from the Summerfield area.

There are several benefits to a good marketing campaign. The word *campaign* refers to the fact that it is a continuous effort until the property is sold. One of the major reasons to market a property is to increase the number of people who know the property is available. We learned back in Economics 101 that the more exposure a product receives, the faster the product will sell. What marketing will not do is get a property more money than the open market will give. Sellers expect that we can use our expert marketing skills to get them more money than they could get themselves. This simply is not true. We can expose a "well-priced" property to the market and get it sold faster than a seller can.

Advertising

Advertising is the most common and widely used form of marketing. Advertising is a passive way to market a property because we run an ad and then wait until a prospect calls us. Advertising can be very expensive. Running a full-page ad in *The Wall Street Journal* could cost $30,000 per issue—not smart on a $60,000 house. Advertising does not need to be expensive, so be careful before you spend.

Writing Effective Ad Copy

When preparing ad copy, you should first determine the purpose of the advertisement. Is the ad to promote the real estate company or to sell a real estate property to benefit a client? The broker should analyze the property or the brokerage firm and decide on the advantages and benefits. Decide to which potential client you are trying to appeal. Adding personal appeal to your ad copy is critical to its success.

> *"If you think advertising doesn't work, consider the millions of Americans who now think yogurt tastes good."*
>
> *—Joe L. Whitley, management consultant*

Every classified ad should carry the reader through four selling steps. In the advertising community, the four steps have the acronym of AIDA, which are:

1. ATTRACT ATTENTION: For example, use a catchy headline. The headline is probably the most important part in writing an ad. You need to catch your prospect within the first few words, or you will lose them forever. Always document your results to determine the best use of your money. Use a lot of white space (that space where nothing is written). White space in print advertising attracts attention to your ad(s). Occasionally ask questions in your ad. People have a natural tendency to be attracted to questions.

2. AROUSE INTEREST: To arouse interest, tie the body copy into the heading. Create interest and desire by listing features and detailing the benefits of those features to the clients. The interest stage is your

opportunity to get them to want to read further. If you do not create interest, the prospect stops reading and moves on to the next ad.

3. CREATE <u>DESIRE</u>: To create desire, list only the best features and benefits. The desire stage creates that intense desire to have the services promised. Writing skill is necessary here to create the right atmosphere for the prospects. The prospects should be able to see themselves living in that house or working at your office. Anything less, and you will not receive a phone call.

4. CALL FOR <u>ACTION</u>: The call for action is a must for advertising. It tells the prospect what to do, such as "better hurry" and "call now." Ads are written and sold exactly the same way, and in order to get the sale, you must ask for the sale. In ad writing, you must ask for the call.

    - Research has found that you will receive a greater response if you close the ad with a request to call, using your full name.

    - Research has found that by using the word *please,* the close is softened and greater response occurs. So *pleeeeease* call for action in your ads.

If your copy tells all the essential facts clearly, holds the reader's attention from start to finish, and makes a specific call to action, it will be successful. The following is a checklist for writing the ad:

1. Organize all the facts from the viewpoint of the reader—not your own.

2. Appeal to emotions, such as love of comfort, status, family responsibility, and so forth.

3. Keep It Simple and Short (KISS). Avoid long, windy sentences; however, do not abbreviate. If it is important enough to put in an ad, it is important enough to spell out. Sometimes we get so close to real estate that we forget what it is like to be a consumer, so let's look at it from another direction. I once wanted to buy a mini-pickup truck. I would read ads in the newspaper that had the word "OBO" at the end. Now what does a musical instrument have to do with buying a truck? Okay, so I knew they were not talking about a musical instrument, but I really did not know what the letters "OBO" meant. Guess what? I never called in response to those ads. It could have been a great truck, but I would not call and be embarrassed by my lack of knowledge. I have a friend who has a used car lot, and I asked him what "OBO" meant. He got a big laugh and I now know it is "Or Best Offer." My point is, don't eliminate your potential client by using cute abbreviations, because someone might not know their meaning.

4. Use meaningful words that stir emotion. If you are recruiting, make the reader "wade through the money they will make at your office," or if you are marketing a property, let them feel the "cool" water across their skin when they jump into their new swimming pool.

5. Inspire confidence. Don't use exaggerated descriptions that are not believable.

6. Write copy just long enough to tell the whole story. Flowery expressions and literary gymnastics will not hold the reader's interest.

7. Avoid clichés and overused words such as "super" and "great."

8. Clients buy houses and real estate; salespeople buy brokers. For effective marketing in real estate, do not mix marketing strategies. Advertise for one or the other but not both in the same advertisement.

9. Stick to the truth. Misleading advertising is illegal and unethical.

10. If you want to use a slogan, keep it to seven words or fewer; otherwise, it becomes counterproductive. For even better results, keep the slogan to three words or fewer.

11. Keep in mind that the average person retains one percent of what he or she sees each day, and that the average person inherently mistrusts and sometimes fears things and people that are not familiar.

12. Advertising campaigns should be no less than weekly for a minimum of three months.

Here are some other questions you should ask:

- Do people like your ad?
- Is your ad memorable?
- Does your ad give you personality?
- Does your ad provide a simple message?

Research has found that the more meaningful the message, the more it is received. Research has also found that there is an inverse relationship between the number of messages in any given ad and the effectiveness of its results.

Once an ad has been run, you should do the following:

1. Change the ad layout and words each time.

2. Experiment with features of the ad. If it isn't working, change it!

3. Document the calls received with each change. This will track the correct changes and the ones that did not work. Don't make the same mistakes twice.

> *Advertising is salesmanship in print.*

The real estate company pays for all of the company print advertising. The broker makes a determination about which publication to use and then specifies which properties to advertise. If the brokerage company has a marketing director, this would be his or her job. The salesperson has the right to advertise separately, but the broker would not participate in the cost.

FAIR HOUSING LAW GUIDELINES

The Fair Housing Law encompasses the notion that you should describe the property, not the seller, landlord, or appropriate buyers and tenants. As a broker, you are ultimately responsible for all the advertising that leaves your office. Your standard policy should be to review the advertising before it hits the media. The law does not look at your intent. Do your actions indicate a discriminatory behavior?

RACE, COLOR, NATIONAL ORIGIN   Real estate advertisements should state no discriminatory preference or limitation on account of race, color, or national origin. Use of words describing the current or potential residents, or the neighbors or neighborhood in racial or ethnic terms, will create liability. Phrases such as "master bedroom," "rare find," or "desirable neighborhood" are not in violation.

RELIGION   Advertisements should not contain an explicit preference, limitation, or discrimination on account of religion. Advertisements that use the legal name of an entity containing a religious reference or those containing a religious symbol standing alone may indicate a religious preference. However, if such an advertisement includes a disclaimer (such as the statement "this home does not discriminate on the basis of race, color, religion, national origin, sex, handicap, or familial status"), it will not violate the act. Advertisements containing descriptions of properties or services that do not on their face state a preference for persons likely to make use of those facilities will not violate of the act.

The use of secularized terms or symbols relating to religious holidays, such as Santa Claus, the Easter Bunny, or St. Valentine's Day images, or phrases such as "Merry Christmas," "Happy Easter," or the like, does not constitute a violation of the act.

SEX (GENDER)   Advertisements for single-family dwellings or separate units in a multi-family dwelling should contain no explicit preference, limitation, or discrimination based on sex (gender). Use of the term "master bedroom" does not constitute a violation of either the "sex" provisions or the race discrimination provisions. Terms such as "mother-in-law suite" and "bachelor apartment" are commonly used as physical descriptions of housing units and do not violate the act.

HANDICAP   Real estate advertisements should not contain explicit exclusions, limitations, or other indications of discrimination based on a handicap. Advertisements containing descriptions of properties, services or facilities, or neighborhoods do not violate the act. Advertisements describing the conduct required of residents do not violate the act. Advertisements containing descriptions of accessibility features are lawful.

FAMILIAL STATUS   Advertisements may not state an explicit preference, limitation, or discrimination based on familial status. Advertisements may not contain limitations on the number or ages of children, or state a preference for adults, couples, or singles. Advertisements describing the property, services and facilities, or neighborhoods are not discriminatory and do not violate the act.

Fair Housing Law Guidelines Acceptable Wording   The following words are directly from the HUD and are printed to aid in writing advertisements that do not discriminate.

- **Acceptable Wording**

Close to schools (or generic places)	One bedroom apartment
Den	Family room
No smoking/drinking	Number of bedrooms
Play area	Private setting
Privacy	School district
Secluded	Security provided
Seniors	Townhouse
View	Square footage
Traditional (style of home)	Walking distance to . . .

- **Questionable Wording**

55 and older (restrictions)	Older persons
Executive	Female roommate
Male roommate	Neighborhood

Remember: Describe the property, not the seller, landlord, or appropriate buyers and tenants.

- **Unacceptable Wording**

Adult (adult building, adult park, etc.)	Adults only/Adults preferred
Age (any specification)	Bachelor/Bachelor pad
Any use of girl, lady, or woman	Any use of boy, guy, or man
Black	(Blank) need not apply
Blind	Board approval
Catholic church	Christian
Couple (couples preferred, only, etc.)	Crippled
Deaf	Drinker(s)
Ethnic landmarks	Executive, exclusive
Family	Female
Gentleman's farm, ranch, etc.	Grandma's house
Gender (except ads for roommates)	Handicap limitations
Hispanic	Integrated
Jewish	Male/Man
Marital status	Mature or mature person
Membership approval	Name of school
Mentally handicapped/Mentally ill	Mormon temple
Nationality (Oriental, Hispanic, etc.)	No children
No family problems	No play area
Number of people	Older person
One child	Oriental
Perfect for two	Private, private community
Physically fit (ideal for, limited to)	Race
Religious landmark	Religious name
Restricted	Retired
Senior citizen, senior discount	Sex

Single, single person	Smoker(s)
Traditional (settings)	Two people
Unattached (referring to a relationship)	White woman
Words descriptive of landlords or tenants	Young, energetic person

ADVERTISEMENTS THAT COMPLY WITH REG Z The Truth-in-Lending Act (REG Z) was enacted in 1969 to "assure the meaningful disclosure of credit terms so that the consumer will be able to compare more readily the various credit terms available to him to avoid the uniformed use of credit." The Act refers to regulations to be established by the Federal Reserve Board. In response to this requirement, the Board came out with Regulation Z.

One of the specific forms of credit requiring disclosures is residential mortgage transactions. Special rules exist for advertising of mortgages, which apply to any ad for the sale of real estate containing financing information.

For several years, REG Z was the final word in determining compliance with the law. In 1976 Congress sanctioned another authority for determining compliance, the "Official Staff Interpretation." Since then, several "Official Staff Commentaries" have been issued to clarify specific issues and make compliance easier.

Facts about Advertising and REG Z

1. REG Z only applies to the advertising on one- and two-unit residential real property.

2. REG Z only applies to advertising where the potential consumer will use the property as a principal dwelling. Advertisements to sell the following types of properties must comply:

   A. Single-family detached

   B. Duplex

   C. Two detached units on one legal description

   D. Townhouses

   E. Condominiums

   F. Houseboats

   G. Cooperative housing unit

   H. Farms and ranches used primarily for residential purposes

   I. Mobile homes and trailers (also applies if these are considered personal property)

3. If your advertisement promotes the sale of the following types of real property you do not need to comply with REG Z:

   A. Vacant land

   B. Business or commercial real estate

   C. Industrial

   D. Residential rentals with three or more units

   E. Farms and ranches primarily used for agricultural purposes

4. For fixed-rate loans, if you advertise you must also advertise:

   A. Annual percentage rate

   B. Simple interest rate

   C. Down payment

   D. Monthly payment

   E. Loan term (length)

These laws and regulations are to protect the consumer from being discriminated against. As the broker, you must be aware of these laws and communicate them to your sales force.

Frequency

Frequency refers to the number of exposures and the amount of time between exposures. Needless to say, the more exposures to the open market, the more chance the *right* buyer will see the property. Real estate professionals continually market a property through a variety of media and have the capital to publish the property with the proper frequency.

Advertising Media

There are a variety of types of advertising media, the most relevant of which are described here.

PRINT

Print advertising is running an ad in any print media. The mainstay for the real estate industry has been the print media, which includes the newspaper (national, local, and special), magazines, and any homes guides. There are several types of print media.

NEWSPAPERS Newspapers are publications that are run on a repeated frequency basis. The newspaper sells itself to readers by printing interesting and newsworthy stories. The way the newspaper makes its money is by selling ad space. The better and the larger location, the more it will cost to run an ad. If you want the front page, you will have to pay dearly for it, because that is the space most con-

sumers see first. If you are willing to have your ad buried in the middle of the newspaper somewhere, you will pay less, but will anyone you want see it? These are the considerations you must make before running a newspaper ad.

International Newspapers International newspapers are newspapers from other countries or that reach international markets. Both are probably too expensive and not conducive to real estate sales in your local market area. The only exception is if you have information about a business move to your area from a foreign country. In this case, you could market your company to people in the affected area in their local newspaper.

National Newspapers National newspapers are newspapers that reach the entire nation. These are newspapers like: *The Wall Street Journal, The Chicago Times, The New York Times,* and *USA Today,* to name a few. Again, these newspapers are too expensive and not conducive to real estate sales in your local market area. The only reason you might want to use a national newspaper is if you are marketing a high-dollar estate and you want to reach top executives. Be careful with your marketing budget on this one. Here is a thought: if the seller demands that you advertise in a national newspaper, tell him or her that you must have an up-front "marketing fee" of $50,000. The fee will be taken off the real estate commission when and if the property sells. This is a brave statement, but it will back the seller off or get you one heck of an advertising budget for that specific property.

Local Newspapers Local newspapers are newspapers that typically reach a local area or region. For example, in Fort Worth, Texas, the major local newspaper would be *The Fort Worth Star-Telegram.* A real estate company will spend most of its print advertising budget dollars in local advertising. This type of advertising not only gets properties sold, but also makes a good and active name for your real estate company. Print advertising is dwindling because of the Internet, but at the current time it is still very popular.

Community Newspapers   Community newspapers are distributed to a limited area, usually a small community or neighborhood. In Azle, Texas, the major local newspaper would be *The Fort Worth Star-Telegram* but the community newspaper would be the *Azle News*. Local independent real estate companies use community newspapers quite effectively. These companies want to create a name for themselves, and the community newspaper is a great place to do that.

Community newspapers tend to be less expensive than local newspapers because their circulation is less than that of the local papers. The cost of a full-page advertisement in a community newspaper would get you a small block ad in the local newspaper.

For Sale By Owner Newspapers   These newspapers are more a kind of specialized advertisement paper or magazine than an actual newspaper. They carry ads for individuals selling small-dollar items like lawnmowers, bicycles, and furniture. Some of these ad magazines specialize in selling cars or real estate. The papers that carry small dollar items are not the best spot for selling high-dollar properties.

MAGAZINES   Actual "interest" magazines are different than newspapers because issues come out less frequently and the content focuses on only a few key topics. Real estate is not best promoted in a magazine; it tends to be more fluid than magazines allow. Running an ad in a magazine may take several months from idea to issue. It would be an incredible waste of money to advertise a property that sold before the issue hit the stands. Sure, you may get calls, but the callers may feel you are misrepresenting the property. Magazine ads are usually for national real estate companies that are advertising for name recognition.

REAL ESTATE MAGAZINES   Real estate magazines are solely dedicated to advertising current active properties for sale. They usually feature pictures of the houses with a small amount of information on the property. These magazines are frequently distributed to airports, grocery stores, and convenience stores. They contain some of the best print advertising space available. The people who pick these up are serious about buying a property. You are directly marketing to the target group interested in your product. The best places in the magazine are the inside front cover and the back cover, and those spots are also the most expensive.

YARD SIGNS

The independent broker must decide the type, size, and layout of the yard signs they provide. There are two basic types:

1. Post—Large wood or composite material post in an "L" shape with the sign panel made of steel and hanging from the arm of the post. The advantage of these signs is their size because they make a statement and can be seen from several blocks away. The downside is that the initial cost is greater, and they are so difficult to install that a sign company is needed to take care of the installation. The sign company charges a fee for each sign that they place on a property. Additional charges from the sign company occur if the signs get damaged or the sign company has to drive out of the city. The real estate company usually pays for the metal panels and then the salesperson pays the sign company to put them up on their listing.

2. Stake—The stake sign is usually all steel or aluminum and smaller in size than its post counterpart. Because of its smaller size, most real estate salespeople can place them in their cars and install them without the need of professionals. The cost of the signs is usually less than purchasing the post sign. The real estate company ordinarily buys the stake signs, and the real estate salespeople will check out one at a time to place on each of their listings. Some real estate companies use both the stake and the post signs. The stake sign is used for lower-priced properties and those on the outskirts of the city. The post sign would be reserved all other types of listings.

SIGN RIDERS Sign riders are the metal information attachments that are placed on yard signs. These can be used to identify a specific number to call, identify the listing agent, advertise a special feature of the property, or announce the status of the property and showing instructions. The riders give additional valuable information to any potential buyer who may be driving by. Riders make the real estate sign more interesting and relate information for that specific property.

Usually the information riders ("lakefront, 4 bedroom, and pool," for example) are purchased and provided by the broker. The riders that identify the salesperson and his or her telephone numbers are provided by the salesperson.

Buyers who drive by will tend to have more interest in calling about a property if the rider identifies a feature that is of interest to them. This is another investment into your office that you should make as soon as possible. Then actually make sure they are put up. I have seen real estate brokers spend the money to buy company sign riders that then sit on the floor in their office because the salespeople are too lazy to put them up. If you are going to leave the sign riders on the floor of your office, don't bother buying them because studies have shown that buyers will not walk into your office and pick up a company sign rider just to call your office.

INFORMATION BOXES   Information boxes or tubes are also attached to the yard signs. Inside the box or tube are information sheets that offer the consumer data on the particular property and usually a picture of the property on a high-quality paper. These are protected from the weather by the box or tube. Most real estate offices require their salespeople to buy these if the salesperson so desires.

KEY BOXES

Key boxes (also called lock boxes) are usually placed on the outside of the front door of a listing providing a key to real estate salespeople with the authorized access codes. The key box is a necessity in marketing a property for sale, but you can also use these to market your office.

Go to any crafts store and purchase 1/8-inch rubber foam board. Cut the board out to match the width of your key boxes, but allow several inches above the key box and several inches left below the key box. Use this space to market yourself. Above the key box have the words, "Professionally marketed by Acme Real Estate." Below the box have your office contact information. Tell the sellers you are placing this foam board behind the key box to protect their door from scratches. Never miss an opportunity to market your company. Your salespeople can do this, but most don't. They don't want to spend the money and take the time to make these.

These boxes come in two basic styles:

1. Electronic—Electronic key boxes allow access by means of an electronic key card. The advantage of this type of key box is that the electronic key box keeps electronic records of all who have gained access and of

all the properties that have been accessed. Both provide immense protection in case of a break-in or fair housing accusation.

2. Combination—Combination key boxes allow access by means of a combination of either numbers or letters. These are like the old "locker" type of lock where you turn the dial and it unlocks with the right sequence of letters or numbers. The advantage of this type of key box is that everyone you allow can get access. The disadvantage is that there is no record of how many times access was given or that someone gained access by illegally obtaining the passcode.

Some sellers are apprehensive about placing a key outside their door. I had a seller who refused to allow a key box on his door. I went to my car and got out a key box and brought it back inside with me. I handed it to the seller and told him if he could get the key out in less than a minute I would give him ten dollars. He struggled, pried, banged, and pounded the key box for a while. I turned to his wife and I casually asked her whether, if she were a burglar wanting to enter the house, it would not be faster just to break the window. She laughed, and he allowed the key box to be placed on the door.

The broker may purchase a few key boxes for emergency use for their salespeople, but most brokers make their salespeople provide their own key boxes. When the salesperson *owns* the key box, they seem to take better care of it.

COMPANY BROCHURES

Company brochures are usually tri-fold brochure-type letters that introduce your company and tell about your office accomplishments. Like the personal brochures salespeople use to market themselves, these are to be used to market to other salespeople to get them to work for your company. These are to be used sparingly. Their cost prohibits mass mailings. You should send them to any potential recruits you may have and leave them with anyone you talk to about a real estate career. The difference between these and business cards is that everyone gets your business cards, but company brochures are to be given only to serious prospects.

You can use your personal computer, if you have that capability, to make and print these company brochures. If you do it yourself, be sure you do it well. A cheap brochure means a cheap real estate company and broker. There are printing companies that do company brochures, but the cost is high.

MULTIPLE LISTING SERVICE

The Multiple Listing Service (MLS) allows a property to be exposed throughout the world. Buyers transferring from out of state can find houses that are currently for sale on the MLS. Some services are more protective and allow only members on the site. Other services allow the consumer on in limited fashion through the Internet. A majority of real estate sales result from MLS, and almost every residential real estate company I know of is part of a local MLS.

The Multiple Listing Service is the best possible way to market your listings. Over 70 percent of property sold is sold through the MLS. Most real estate brokers take for granted the power of the MLS to market their company. Many real estate companies input the listing data into the MLS for their salespeople. If this is true for your company, be sure to make some comment in the "Remarks" section to help market your company. Such things as the following are appropriate:

- "Acme Real Estate professionally offers this property for sale."

- "For a personal tour, please call Acme Real Estate."

- "For additional information on this property, please call Acme Real Estate."

- "For information on similar properties, please call Acme Real Estate."

Any way you can mention what you do or how you do it is helpful in marketing. Your company name in the industry is your marketing brand. Almost all real estate companies are part of their local MLS, but very few pay for the access fees for their salespeople.

PROPERTY BROCHURES

A *property brochure* is a brochure that tells of a specific property. The brochure is a minimum of four pages and is usually in color on high-quality paper. The cost of a property brochure usually prohibits its use, except for fine homes and estates. I know one real estate broker who only deals in elite executive homes. She publishes brochures for her office's properties that have a blank for the selling salesperson to staple their business card. She does this in an effort to encourage distribution to potential buyers.

Because the property brochures market one specific property, most real estate companies require their salespeople themselves to publish these for their clients.

PROPERTY PROFILE SHEETS

Property profile sheets are also called *property graphics.* The property profile sheet is usually a single sheet of paper that describes the property and has a picture of it. Property profile sheets are much less expensive than property brochures and should be used on almost all your company's listings.

The profile sheet contains information about the number and sizes of rooms. List all the best amenities of the property and information about schools and taxes, as well as information about your company and how to get in touch with the listing salesperson for a showing.

Graphics should be professionally done. I say professionally because these should be of high quality. If your office has the print capability to do these, you certainly may. There are several printing companies that will print these out for your office for a fee. The fee is usually reasonable. Have them print your two sets of flyers for your salespeople: one set in full color and another set in black and white. The colored ones are to be passed out by your salespeople to potential clients. Your salespeople will want to place some of the colored ones on the kitchen table at the property. The black and white ones should be used to fill up the information box on the yard sign. These are for passersby. You will lose a lot of the ones out front, which is why they should be black and white. If you are real clever, you will teach your salespeople to have them mailed directly to the seller and have the seller put out only a few in the information box. The seller then monitors the box and fills it up when necessary. They are glad to help. Whether you provide these for your salespeople or they provide them on their own, be sure they are of top quality.

RESIDENTIAL SERVICE CONTRACT: THE HOME WARRANTY

Home warranties are basic insurance policies that protect buyers for one year after the purchase of a home. They can also be used as marketing tools. The number one fear of any buyer is that of having purchased a lemon. Most lawsuits result from a buyer feeling he or she was lied to about the property condition. A home warranty can remove a lot of these problems. They cover most mechanical items in the home. Check each policy for terms, or better yet, provide the buyer several so that he or she can choose the home warranty company.

You should set an office policy that each of your salespeople must offer the Residential Service Contract to both the sellers and buyers in a transaction. If the clients refuse to purchase a contract, they should sign a disclosure statement that confirms that they were offered the service. A Residential Service Contract can save your brokerage company from being tied up in a long court battle when a property condition problem occurs.

TELEPHONE DIRECTORIES

Telephone directory ads are best used for real estate companies to get calls from sellers. As always, the larger the ad, the more exposure and the more cost.

The real estate broker should have an advertisement in the telephone directory to solicit real estate salespeople. When a person begins to get inquisitive about a real estate career, he or she may begin their search in the telephone directory. If your advertisement is sizable and in the advertisement you mention that you are willing to interview potential real estate professionals, you may get more recruits.

RADIO

Real estate salespeople rarely use radio advertising for recruiting or advertising specific properties. When used, radio is best for advertising multiple tenant or multiple property sales. Radio is frequently used to advertise newly built apartment complexes desiring a significant number of tenants immediately. Radio is also used for builders that have just opened a new subdivision.

One way a real estate broker can get on the radio without the cost would be to volunteer for a real estate information radio show. Usually these are promoted and paid for by the participants, but it is worth investigating because of the immense creditability you will receive from doing radio.

TELEVISION

Television is very impressive but very expensive. National television is reserved for national real estate companies that are promoting name recognition. Local television can be an avenue for real estate brokers as long as the costs are in line with the marketing budget.

THE INTERNET

The Internet is well on its way to replacing print advertising as the most used real estate medium. Real estate–related advertisers are one of the Internet's fastest-growing advertiser segments, with local real estate companies being the most active advertisers with the purchase of local search phrases. Web-based companies and individual brokers make up most of the real estate advertisers, with "For Sale By Owners" trailing far behind. The Internet is where a majority of buyers now begin their research for their next home. The most important reasons for a consumer to use the Internet include ease of access, ability to search by criteria, personalized searches, and availability of online preliminary qualifications.

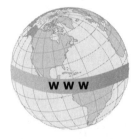

Do not think the Internet is a savior for all your real estate office problems. Some real estate brokers pay thousands of dollars per month for web sites that no one sees.

The real estate broker should also be keenly aware that real estate salespeople from competing companies are watching your presence on the web. An incredible site may be enough to get a call or e-mail. Those that are considering a career in real estate generally search the web first before calling a real estate company to seek employment.

Conclusion

Real estate marketing is a large part of the real estate brokerage business. A real estate broker must take great pains to be sure the efforts are rewarded. A broker that lets real estate marketing take a backseat will be driving a car heading for a cliff at top speed.

Chapter Five Review Questions

1. Commercial brokerage includes all of the following *except*
   A. big box.
   B. high-rise.
   C. multi-family.
   D. industrial.

2. Which of the following is not a duty that a property manager is expected to perform?
   A. Leasing
   B. Complaining
   C. Rent collection
   D. Marketing

3. What is a real estate company's overall marketing direction called?
   A. Marketing plan
   B. Marketing budget
   C. Marketing direction
   D. Marketing strategy

4. A real estate company's marketing strategy should be
   A. written in general terms.
   B. used to monitor expenses.
   C. aligned with your goals.
   D. all of the above.

5. The company marketing plan should meet all of the following requirements, *except*
   A. be written in general terms.
   B. have a beginning date and an ending date.
   C. should align with the marketing strategy.
   D. provide analysis of all costs.

6. What is prospect generating advertising?
   A. It is the advertising that gets people to know your name.
   B. It is the advertising that gets people to know what you do.

   C. It is the advertising that gets people to call you.

   D. All of the above are goals of prospect generating advertising.

7. Which of the following is *not* name recognition advertising?

   A. Television

   B. Print advertising specific properties

   C. Bus stop benches

   D. Name badges, career apparel, and car signs

8. All of the following are important aspects of a marketing budget *except*

   A. should be written by the Chief Financial Officer, not the Marketing Director.

   B. spells out the money to be spent in the marketing plan.

   C. needs to be disciplined.

   D. at least 10 percent of earnings should be allocated to the marketing budget.

9. What advertising term refers to the number of exposures and the amount of time between exposures?

   A. Incidence

   B. Prevalence

   C. Occurrence

   D. Frequency

10. Which of the following print media makes the most sense for "niche" type real estate companies?

   A. International newspapers

   B. National newspapers

   C. Local newspapers

   D. None of the above is appropriate

11. What are the four selling steps in advertising?

   A. Attention

   B. Interest

   C. Description

   D. Action

12. All of the following are good ideas when writing advertising for real estate, *except*

  A. avoid white space: use the entire ad.

  B. keep it simple and short.

  C. appeal to emotions.

  D. inspire confidence.

13. Which of the following is not a protected class under Federal Fair Housing laws?

  A. Race

  B. National origin

  C. Age

  D. Color

14. Which of the following phrases would violate the Fair Housing Laws?

  A. Family room

  B. Adults only

  C. Private setting

  D. Walking distance to mall

15. What law was enacted in 1969 to assure the meaningful disclosure of credit terms?

  A. Truth in Lending Act

  B. Sherman Antitrust Act

  C. Deceptive Trade Practices Act

  D. Real Estate Settlement Procedures Act

16. Under Regulation Z, for fixed-rate loans, if you advertise the loan term and monthly payment you must also advertise the

  A. annual percentage rate.

  B. simple interest rate.

  C. down payment.

  D. all must be included.

17. What are the two basic types of real estate yard signs?

    A. Wood and composite

    B. Post and stake

    C. Inverted L and H

    D. Flat and big screen

18. What are the metal information attachments that are placed on yard signs?

    A. Informational tags

    B. Sign adaptations

    C. Real estate name panels

    D. Sign riders

19. What are the two basic types of key boxes?

    A. Electronic and combination

    B. Drop down and flip up

    C. Member and affiliate

    D. Mono and duo

20. What is the purpose of a company brochure?

    A. To introduce your company

    B. To tell of your office accomplishments

    C. To demonstrate a quality product

    D. All of the above

21. What service allows a real estate property to be exposed throughout the world?

    A. The Real Estate Property Service

    B. The local daily newspaper

    C. The Multiple Listing Service

    D. The International Property Search and Data Service

22. Advertising on the radio is best suited for which of the following?

    A. An expensive estate

    B. Newly built apartment complex

C. A church

D. Radio is never appropriate for real estate sales

23. What medium is replacing print advertising for real estate sales?

A. The Internet

B. Billboard signs

C. Airplane banners

D. Cafeteria menus

6 Additional Marketing Ideas in Real Estate

Marketing My Office

These marketing ideas are less well known but are additional ways to get people interested in your office or sell your office inventory. Do not consider the following ideas first, but put them in your basket to use later.

Name Recognition Advertising

There are a variety of ways to publicize your real estate office through name recognition advertising.

BUS BENCHES

The benches that you wait on for the bus now have advertising on them. This is strictly name recognition advertising, and for the real estate industry may not be the best place to use the money in your marketing budget.

GROCERY STORE PLACE-CARD BOARDS

These place-card boards, usually on a wall at the front of the store, hold place-cards with advertising on them, but the public rarely scrutinizes these. Generally, people going into a grocery store want groceries, not real estate brokers.

SHOPPING CARTS

Shopping carts have an advertising spot on the front of the cart that a real estate broker can purchase. This is merely name recognition advertising, and I believe there are better places to be if you want your name out to the public.

MOVIE SCREENS

Movie theaters sell a few seconds in front of a captive audience. The people waiting to see the feature film will watch the advertisements pass in front of them. This is also strictly name recognition advertising. Again, real estate brokers seldom use this type of advertising.

BILLBOARDS

Billboards are those giant boards located along the highways of the world, another form of name recognition advertising. Some real estate brokers have used these billboards with great success, but most cannot afford the enormous expense to make this type of marketing to work. One real estate professional has had the same billboard in her market area for over ten years. She has said that she has not received much business from the sign but that people do recognize her at appointments, and that recognition does help her convert the appointment into a listing. Is it worth it? She has spent thousands and thousands to get that recognition. If she canceled that billboard, she would lose that recognition within a few months.

BATHROOM AD CARDS

Can you believe this one? Yes, when you go to the bathroom at many public restrooms there are ad cards on the wall in front of you. I don't know about you, but that is not when I want to be thought about!

CAR SIGNS

Car signs feature your real estate company on magnetic signs to be placed on your door panels or the back of your car. These should be purchased as soon as possible. You need to let everyone know that your company sells real estate. The car signs are always marketing your company and what you do. These are another form of name recognition marketing, so you should not expect to get business from them. However, I have gotten business based on car signs in the past: I was driving really slowly, looking for investment properties. In my mirror I saw a man running after me. Turns out he needed to sell his house, and he had seen my signs. Those signs paid for themselves ten times over! You can also paint or use vinyl lettering to have your company name on your vehicle permanently.

MOVING TRUCKS

I have seen real estate companies buy a box truck and allow their clients to borrow the truck to help them move. Be careful about liability on this one and be sure to have insurance protecting the company. The company can then advertise that "we *really* help you move!" There are now moving billboards on the outside of the trucks—a really neat idea, but relatively expensive to buy, customize, and maintain.

Name Tags/Name Badges

Your salespeople should wear their professional real estate name tag at all times. A name tag is usually plastic or vinyl and has the salesperson's name across it with the note indicating that he or she is in real estate. The name tags come in a wide variety of shapes, colors, styles, and customized options. Don't overlook attachments such as award pins and ribbons— they're a great way for the broker to recognize a real estate salesperson who has done something beneficial for the company and at the same time encourage salespeople to wear their name tags. The name tag is a silent salesperson. If a salesperson somehow fails to introduce him- or herself, the name tag will do the talking.

> *"I have had conversations with thousands of people I would never have met had I not been wearing my name tag. It's truly amazing how one small action can have such a profound and consistent effect on human behavior."—Scott Ginsberg (has been wearing his nametag for the past five years everyday and everywhere)*

Salespeople should wear the name tag on the right side of the chest so it can be read when they shake hands in a greeting. Some brokers will buy new real estate salespeople their first name tag for them. Be sure to pay a little extra and get your salespeople professional name tags to demonstrate their professional image.

SCHOOLBOOK COVERS

Elementary schools provide paper book covers for their students. Your company can provide those book covers for the students printed with the name of your company and contact numbers. It is expensive, but just think: your office's name will be in front of every one of those parents every day. Maybe several of your affiliates (title, mortgage) would be willing to participate to spread out the cost.

BUSINESS CARDS

If your salespeople are not carrying their business cards, they are out of business. I have had real estate "professionals" tell me they have "run out" of business cards but they will be ordering more soon. What? Why weren't those ordered months ago? Be sure you train your salespeople to always have on hand more than they will ever need (they're cheap) and then have them make every effort to pass them all out immediately. Have them pass them out to everyone. Teach your salespeople that they should never shake a hand without a business card in their hand. They should place their business card in any of their outgoing mail—even bills—no matter to whom the mail is sent. That piece of mail has now become a marketing piece.

I challenge you to teach the following philosophy:

> *Never give your money*
>
> *Without giving your card*

I did this and found I gave out a lot of cards and received a lot of money. If you are supporting them, they should support you. I gave my business card to the gasoline attendant and he bought a house through me. I gave a card to my waitress and she bought a house through me. I got on the elevator with a student of mine and he handed a business card to the next lady that got on the elevator and she bought a house through him!

Here is one thing you can do as a broker: have a broker card with the question, "Have you or someone you know thought about a career in real estate?" Develop the policy "I must hand out at least ten of these business cards per day." Rules are you must actually *hand out* the card. You cannot leave a stack on some office table and think you are done for a month. You must give your card to someone *new* every day. I don't care if you give your card to your spouse, that's fine, but you can only count that once. Now how hard is that? Piece of cake! The first day it is no problem. The first week, it is still no problem. After the first month, it begins to get tougher. The second month you are scrambling to find anyone to take your card. You will be dreaming of people to give your business card to. You will give one to your neighbor that you have known for ten years. You will give one to your daughter's teacher. Heck, you will give one to the person in line in front of you at the convenience store. Watch how your mind changes. You now are desperately seeking anyone to give your business card to. That is a moneymaking mind-set. Now that you have this down, teach it to your salespeople!

GIVEAWAYS

Giveaways are small items with your company name and contact information on them. You should give these away anytime you are doing recruiting or any other time you want to market your company in a unique way. Here are some helpful ideas:

CALENDARS   Many real estate professionals use calendars as part of their giveaways. The good thing about calendars is that you are in front of potential recruits and clients every day for a year. The bad thing is that you must do these every year to work. If you do these every year, people will begin to look forward to receiving them. If you do these once and never again, it was a waste of money.

SPORTS SCHEDULES   You can print high school, college, or professional game schedules on a small card. You have your office name and contact information on the back. Be sure you have the authorization to publish this information.

FRISBEES   You can get your company name and contact information printed on the back of frisbees. You can give these to youth groups to use and keep. You can give them to high school cheerleaders to throw at football games (small plastic footballs are good too).

These are just a few ideas—you can put your company name and contact information on about anything. Be creative here. Think about your office and your objectives, and use that as your guide to giveaways.

Home-Buyer Seminars

Home-buyer seminars are given to attract members of the public that are in the market to purchase a home. You will also find that there will be people in attendance who want to make real estate their career and do not know where to start. During the seminar, you demonstrate the process of purchasing a home. Be sure to give good and helpful information—that's what you promised, and that is what you should give. This does not limit the possibility of emphasizing the benefits of using you as their brokerage company to buy their next home, nor does it keep you from demonstrating the benefits of real estate sales as a business.

The seminar should be scheduled for once per month. It should be as good and as simple as possible. You should develop a notebook of about twenty-five pages for each participant to have the information to take home. Be sure your name, office name, and contact information is in every manual. It would be best to have your important points written up in a computer presentation to project onto the wall or projection screen from a data projector. Then market this seminar through whatever means you feel is appropriate. Different marketing will bring different clientele.

Do all the speaking yourself—no need to bring in any "experts." There are two reasons for this: first, you want to be the expert because you're the person they came to see. You can have some of your salespeople there to handle those who want to buy real estate. Second, it is very embarrassing to have three or four experts in real estate show up to speak when only two couples show up to participate. On the positive side, you now have two couples you did not have before the seminar, but this is diminished by your humiliation at having more speakers than participants. If you are the only speaker and two couples show up, you can sit down with them and make it more of a question-and-answer session.

You should charge the participants some fee for attending. We like to believe that if the seminar is free, more people will attend. The opposite is true. What's the first thing that would cross your mind about free stock investment seminar? Answer: They are trying to sell me something. You probably would not go. People feel that if they have to pay for something, it must be worth something. You could say the cost is $15 per person or $25 per couple. They can get discount (or free) tickets at a mortgage company that is helping you with the cost of the seminar. You could work with local real estate schools to offer the same discount tickets.

You should hold these in your office if at all feasible because of the cost. You should hand out a seminar manual with important topics summarized, but not much else. Do not cater these events. If you want to, you could provide them drinks.

When the participants enter the room, have music playing, or better yet have an introductory presentation playing from the data projector on a continuous loop.

Before you dismiss the seminar, be sure to ask for the opportunity to represent the buyers in the purchase of their home. If they are interested in real estate as a career, you should set up a time for a more formal interview. You are the broker, and it is expected for you to ask for the business.

Home-Seller Seminars

Home-seller seminars are exactly the same as home-buyer seminars except that instead of helping the buyer *buy* a home, you will help a home seller *sell* a home. The preparations are the same. There should be seminar manual to pass out, and you should make your presentation using a computer and a data projector. Remember, not everyone there will have real estate to sell; some may be looking to better their lives through the profession of real estate sales.

Trade Shows

Trade shows are gatherings of vendors and tradespeople to offer their wares from a central location. Usually they feature industry updates in a stadium-like locale and skills training in "break-out" sessions. Some trade shows combine with conventions to draw individuals from the convention. Trade shows having anything to do with real estate are worth attending.

Most of these shows provide you with a table and very little else. Become self-sufficient. The first thing you should develop is a "trade show checklist." The checklist should list everything you need to bring to these shows, and will save you from forgetting an item that you may desperately need.

Have a tablecloth to put over the table. The tablecloth should have your company logo in the middle front so that people can see your company name from across the room. You should develop some type of backdrop to display items you feel are important to the people that will be passing by. Bring lots of giveaways and print material. Most importantly, have some type of sign-up sheet for customers and potential recruits.

Conventions

Real estate companies love to have their conventions. I have no problem with conventions if you use them to recruit your competition's real estate salespeople or to retain the salespeople you currently have in your office. Each real estate professional expects some sort of award for his or her contribution to the business. Almost every major real estate franchise has at least one awards convention where it presents production awards to its salespeople. There are conventions for the NATIONAL ASSOCIATION OF REALTORS® and all of the state and local associations.

When you attend these conventions, be prepared to press a lot of palms and pass out hundreds of business cards. It is probably not the best place to openly recruit, but your presence alone can be a form of recruiting. If you have company brochures, bring a bundle to pass out when you talk with future salespeople. Not only can you can give it to them and ask for referral business, but they now have your company brochure just in case they ever think about switching offices.

Home Improvement Shows

Home improvement shows feature the latest in home improvements. The show has vendors that promote home improvement items, such as gazebos, spas, gardens, and decking, to name a few. Sellers may want to improve their property before they actually put their home on the market to sell. This would be a great way to meet these sellers before they call in your competition.

Any time you get in front of people, you should be recruiting. You may meet someone at home improvement shows that you would never meet otherwise. This person may become your top producing real estate salesperson. The more exposure you get for your office, the better chance you will have to get new recruits.

Career Days/Career Fairs

Colleges and universities have career days for their students. As a broker, you should have booths at these events. You can ask to be added to a mailing list to receive invitations to these events. Some events have nominal fees, while others are free. The arrangement is the same for a trade show, so review that section for more insight. These career days can yield twenty or more potential recruits. Most don't pan out, but the effort is well worth it.

I don't go to high school events simply because most high school students lack the maturity for a career; they are simply looking for a job. I love young people, but recent high school graduates do not seem to work out in this business.

Colleges and universities usually will also allow you to post job listings, accept résumé submissions, and hold on-campus interviews. Be sure to go through the "Career Center" or "Placement Office" before entering campus to recruit. Most colleges will not allow you to recruit for sales positions, but you can instead recruit for management positions. Every real estate company needs to be recruiting for better managers. If you are your only manager, recruit to replace yourself so you can do bigger and better things. Anyhow, no manager would be considered without real estate sales experience. So you may be hiring for managers, but they must start working as salespeople.

Some colleges will allow a business to hold an "information session" or "information luncheon" with their students. The information session is to inform the students about you and what you do. Although they want you to educate rather than to recruit openly, they know and expect you to recruit afterwards. Provide the students with take-home material and have visual aids to facilitate the presentation. After the presentation, students will wander up to the front to ask specific questions. This is a great time to recruit, so have a registration form handy.

Flyers

Flyers are photocopies with information about careers in real estate and usually a picture of the office. The flyers are distributed in an area where the real estate company wants to have real estate salespeople. Keep these inexpensive so that you and your salespeople can pass them out to everyone in an area. The best way to distribute them is door to door. Here is a typical flyer wording:

> *Have you ever thought about real estate as a career? Currently, a local real estate company is looking for self-starting individuals interested in making a difference in their lives as well as the lives of others. The income is only limited by the effort of the person. No experience necessary, all training is provided. Call Today!*

I used to combine duties to get more done in less time. Instead of working out and then hiring someone to pass out flyers, I did both at the same time. I would start in the morning in my running outfit clothes and run from house to house in the area distributing flyers. I would not talk with the owners because I was all sweaty. But I distributed a lot of flyers and also got a decent workout.

Word of Mouth

You should tell everyone that you are a real estate broker. The more people you tell, the more they tell, and so on and so on. Word of mouth is one of the best forms of marketing, and by far the least expensive. Here are some examples of opportunities to use word-of-mouth marketing:

ANNOUNCE AT LOCAL ASSOCIATION OF REALTORS®

You pay money to belong to your local ASSOCIATION OF REALTORS®. You should become well known in that association. This is a natural way to promote your company. Your association will also give you access to many real estate professionals from surrounding areas and maybe regions. Affiliates of the real estate industry, such as title and mortgage companies, make good recruits. The best way to get to know the affiliates is through the ASSOCIATION.

NETWORKING GROUPS

There are professional networking groups in your vicinity that meet and discuss current topics, but the major emphasis is on building referral business. Being active and marketing your company to these groups gives you exposure to a wide range of potential recruits.

SPHERE OF INFLUENCE

Your sphere of influence is the group of people that know you and what you do. You want to help your friends, and they want to help you. You must let this group know that you are in the real estate profession and you looking for potential recruits. Do not tell them once and expect them to remember. You must be in contact with them monthly so that you will immediately come to mind if anyone talks to them about real estate as a career.

REFERRAL NETWORKS

A referral network is a way for a brokerage firm to get individuals to earn referral fees from the real estate business without actually practicing real estate. Some real estate salespeople do not make a career of the real estate business. For one reason or another, they give up selling and just let their real estate licenses expire. This is a tragedy because these people can help your business. As a broker, you should develop a referral network. The members of the network do not sell real estate, but they have an active real estate license. Anytime they hear of a buyer or seller of real estate, they call the lead coordinator and pass along the referral. The lead coordinator will assign the lead to a salesperson from your company. Once the property closes, the referral salesperson will receive a portion of the commission. By forming a referral network, the broker can have the benefit of additional real estate sales.

You can search your real estate commission's web site or subscribe to a list of "sent back" licensees. You can call them, write them a letter, or e-mail them. If you want to call them, use the following script:

Broker: "Mr. Jones?"

Jones: "This is Mr. Jones."

Broker: "Mr. Jones, this is Dan Hamilton with Acme Real Estate and I noticed you have turned your license back to the state real estate commission. May I ask why?"

Jones: "I have another job."

Broker: "I see, that is a shame to have earned the license and now have it be useless to you. Let me ask you, can I show you a way that the license could still make you some money without your ever having to actually sell real estate?"

Jones: "What do you mean?"

Broker: "We have a referral network you could join. The referral network would allow you to refer your friends and relatives to us for their real estate needs, and once the transaction has closed you will receive a referral fee. Does this make sense?"

Jones: "That's great!"

Broker: "Why don't you come to my office, and we can take care of the transfer."

RULES OF THE REFERRAL NETWORK   Upon forming a referral network, you should follow some simple rules:

1. The referral person does not sell any real estate at any time for anyone. This is a must, and they need to sign an affidavit to that fact. You cannot have loose cannons out there with real estate licenses, outside your control.

2. The referral person must keep his or her license active.

3. The referral person must stay only with your referral network.

4. The referral person must only receive money from real estate business through his or her designated broker.

5. The referral person must act with the utmost in professionalism when representing the company.

The referral network can grow to have several hundred licensees working within it. Take this slowly. Some brokers establish the entire network under a different broker's license to avoid additional fees associated with the real estate industry. Be sure to check with state and local laws and regulations for this type of business.

AFFILIATES

Affiliates are people who do business related to the real estate industry but outside of sales. These businesses need your company's ability to generate clientele. If you help these affiliates with their business, they should reward you by helping you with yours. They should send potential recruits your way. You should not only network with these affiliates but also market to them for business, and you will find they market to you. Some of the following are affiliates that fall into this category include:

INSPECTORS   Inspectors take a look at real property and give their expert advice on the condition of that property. These people are absolutely necessary to limit the real estate salesperson's and broker's liability in a real estate transaction. Who selects the inspector? Of course, the buyers should, but they want our advice to help them choose. Be careful here— you could create some liability by your recommendation. If you do this correctly, you can recommend a qualified inspector. First, you should know the inspector and be certain that he or she has the expertise and integrity to do a good job. The inspector should have a license number from the state in which he or she does business. Second, the inspector should be bonded and have errors and omissions insurance. Both of these will protect the buyer just in case the inspector won't.

TITLE COMPANIES   Title companies provide the owner's policy of title insurance for the buyer of real property to protect the buyer from claims against the property that were undiscovered. A title policy should be issued for every real estate transaction your company is involved in. As a result, your company can direct a great deal of business to a title company. Regulations prohibit referring business to companies expecting to get monetary return, but nothing prohibits you from marketing your services to these title companies for their referrals of real estate salespeople. Occasionally, these title officers will hear of an unhappy real estate salesperson. They should call you and give you the information. If they feel uncomfortable doing that, then you may want to find another title company.

MORTGAGE COMPANIES   Mortgage companies provide the funds necessary for the buyer to purchase real property. When buyers begin the process of finding a home to purchase, they look to a real estate professional to help. As a result, we can send business to the mortgage company that provides our buyers the best options. We should get business back from the mortgage company when a customer also wants to become a real estate salesperson—that's a fair trade.

APPRAISERS   Appraisers are professional property evaluators. Their job is to determine the worth of a real estate investment. Generally, they are to protect the mortgage company from lending money on an inadequate property. Appraisers usually work as "staff" appraisers, meaning they work directly for that particular mortgage company and are usually on salary with that mortgage company. But some work as "fee" appraisers, meaning they work independently of a particular mortgage company and get paid in fees from their clients. Your recommendations of a particular appraiser can be very valuable to that appraiser. Those same appraisers should recommend your company when a client asks them about the real estate profession. You must let the appraisers know that you will appreciate their recommendations and have a system to market to each appraiser with which your company does business.

STRUCTURAL ENGINEERS   Structural engineers evaluate the property's structure to determine its soundness. Most structural engineers cherish recommendations from real estate professionals. You should market to these engineers, because sometimes owners will seek out a structural engineer before putting their homes on the market.

SPEAKING

Most people are afraid of public speaking, but those who practice it garner a great deal of respect. Speaking for groups on the subject of real estate allows a person (and company) to demonstrate expertise. Make sure you ask plenty of questions before you accept a speaking engagement. You will want to know the following details:

- Exact subject matter
- Length of time for speech
- Number of people in attendance
- Seating arrangement and speaker platform
- Sound and lights, if provided
- Marketing of the event

You will want to ask these questions before you agree to speak. Keep a file on all of your speaking engagements and form a checklist of questions to ask and items to bring.

A speaker does not need to know all about the subject, but should be able to find the answers to participants' questions and follow up with them after the event. Script would go something like this:

Speaker: "That is an excellent question, and I want you to have the best answer, so let's do this: I will research that and follow up with you after this event to discuss the solution. Will you please leave me some way to get back in touch with you?"

Notice how helpful that sounds? Another way to defuse a question is to solicit responses from the audience. For example:

> *Participant:* "What is the most popular loan program available right now?"
>
> *Speaker:* "All right, let's find out from the rest of you what type of loan programs are you using currently or have used in the past?"

See how you can buy time and maybe avoid sole responsibility for answering the question? This all depends on the responsiveness of your audience. The fastest way you can lose respect and credibility is to answer a question incorrectly, trying to look like you know everything.

This is not a speech-coaching course; I just want to demonstrate how effective a speaker you can be even if you do not have years of experience in the business. Remember: You do not need to earn respect and credibility, the audience will *give* it to you; all you have to do is not lose it.

Here are a few places where you might want to speak and groups you might want to speak to:

HOUSES OF WORSHIP Local places of worship want informative speeches for their congregations. It is usually difficult for them to book talent because most want to be paid, and these places generally will not pay for talent.

CIVIC GROUPS Civic groups tend to specialize in certain groups of people with similar interests. Speaking to a quilting group would be quite different from speaking to a group of handymen. So be prepared to handle the different types of groups.

SCHOOLS Sometimes high schools and colleges will want you to speak on career nights. These are different than recruiting events. During your speech, you will explain to the students the benefits of being in the real estate business. This service will land you in good favor with the campus counselors and other faculty, as well as the parents of the students, all of whom could be potential clients. Be sure to market to these people when appropriate.

COMMUNITY SERVICE

Community service is working with worthy causes for the benefit of all. You should not prospect these entities, but you can market your company by being active in the charities you choose. People want to help those that contribute. Again, you should not be involved with these groups just to market to them; you should be working because you want to give back.

My office did a project with several other individuals and groups in our community to rebuild a house for a homebound woman. All of the real estate salespeople from my office wore T-shirts with our company's name on them. We never asked for any business, but several members of the community came to us and asked for real estate help.

SHOPPING MALL KIOSKS

Indoor regional malls offer small kiosk booths that your office can rent out to provide services to passersby. This unique idea gets a lot of exposure but very little actual business. The benefits are simple: the more people you can get in front of, the greater chance you have of finding someone who wants to buy or sell real estate. However, not too many people seeking a real estate professional would head to the mall. The disadvantages are the expense of rental, the length of time for rental, and the time it takes to "man" one of the kiosks. A better idea would be to see if the mall would allow you to rent a kiosk once per month. Probably not, but it doesn't hurt to ask.

The cost of a kiosk cart can range from two to ten thousand dollars. You can set up a small booth with tables, which can save you additional money and will probably work better, depending upon the mall. You can add large plasma screens for spectacular multimedia presentations to draw additional interest. To attract potential salespeople, you will need information about education, services offered, and financing options for schooling. You do not need to have anything there for them to buy, but you will need information sheets for them to fill out to track the potential recruits.

The most popular site for kiosks is shopping malls, but you may want to check out airports and other transportation facilities, sporting events, festivals, and other creative venues.

CLOSING GIFTS

Closing gifts are things your salespeople give to their clients at the closing of the transaction. Closing is a happy time, and a gift just adds to the joy. Closing gifts are a nice way for your salespeople to say "thanks" to their clients by purchasing them a gift, but you should also use this as a marketing tool. Don't give gifts that are disposable, can be used up, or could potentially die, because if the client gets rid of the gift, they get rid of you. Your job as the broker is to insure that your salespeople are presenting gifts to their clients so that your brokerage name is respected and recommended in the community. Most real estate companies do not buy the gifts but rather insist that this is the salesperson's expense. Some real estate brokerages do buy the gifts to make sure that they are given, because if the salesperson is left to purchase the gift, most won't do it. These brokers keep a supply of the gifts in the office for use. The following are examples of some closing gifts:

BRASS DOORKNOCKER WITH ENGRAVED NAME The doorknocker should have "Presented by: _____," with the salesperson's name engraved in small letters below the buyer's name. These are great because they will remind the owners of your salesperson every time they open their front door. You might hire or suggest that your salesperson hire someone to deliver the gift and actually install it, because otherwise they might never get around to hanging it up.

LEATHER BINDER TO HOLD IMPORTANT PAPERS The buyers, now owners, will have many important papers they will need to be able to retrieve at a moment's notice, including the closing papers, deed, purchase agreement, insurance papers, note and mortgage, title policy, and many others. Your salespeople could provide the buyers with a leather binder to hold all of these papers. The binder should look very professional, and should have your company's name and the real estate salesperson's name embossed on the inside so that if the buyers ever want to sell, they will know whom to call.

Some companies have these binders for sale, or your office may have its own custom-made. Remember: Be sure the gift looks professional, because it is a reflection of you and your company. So spend the money to make these look good.

You do not need to spend a lot of money to purchase your clients a gift. Use your imagination, and you may think of other gifts.

REFERRAL GIFTS

A major portion of your business should come from referrals. Referrals occur when people you have worked with recommend you and your company to their friends. This is the easiest and best business. With these people, your salespeople have no competition. You will be the only real estate professional the clients talk with, because their friend recommended your salesperson. The client will think, "If my friend believes your salesperson can do the job, I believe the same."

These referrals don't just happen; you as the broker must market to get them, and once you get one, you should want more. The best way to do that is to make certain your salespeople do an excellent job for the referral and then give a referral gift to the person who provided the referral. This gift can be of any nature. By cultivating your relationship with this person, you insure that they will continue to give referrals. Make certain you comply with your state's real estate commission.

SPORTS TEAM SPONSORSHIP

Local youth sports teams are always seeking sponsors. By sponsoring one or more of these teams, you can market your office to the coaches and to the players' parents. Your office can simply donate money, or you can go as far as sponsoring uniforms with your company name and contact information on the back. I used to sponsor my personal softball team. How great is that— I got great exposure for my company, and we all had "cool" uniforms!

SCHOOL PROGRAMS

Educational institutions, from elementary schools through colleges, have events they want to print programs for so that the participants and audience know the players and the schedule of events. By paying to have these programs printed, you can be sure to include (with the school's permission) your company's name and contact information.

Rarely will these programs be thrown away, because the parents want to keep the mementos of their children playing in a sporting event or scholastic event. The following are a few examples of events that might require a program:

- **Football program**

  This program lists all of the players and coaches, the cheerleaders, the opposing team, and any additional interesting information that might be included.

- **Graduation program**

  This program lists all the students that are graduating and the faculty that are important to the school.

- **Music programs**

  This program lists all of the students that have a part, the instruments they play, and the music they perform. It would list all of the music teachers and the people that helped put the program together.

- **Play programs**

  This program lists all the student actors and actresses, the acts, the director, and all other people that helped to put the play together.

You might want to get additional help from other sponsors (title, mortgage) for these programs because of the expense.

EVENT SPONSORSHIP

You should select some type of event to do at least once each year. This type of marketing can be expensive, but it can also make a name for your company. The event does not have to be huge, just memorable. Take a look at some of the following and see if any strike your fancy:

CHEERLEADING CHAMPIONSHIPS Many cheerleaders cannot afford to go to national championships, so why not hold local championships? Invite all the local cheerleader groups to participate. Provide necessary items like water, trophies, and stipends for judges. You, your office personnel, and your office salespeople will need to plan this one out to be sure of a quality event. Have the local media on hand for the awards. As with all events, you should be the coordinator, but you do not have to do everything yourself.

PARADES Get involved in your local town's annual parade. Almost every town will have a parade at least once per year. Sponsor a float, ride on a float, or be a director. Working on the parade committee puts you in touch with very influential people. Don't let it slip your mind that you should use these events to do marketing for your company. Throw out bags of candy with your business card attached. Have banners with your company's name and contact information along the side of the float. Sponsor part of the program. Have banners along the parade route. You should always be thinking of ways to market.

EASTER EGG HUNT This is one of my favorites. I decided one year to hold an Easter egg hunt for the surrounding neighbors of our office. My office people and I marketed by posting flyers throughout the area. We designed a registration form to be filled out in advance or at the event. The form gave us names, addresses, and telephone numbers to continue our marketing after the event. I got an Easter Bunny outfit. The other real estate salespeople from my office bought plastic eggs, candy, and small toys. We then had a party and stuffed all the plastic eggs. We expected four hundred people and eight hundred showed up. We madly ran to the store and got more eggs. In the end, everyone was very happy and appreciative.

The successful marketing during and after the event was not the best part—the best part was that I got to wear the Easter Bunny outfit. The Easter Bunny seemed to love my daughter because he carried her all over the event and helped her find eggs (she did not know I was the Easter Bunny). Her smile was worth all the money and effort! How about that— we get to do wonderful marketing programs and create memorable events for others and ourselves!

FLAG DISTRIBUTION ON INDEPENDENCE DAY   A favorite of real estate salespeople is to distribute little plastic U.S. flags on wooden sticks with the salesperson's business card attached. Salespeople go up and down the streets placing the flags in the yards of the houses by the edge of the street. This creates a great effect when you drive down those streets—flags blowing in the wind all in a line. Impressive!

When my office did this, we received numerous telephone calls indicating how appreciative the owners were to have the flags. We even received calls asking me to place flags in their yard next year.

Many companies print up the flags. Organize with the salespeople in your office to order as a group at volume discounts. You could buy the flags for your salespeople if in return they would be willing to put them out.

Placing flags on Independence Day is so popular, your office might want to think of placing the flags out on September 11th. Being different in marketing sets your company apart. How about placing the flags on both days?

PUMPKINS ON HALLOWEEN   Another great idea that's often used is placing pumpkins with your company's business card on owners' doorsteps. You should make an attempt to find a seller of pumpkins with an oversupply and make a deal to buy all of them. Again, you could buy these for your salespeople if they would be willing to put them out, or leave the purchasing up to them.

BOY OR GIRL SCOUT CAMP-OUT   Find the local Boy Scout or Girl Scout troop in your area and offer to sponsor its next camping trip. Your company will provide the money for food and maybe buy some piece of outdoor equipment with your company's name and contact information to give it to each scout. How about frisbees? They are inexpensive and popular. You don't need to have a son or daughter in scouts, but don't expect to go on the outing.

MEMBERSHIP IN CIVIC GROUPS

You should be a member in at least one civic group and actively participate. Civic groups allow you to give back. As always with community service, you should be a member for the right reasons, not just as a marketing strategy. However, civic participation can be a good vehicle for earning respect in your community, and is therefore one of the best types of marketing.

LOCAL HOMEOWNERS' ASSOCIATIONS

Generally, homeowners' association leaders get little respect. Their members don't think they do enough, but their spouses think they do too much. These people are seldom paid and often berated. Call up the nearby homeowners' associations in your area and ask to be an honorary member or an affiliate. The president will be shocked and pleased to have a respected member of the real estate profession interested in the association. You now can market your office directly to all of the owners. You must do this subtly, but it can be done. Volunteer to maintain the association's roster and mail out the monthly newsletter. The president will be so glad a professional is now handling the newsletter that he or she will let you put a business card-sized note in the corner about your company. The note could read:

> *Have you ever thought about real estate as a career? If you have please contact the editor of this newsletter at:*
>
> *Dan Hamilton*
> *Broker/Owner, Acme Real Estate*
> *817-555-1212*

If the group doesn't have a newsletter, be the hero and volunteer to make one up. I suggest an electronic newsletter on the Internet rather than a print newsletter sent through the postal service. People will come to you if they want something in the newsletter, and you will also have the roster of every one in the association. You may want to consider having your office staff put the newsletter together.

SCHOOL PTAS (PARENT-TEACHER ASSOCIATIONS)

School Parent-Teacher Associations are always in need of a helping hand. Volunteer to collect money for new textbooks or make arrangements to have your office to purchase them. This may be very expensive, but think how long a school will keep the books you buy. Whether you buy books or simply participate in the local PTA, it helps. When you make yourself available to these people, you also make yourself available to entire community. You want to help them, and they want to help you.

CLUBS

By club, I do not mean a nightclub, dance club, or billy club; I am talking about civic clubs such as Lions clubs, chess clubs, and sewing clubs. These groups usually have a theme, and if you enjoy their theme, you will also probably enjoy the company of the other members. Marketing to these people is best accomplished by "word of mouth."

OPEN HOUSE

There is a great deal of information out there on how to market a property and your company by conducting an open house. The information we will cover here is merely a summary and should be treated as such.

Open houses attract people interested in buying in that particular area. They also attract people that live in the area who may want to sell. The best part for a broker is that they can also attract a recruit who is considering real estate as a career. The more marketing flash and publicity your salespeople put on at an open house, the more potential clients it will attract.  Banners, flags, and signs should be displayed at the house on the open house day. Your salespeople should place open house directional signs at the corners of all major traffic intersections in the area. Be sure to check local laws for sign placement, and if a sign is to be placed at a corner of someone's yard, be sure to ask permission.

Your salespeople should market at least two open houses per week. Yes, this is work, but isn't that what they are supposed to be doing? Open houses are traditionally held on Saturday and Sunday—both great days for buyers to be out and looking for property. You could hold an open house during the week to seek out the buyers and sellers who may not have the ability to go on the weekends. You could also hold the weekday open houses in the evening or maybe provide a light lunch to get the working crowd. If your salespeople don't have any listings or too few hold open every week, they could ask real estate professionals in your office if they could hold one of their houses open. They could contact a builder of new houses to see if they could hold one of their newly built houses open. Salespeople could even call a FSBO (For Sale By Owner) and offer to hold the house open. This helps your salespeople in two ways: first, they get all the leads into that FSBO during the open house time, and second, they build a rapport and respect in the FSBO's eyes.

No matter what your salespeople do, they should consider open houses as one of the best ways of marketing to the public.

BROKER'S OPEN HOUSE

A broker's open house is marketing a property and your office to other professional real estate salespeople. A salesperson in your office uses one of his or her new listings on the market and provides lunch for all that come to look at that property. You market this exclusively to real estate professionals—no outside marketing to the public. Do not put up yard signs. Market the broker's open with flyers to the local real estate offices. These flyers can be hand delivered, faxed, or e-mailed, although these last two methods are less effective and you must check the "Do Not Fax" and "Anti-Spam" laws in your area.

Broker's opens can be a way for real estate salespeople to get a free lunch. I have been to broker's opens where the real estate people walk in the front door and then head straight for the food. They never bother to look at the property, and when they finish eating they leave. You cannot stop this behavior, so don't try. You hope the "professional" will respect your salesperson's efforts to market this property.

The more talented your salespeople are at preparing a meal, the better the broker's open will be. Some real estate salespeople have special items they can prepare that are hits and always bring a crowd. Some offer drawings for free "stuff" to add to the attendance.

You could organize a bunch of salespeople with listings in close proximity and hold the broker's open together. This cuts down on the marketing and increases the attendance. Appetizers could be offered at the first house, the main course at the second house, and dessert at the third house. At the fourth house, you could hold a drawing for prizes for those who attended all four houses.

At the broker's open, your function as a broker is to greet the real estate salespeople from other offices. Here you are at one of your salesperson's broker's open, shaking hands. The other salesperson thinks that his or her broker would never do that. If that salesperson is unhappy, he or she might seek you out because you show support for your people. By the way, your second function is to retain your current salespeople by supporting their efforts to generate sales.

One last comment: some broker's opens offer wine and cheese open houses in the evening. I cannot recommend this because of the liability. Be sure you consult a lawyer before you offer alcohol at any event.

OFFICE TOUR (CARAVAN)

A very effective way to market your office and to retain your salespeople is to take them to see the new listings acquired over the past week. In most offices, this is a scheduled time to go and preview the new listings. Be sure to set time aside to go on these tours. It will allow you the opportunity to see the inventory your office is carrying, but it also shows your dedication to and support of the people in your office. Do not become a prima donna and expect everyone to look at your office's property if you are too good to look at theirs. I understand you are busy and have things to do as a broker, but you should attend these office tours.

Some refer to this as a jailbreak because the real estate salespeople almost run through the houses. The objective is to be familiar with the office inventory so that if a buyer calls in to the office your salespeople will be more helpful. Most sellers appreciate an office tour to show support for their sale.

The listing salespeople should give everyone a card with a couple questions on it to answer as they view each listing, such as

- What was your overall opinion of the house?
- How did you feel about the price?
- What improvements could be made to help the salability?
- Any additional comments?

Keep the questions to a minimum and leave enough space for the real estate people to write their comments. Use these cards as information on the marketability of the property. When the seller insists on overpricing the house, these cards could indicate that all the other real estate professionals agree and the price should be lowered to get the property sold. It also shows the seller that your company is professional.

154

Be sure the seller has made the property "show" ready. All the windows should have the curtains pulled back, all the lights in the house should be on, and the house should be clean and smell fresh. Providing a snack like cookies is a nice touch, but not necessary.

Some real estate brokers are trying virtual tours of the properties instead of actually touring them. I will wait to see the results, but I do not believe this is effective because the real estate salespeople will not be able to remember what they saw on a movie as well as they can by walking through.

The local ASSOCIATION OF REALTORS® typically offers property tours for its members. These are similar to office tours, except that the entire association is invited. You should participate in these if you are a member. This is a spectacular way to market your company and actively recruit other salespeople. You have uninterrupted time to talk with other salespeople and invite them to a one-on-one lunch to discuss their future. If you do go, you may be the only other broker to attend. That sends a tremendous message about your dedication to this business. If you don't go, plan on watching your salespeople be recruited by the brokers that are attending.

CAREER APPAREL

Career apparel simply means the clothes you wear have identification that indicates you are in the real estate industry and are proud of it. You should always wear your name badge as a silent and constant marketing item. You should dress professionally with career insignia on the left-hand side, and you should encourage your salespeople to do the same. I have seen numerous brokers that press their salespeople to always wear their name tag without wearing one themselves. Don't send mixed messages: wear your name tag first, and others will follow your example. Any way you can think of to market yourself and your company will benefit you in the long run.

MAIL-OUTS

Mail-outs are a great way to prospect. Your office should buy custom envelopes and letterhead with your company's name and contact information. Any correspondence should use this custom stationery. If your staff mails the monthly office bill to the electric company, put it on company stationery and include a business card. Who knows in whose hands that information will land? If you send your mother a birthday card, do it on your company stationery. Constantly market to all your personal contacts using your custom stationery.

PUBLIC RELATIONS

Public relations encompasses all aspects of letting the public know you are in the real estate industry. Public relations includes doing editorial pieces for print media, speaking at public engagements, and issuing of press releases.

The term *public relations* means getting the media to notice you and your company in a positive light, at least once a month. When a newspaper publishes an article about one of your company's achievement, it becomes truth to the reader, whereas the same reader would discount an ad because it was paid for.

You should submit public relations stories weekly to the newspaper. The worst that could happen is the article is not used. Newspapers need to fill in sections in their newspaper with stories. If you have stories handy for them, they might use your company story to complete the newspaper.

You should submit public relations stories on virtually any subject. For instance, I once submitted a story about how our real estate office rescued a trapped kitten; no kidding—it made the front-page news complete with pictures, and we got many calls thanking us for our kindness and concern.

You never know what will be taken or rejected; your job is to submit. You do have to do certain things to make this happen, however. First, you must do newsworthy things; however, almost anything is newsworthy if worded correctly. If you are reading this, you are probably attending a career-building class for brokers. Send this in as a press release. Have you helped at a charity event? Have you won an office production award? Were you selected as the real estate broker of the month? All of these could be uses as press releases. Here are some suggestions for PR stories:

- New associate
- Top-listing salesperson
- Top-selling salesperson
- High-dollar listing
- Any charity event
- Any award or recognition

The correct writing of press releases tends to be generic, and yet you want to be sure that the particular print medium to which you are submitting your press release will accept it in the format you have written. The best way to know is to invite the editor out to lunch and ask for the correct format.

Why will the media print something for free when they get paid for advertising space? The reason is that at fifteen minutes to print time, the editor cannot always fill a certain space with paid advertising. The editor must do something, and that is when he or she will pull out the press release folder and choose whichever one strikes him or her first. Great reason to take the editor to lunch!

You should encourage your salespeople to submit these press releases, too. When their names are mentioned, your office is as well. The best way to be sure that these press releases go out on a regular basis is to assign this task to one of your office staff persons.

RADIO BROADCASTING STATION

I threw this one in here to show there is almost no limit to marketing if you keep your eyes and ears open. Certain companies produce a small briefcase-sized radio broadcasting station. It's true! I owned one!

All right, this did not make me a disc jockey, but the radio station could broadcast about 400 feet in every direction. The radio station would run on a digital continuous loop of about four minutes of information. You could record the message about a particular house and broadcast it from that house. On the yard sign a rider would indicate which frequency to turn to to listen to the message. You could also put these in your office window and broadcast information about the next real estate career seminar.

The great thing about this was that it broadcast 24 hours a day, and it was a very unique way to market. The problem: each one costs several thousand dollars.

RECORDED MESSAGES ABOUT PROPERTIES

Some offices offer recorded messages about properties through a toll-free telephone number. The prospect can call in to the number and then dial in the property code and listen to the information. The number is marketed by posting a name rider on the yard sign. Another way to market the number is by posting graphics in the window of the real estate office. Passersby can stop and look at the graphics, and if they want more information they can call the toll-free number. Be sure that the recording also offers advice about how to start a real estate career.

Conclusion

After reading this chapter, you as a broker/manager should be able introduce new ways to reach clients and salespeople. You should be able to add any or all of the following to your marketing efforts: bus benches, place-cards, movie screens, billboards, car signs, name tags, business cards, fly-ers, open houses, and giveaways, to name a few. The reader should also be able to hold seminars to attract clients and salespeople. With all of the ideas listed in Chapter 6, a real estate broker should be able to extend his or her reach and market share.

Chapter 6 Review Questions

1. Which of the following, if placed on a car, would help attract real es-tate business?
   A. Carnauba wax
   B. A supermodel
   C. Car signs
   D. None of the above

2. All of the following are true about business cards, *except*
   A. you should not overstock business cards because they are expensive.
   B. business cards should be passed out to every contact.
   C. you should place one or two business cards in every piece of mail you send.
   D. you should have a goal to pass out ten business cards out per day minimum.

3. All of the following would be good items to give away as marketing pieces, *except*
   A. calendars with your name imprinted on them.
   B. cases of Scotch whiskey with your labels on them.
   C. sports schedules with your name engraved at the bottom.
   D. frisbees with your logo in the middle.

7 Real Estate Brokerage Compensation Structures

The compensation structure is a critical part of recruiting and retaining real estate salespeople. If you pay your salespeople too much money, you will go broke. If you pay yourself too much, your salespeople will leave. Do not look to the compensation structure to blame for all your salespeople leaving, however; studies show that the main reason salespeople leave is lack of management guidance.

Multiple Plans

Some companies will offer their salespeople multiple plans, hoping to strike a deal that is best for both parties. These plans can range from 100 percent (discussed later) to a split of the commission between the broker and the salesperson with all expenses paid by the broker. The brokerage company that offers multiple plans to its salespeople is basically telling its salespeople, "We want you working here, so let's work a mutually beneficial system where you can make the money you deserve, and the real estate company can survive and thrive."

Single Plans

Some companies only offer a single plan. Because the single plan does not work for all salespeople, usually the broker will customize certain aspects of the plan to fit a particular salesperson (now resembling a multiple plan system). Single plans are quickly fading as a brokerage strategy. When a salesperson is offered multiple plans, any of which would be better than the single plan his or her current broker is offering, that salesperson may leave.

The reason brokers are hesitant to offer multiple plans is usually because they don't understand them, and they fear the unknown. What if I offer a plan that makes me go bankrupt? My response is to analyze your office and expenses (include a profit as an expense), and then develop plans to offset those expenses and provide for a reserve account. With this mind-set, many plans can be offered. I would offer the salesperson 100 percent of his or her commission if that same salesperson paid a monthly fee to offset those expenses the office incurs. I would pay for everything for a salesperson, if he or she would allow me to keep most of the commission to offset the expenses the company has incurred.

Splits

The most common way to compensate real estate salespeople is the *split,* which involves the dividing of a commission between a real estate salesperson and the broker. You will hear of the *50/50 split,* which means the salesperson receives 50 percent of the commission and the broker the other half. Generally the salesperson's split is mentioned first. As the salesperson increases production, he or she also increases his or her split. The reason for this is twofold: first, the salesperson needs the broker/manager less, and as such deserves more of the commission; and second, the best advertising a brokerage can get is yard signs. The more a salesperson lists, the more advertising the brokerage has, so the salesperson should be compensated for that advertising.

Generally, a real estate salesperson on a split will be rolled back at the end of a calendar year. If a salesperson has earned the position of 80/20 and December 31 hits, he or she will be "rolled back" to 50/50 at the beginning of the year. This is dangerous, because not only are you telling your people to leave your office; you are telling them *when* to leave your office. Your competition will heavily recruit your salespeople near the rollback time. If you don't roll back, your office could go broke. Without rollbacks, a real estate salesperson could do really well one year and then coast from there. The brokerage company would have a great number of high-split, low-producing salespeople, and *would* go broke.

A large number of brokerages are now implementing the *rolling rollback.* The rolling rollback is evaluated each month through a review of the previous twelve months. Basically, this calls for looking at a twelve-month period at the beginning of each month and then determining the split based on those twelve months. The following month, the salesperson

TABLE 7.1	Example of a Split System	
STAGE	COMMISSION EARNED	SPLIT FOR STAGE
1	$0–$20,000	50%
2	$20,001–$25,000	55%
3	$25,001–$35,000	60%
4	$35,001–$50,000	65%
5	$50,000–$70,000	70%
6	$70,001–Unlimited	75%

is reevaluated, and so adds the previous month and drops off the thirteenth month. If the salesperson should be on a 50/50 split one month and then produces really well the next month, his or her split could go up. This means the salesperson could be rolled back in any given month, or may never be rolled back if he or she maintains or increases production. This arrangement is probably the fairest and most motivating of any split system.

Table 7.1 is a *rough* look at a split system. Do not use this system for your office until you know your break-even numbers and what you need to earn for a profit.

A salesperson can start on a higher split, but to reach the next stage, he or she must qualify at a higher amount. For example, a salesperson may desire a 60 percent split. The broker could start the salesperson out on 60 percent, with the first stage being $50,000 before he or she moves up. The salesperson gets a higher starting split, but it takes longer to move up. With this system, a salesperson can reach and attain any stage he or she desires. If a person wants a higher split, he or she can also compensate the broker by paying a desk fee. A desk fee is the costs of the office divided by the total number of desks the office holds. If the broker can get a fee per desk, then he or she can make a profit. The desk fee can be a prorated amount, depending on the split the salesperson is willing to take. One hundred percent commission can be obtained with the compensating desk fee.

One Hundred Percent

The 100 percent concept is just that—a concept. In reality, no real estate office could offer all of its salespeople 100 percent of their commissions and stay in business. The concept is basically that the agent keeps all the commission and pays the broker a fee to do business. This concept works well for the *trained, experienced, and independent* real estate salesperson. It is not the best avenue for the real estate neophyte who needs broker support.

I was once at a real estate conference where I heard the keynote speaker talking individually to attendees. One person told the speaker that he was new and hired on at a 100 percent office. The speaker advised him to find another broker. That was not what the new person wanted to hear, but the speaker was correct because at a true 100 hundred percent concept office, the salesperson will get very little help or training. The alluring chance to make more money and to run one's own business with limited management interference is the draw for the 100 percent office.

The 100 percent concept works well for the real estate salesperson who has an established business and does not want interference from the broker or other real estate salespeople. The downside for the salesperson is that he or she must pay for almost all expenses related to the brokerage business. In other words, the 100 percent salesperson is basically operating his or her own real estate company under the name of the broker. To the brokerage company, paying a salesperson 100 percent of the commission with a monthly desk fee and paying for none of the salesperson's business expenses is roughly the same as paying a salesperson 70 percent of the commission and paying for the salesperson's business expenses.

From the broker's point of view, the 100 percent concept works well for the salespeople that are tired of telling the "rookies" how to fax contracts. Be cautious, though; this concept can get out of hand quickly. I worked with a brokerage once that was 100 percent concept and had more than eighty real estate sales people on board. The broker/owner was doing *really* well. The office was supposed to have "votes" on any changes. The brokerage would then follow the voted changes. At the time I joined, it was the number one office in the great state of Texas for that particular franchise. I was paying the brokerage a relative large amount per month to be associated with that office. Well, the "big dogs" (major money producers) wanted a new telephone system. The key to a new telephone system is that the cost would be spread across the total number of associates, and their monthly fee would increase. That did not matter to the money producers, but I was a little over my head at the time, and it really hurt. Things continued on and the money producers wanted more and more. Up and up went the fees. More and more agents left, meaning the fees were spread across fewer salespeople. Within a year the office collapsed on itself and had to surrender. The concept is sound, but management cannot abandon its rights to direction.

In the 100 percent concept offices, a new salesperson can be hired at a traditional split and then move to a 100 percent split when he or she is capable of handling it. In the beginning, the salesperson needs a great deal of the broker/manager's time. As the salesperson improves, he or she needs less and less of that time and eventually becomes completely independent and able to be at 100 percent.

Profit Sharing

Some real estate brokerage firms offer a type of profit sharing. However, as mentioned before, the brokerage firm has to make money somehow, and a majority of the terms are just another way of dressing up the same concepts.

Profit sharing generally works like this: a current salesperson recruits a new salesperson to the office. The recruiting salesperson will get a portion (profit sharing) of the new salesperson's commission. Most real estate companies offer a bonus for recruiting new, productive salesperson, and this works as a modified bonus.

Be careful if you hear of a new "concept," because there aren't any. I do not bury my head in the sand, but I have been around long enough to see how one concept is like another, except for the words used. My advice here is that before you invest in a better way to broker real estate, take the time to investigate all angles and get some insight from those in the industry.

Teams

Teams of real estate salespeople sometimes want to work together and form a team. The thought behind teams is a great concept, except that, like Marxism, in actual practice it is not so great. We will discuss teams at a later time, but now we will look at it in the context of compensation. When planning your compensation plans, you must include the team concept, or else you might be taken for a loss. A real estate salesperson earns his or her way up to a high split and then forms a team that operates under him or her. All production goes under the salesperson with the higher split, and the only loser is the broker. The broker bears the expense of the team, but instead of each salesperson on a different split, they are all paid based on the one person's high split.

Home Office

Another way a real estate salesperson can get a higher split is to work from his or her home. Without the cost of the desk, the broker can offer higher splits. The only problem is that most salespeople have a problem being disciplined enough to work from home. An additional problem is the disconnect that might develop between the broker and the salesperson. Without the aid of the broker, a salesperson must be independently knowledgeable.

Employee

A few real estate companies offer their salespeople the position of employee instead of independent contractor. They pay their employees a salary instead of commission splits. Very few real estate companies actually do this. The up-front costs for a real estate brokerage make salaries almost prohibitive.

Bonuses

A bonus is extra incentive to sell a particularly difficult property, such as those with foundation problems, fire damage to part of the structure, failure to fit in with the surrounding area, location near industry or busy streets, or a so-called "bad" area of town. The property could have a *psychological stigma* associated with it, as happens when an event occurs on a property that creates a positive or negative "feeling" about the property that has no basis in actual condition. For example, if someone had been murdered on a property, the murder would have to be disclosed to any potential buyer and could hinder the sale. Why? No damage occurred to the property, yet many buyers will shy away from viewing a property with a psychological stigma associated with it. Any of these reasons could make a property difficult to sell. Some brokers will offer a bonus to the selling salesperson who can find a buyer. Most bonuses range from a few hundred dollars to paid vacations. I once saw a $120,000 Ferrari given away as a bonus!

The discussion here is whether or not the broker should take these bonuses or allow the salesperson to receive them. All monies earned in a real estate transaction must be paid through the broker, but the broker can pass the money on to the salesperson involved in the transaction. Some brokers allow the salesperson to receive all of any bonuses paid. This money does not count as dollars earned, since it could change a commission split. The problem with allowing a salesperson to receive bonuses is that an unscrupulous salesperson might rig a portion of his or her transactions to be paid as a bonus. The downside of splitting the bonus according to the salesperson's agreed split is ill will. If another broker does not split bonuses and you do, will that have a negative effect on recruiting and retaining salespeople for your firm? Most real estate companies allow bonuses to be paid to the salesperson, but they are monitored closely to avoid abuse.

Conclusion

Compensation structures should be thought out by the real estate broker to avoid losing real estate salespeople to other brokerage firms. The broker needs to find out what is being offered at those competing firms. If the broker reacts too late on compensation issues, his or her salespeople could disappear.

Compensation structures should also be examined from the point of view of the broker. A broker is due a profit for operation, and if consideration is not taken the broker could lose money and still have the risk of the real estate brokerage.

A broker can hire consultants to help in making the correct compensation decisions.

Chapter 7 Review Questions

1. What compensation structure allows a real estate salesperson to retain all of the commission and pay the broker office fees?
   A. One hundred percent
   B. Broker-out
   C. Table fund
   D. Commission draw

2. A bonus to a selling real estate salesperson could come in the form of
   A. cash.
   B. vacations.
   C. new cars.
   D. all of the above.

8 Real Estate Brokerage Staff Relations

Staff relations refers to the care that needs to be taken when hiring and firing both salespeople and staff. Violation of employment laws and regulations can result in severe financial loss. Consulting with an employment law attorney instead of steaming ahead by yourself could save you a great deal of money.

Employment Law

Employment law consists of thousands of federal and state statutes, administrative regulations, and judicial decisions. To keep informed about local laws and regulations, you may want to check with your city's human resources department and your state's workforce commissions or departments of labor. These entities are around to help you understand your rights and your employees' rights.

Independent Contractor versus Employee

Most people consider real estate salespeople to be independent contractors. An independent contractor is someone who is contracted to complete a task but is not hired for a job. An employee is hired to fill a job position. The difference is how they are handled. An independent contractor

1. Must have a written independent contractor agreement
2. Can be told what but not how to do a task
3. Must pay his or her income and social security taxes
4. Cannot receive any company benefits

The real estate broker/owner must determine how to manage real estate salespeople. Some believe that salespeople should receive a small salary and commissions and be considered employees. This would give the manager much more control over their activities. Most brokers require their salespeople to be independent contractors, and then they only get paid what they earn. This decision must be made before any real estate salespeople are brought on board because of the difficulty of changing hiring policies once a hire has been made.

Manager

A manager is usually someone other than the designated broker, broker of record, or owner. In multi-office type systems, a manager is hired to manage an office for the owner. Hiring of the manager is critical.

Most feel that a manager should not compete with his or her salespeople. This means that the owner will have to pay the managers a great deal of money so the manager can manage and not have to worry about personal sales to survive. Other owners offer managers a small salary and then bonuses when the office is in the black. Some owners cannot afford to offer a full salary, so they opt instead for a combination of salary plus commissions. The commission split is highly favorable to the manager, but it still distracts from the managerial duties. However, it does keep the manager active and therefore up-to-date on the current market.

Management Development Program

A broker who intends to have multiple offices and be hiring managers should have a Management Development Program (MDP) to determine whom to hire and to monitor their progress. The MDP should be handled by the Training Director and reviewed by the owner. This program will be discussed in greater detail later.

Sources for Managers

Managers can be from your current sales group or hired from the outside. Here are some ideas on where to look for your next manager:

EXPERIENCED SALESPEOPLE

Current experienced salespeople from your office are the easiest source to fill a manager's position. You have seen these people handle real estate transactions and potentially difficult situations, and you have determined they are ready for management. These manager recruits are not necessarily your top producers. Some real estate companies believe it is best to promote the top producer of an office to the manager of that office when a management position opens up, but this can create a lot of problems for the office. First, you have taken your top producer out of production, and a drop in the office's overall production is bound to follow. Second, you have taken a salesperson with no management experience and promoted him or her to manager. I have actually seen this happen. In one real estate office, the manager quit and the top producer was promoted to manager. She had no idea how to manage an office. The office lost the income that she had been bringing in as top producer because she had been taken away from production. Within a few months, the office doors closed, and the manager went to another real estate company and got back into production. The end result was the collapse of a viable real estate company and the destruction of a potentially great career (the top producer never got back to where she was before the promotion). I understand the theory behind promoting top producers: the company wants to "reward" its producers, but is being a manager a true "reward"?

This problem can be resolved if you have a Management Development Program for salespeople who want to manage. The program will allow them to find out if they enjoy and are good at management without the commitment and loss of production.

COMPETITORS

Pay attention to up-and-coming real estate salespeople from other real estate offices. These salespeople may make good candidates for your Management Development Program. The program is designed to train individuals to become managers of a real estate office. You will find is that the MDP is a great way to eliminate managers. Most real estate salespeople think about managing or owning a real estate office themselves. I interviewed all of my salespeople about this topic, and over 60 percent said they have thought about it. You do not want to tell them, "No, you would make a terrible manager!" even if it is true, because they may get mad and go to your competitor. Your new script is, "Great, you can start in the Management Development Program immediately." Once in the program, they figure out on their own that they are not cut out to be managers and fade back into real estate sales. No harm, no foul. If it is one of your competitor's salespeople, and he or she doesn't work out in the management program, you still have a new salesperson.

COMPATIBLE BUSINESSES

Other businesses, such as banks, retail stores, insurance agencies, and especially the sales professions, make great places to look for management recruits. These people already have some management experience; however, they lack real estate experience. Each of these management candidates must go through the Management Development Program to learn about real estate. It is difficult for me to believe anyone outside the real estate industry would have the respect of their salespeople without knowing about the business.

MANAGEMENT STUDENTS

Most areas have a local college or university. If these educational facilities offer management degrees, look to them to provide management candidates. Colleges and universities want to place their students into fields that relate to their course objectives, and they usually have career days during which businesses that are recruiting put up informational booths to hire the students. Generally, they don't let "sales" companies attend. You are not there to hire salespeople (at least, ostensibly not); you are there to recruit for your Management Development Program. To be eligible for the MDP, one must have a real estate license and currently be selling real estate for a career. The student must therefore obtain a real estate license and join one of your offices. Once the student begins selling, he or she enters the program.

Management Development Program Model

This model is an overview of the levels in the Management Development Program. These levels can be modified according to your wants and needs.

LEVEL ONE—OFFICE RECRUITER AND TRAINING COORDINATOR

At the "Level One" stage in the Management Development Program, the management candidate will learn the basics of managing a real estate office. Very little time will be spent learning the back office workings; instead, most of the time will be spent on learning how to recruit new salespeople to the office. The second most important thing the candidate will learn is how to retain the salespeople they already have in their office. Here are the limited duties of the Level One candidate:

CONTINUE TO PRODUCE REAL ESTATE SALES   The management candidate must continue to produce real estate sales to survive. Few can make a living only on recruiting bonuses. The more experience in the actual practice of real estate sales, the better real estate manager he or she will be.

RECRUIT REAL ESTATE SALESPEOPLE   We start the candidate out with recruiting because it is the most important factor in being a successful real estate manager. Nothing else comes close. If you cannot recruit, you cannot manage—simple as that. Some managers and brokers hire recruiters to help in this endeavor. Maybe that will work, but more often than not the manager must get involved in recruiting for the process to work effectively. If you don't recruit, how can you establish a relationship with the person who will be making you money in your future? It is here you will find that most management candidates will fall out; they hadn't realized that you actually have to work when you're a manager. Because of fear, most individuals are poor recruiters. The fear comes from lack of knowledge; this book was written to provide that knowledge.

ASSIST IN TRAINING HIRED SALESPEOPLE   The second important training aspect of Level One focuses on retention of salespeople. The best way to retain a salesperson is to make sure that he or she has the proper training. Some fear getting up in front of people and speaking; this is important information for you as a broker to know because public speaking is an integral part of managing. You can avoid public speaking in real estate sales, but not in management. As a manager, you are expected to lead training classes, hold sales meetings, and speak in front of hundreds if asked.

The manager of a real estate office should be training salespeople almost all the time. He or she should conduct "just-in-time" training when a salesperson needs a boost. Managers should also conduct weekly new salesperson training, and they should be able to "field" train on a real listing appointment. And these are just a few training opportunities.

Some people are born trainers. Any training conducted by the management candidate must be reviewed and approved by the acting manager. Some people need training to become good at training, and some will never improve. The Management Development Program provides a good way to weed those out that cannot or will not train.

ADDITIONAL COMPENSATION   I mentioned above that the management candidate should continue to sell while going through the training. That is true; however, the candidate does deserve some kind of additional bonus for recruiting. Generally, the bonus is based on the recruit's production. Once the recruit closes a transaction and the company is paid, the management candidate might receive a set amount of cash. For example, the candidate may receive cash bonuses for the first three closings and then nothing more. The candidate is an independent contractor during his or her entire time as a Level One management candidate. The bonuses give the candidate an incentive to recruit as many salespeople as possible.

MONTHLY REVIEWS WITH CURRENT MANAGER/OWNER As long as a management candidate remains in the Management Development Program, he or she should get a monthly review from the current manager or owner. This review could be short or long, depending on whether additional training is needed. The review is also the time to weed out the candidates who will remain even though they aren't doing anything. And finally, the review is the time to promote the best management candidate to manager trainee—but only if a position is open.

LEVEL TWO—OFFICE MANAGER TRAINEE

The manager trainee must continue to perform the duties assigned during "Level One" plus the following additional duties:

REVIEW CONTRACTS The manager trainee will begin to review any purchase agreements and employment contracts completed by the salespeople in order to discover any mistakes in the contracts and to correct (through training) the mistakes before any damage can be done. This is a very important responsibility and the person assigned to complete the task must be very trustworthy. The manager of record must be sure to have trained the candidate well.

ATTEND MANAGEMENT MEETINGS The manager trainee should attend any company management meetings, conference calls, or training sessions. These may vary by the size of the organization. If the company only has two offices and the training is for the manager of the other office, most likely no management meetings will be held. If the training is for the manager of a multi-office company, then management meetings are much more likely. The company may be a part of a real estate franchise or group of real estate brokers in an area. These people meet frequently, and the manager trainee should attend. Additionally, real estate management training is sometimes offered at local colleges or by some nationally recognized speaker, and in such cases the manager trainee should attend this specialized training.

LEARN TO MANAGE OFFICE SYSTEMS The manager trainee should begin learning office systems and how to manage them effectively. These tasks include accounting, billing, collecting, record keeping, charting, reporting, inventory management, advertising, public relations, and all the other office systems that are relevant to the tasks that managers will face.

ASSIST CURRENT MANAGER WITH MANAGEMENT TASKS   The time will come to let the manager trainee walk in the shoes of a real manager. The manager should be sure that the trainee is ready and prepared for the steps he or she is taking. Do not allow yourself or your managers to take advantage of trainees and get them to do all of the manager's "dirty work." The trainee should be assisting with valuable and important work.

ATTEND INTERVIEWS WITH POTENTIAL RECRUITS   The manager trainee should attend as many interviews with potential recruits as possible. This experience will be very valuable later when the manager trainee will be handling these interviews him or herself. The manager trainee should not be involved in the interview, but should watch and take notes on the interaction. In addition, the manager trainee should be involved in the planning and execution of any recruiting events, such as career nights.

COMPENSATION   Typically, the compensation for a manager trainee is the continuation of recruiting bonuses and then a small monthly bonus for the additional performed services. Because this is paid as a bonus, you may be able to keep the trainees as independent contractors (see an employment attorney). You may want to begin to pay these manager trainees a little better and give them a salaried position. If they are good, they are worth it. If they are not good, eliminate them from the program. By not paying your manager trainees well, you invite your competition to pay them better.

MONTHLY REVIEWS WITH CURRENT MANAGER OR OWNER   As mentioned earlier, the monthly reviews will continue throughout the Management Development Program. The review ends with termination from the program, a continuation at the manager trainee stage, or promotion to assistant manager. Promotions can only be made if a position is open.

LEVEL THREE—ASSISTANT OFFICE MANAGER

The assistant office manager must continue to perform the duties assigned during Level Two, plus the following additional duties:

MANAGE OFFICE ADMINISTRATIVE STAFF   The assistant manager now begins the real tasks of managing: overseeing office administrative staff and managing their performance. The assistant manager should be familiar with the duties of the staff based on his or her experience as a manager trainee. The assistant manager does not hire or fire staff but should be fully involved in the decision-making process.

MANAGE THE OFFICE APPEARANCE   The assistant manager should take over the task of making sure the office appearance meets the public's expectations. This includes everything from having enough contracts on hand to having the lawn trimmed and the parking lot swept. The assistant manager should make the "rounds" every few hours to check the office appearance and should pay close attention to salespeople's desks, conference rooms, break rooms, and bathrooms.

CONDUCT POTENTIAL RECRUIT INTERVIEWS   During the manager trainee experience, the assistant manager should have learned to conduct an interview with a potential recruit and to get that recruit to commit to working with the company. The manager should monitor these interviews closely because if the assistant manager does a poor job, the company could lose a good recruit.

ASSIST MANAGER IN TRANSACTION ISSUES   The assistant manager should be present during discussions with salespeople on transaction issues. These discussions can become heated, and the assistant manager should learn how to handle these tense situations. It is important for the assistant manager not to get involved but to be an observer. The assistant manager can handle less difficult tasks with the manager's guidance and direction.

COMPENSATION   At this point it may become necessary to have all assistant managers on a salary. Their production in real estate sales has probably dropped off because of all their duties as an assistant manager.

MONTHLY REVIEWS WITH CURRENT MANAGER/OWNER   The monthly reviews will continue throughout the Management Development Program. The review ends with a termination from the program, a continuation of the assistant manager stage, or the promotion to office manager. Promotions can only be made if a position is open, and promotions are never made to an office where the candidate served as assistant manager.

LEVEL FOUR—OFFICE MANAGER

The office manager must continue to perform the duties assigned during Level Three (except that office managers are not expected to conduct real estate sales), plus the following additional duties:

RECRUIT REAL ESTATE SALESPEOPLE   This is still the most important aspect of being a great manager. Recruiting will be covered in more detail in Chapter 9. The biggest mistake a manager can make is to delegate recruiting. The most effective recruiting comes directly from the manager.

RETENTION OF REAL ESTATE SALESPEOPLE Retention of salespeople who are currently working with a real estate company is the second most important responsibility of the manager. Give me a manager who is a great recruiter and a great retainer, and I could make a fortune and pay for everything else to be done by others. There are many factors to retention, but the main one is caring. Most real estate salespeople leave one office for another because of management, not because of money. They don't feel management "cares" about their situation. The manager should care enough to have the proper office structure, training, and so forth to aid in real estate sales. The manager should monitor the activities of other real estate companies to be sure they are not providing something your salespeople may want badly enough to leave you.

COACHING The manager becomes a coach to experienced salespeople. These salespeople tend not to need typical training because they are already experienced in real estate. What they need is a coach, someone to make them accountable for their goals and to help them with unique problems at work and in their personal lives.

UPGRADE STAFF AND SALESPEOPLE A good manager is never satisfied with the talent in the office but is constantly on the lookout for the next superstar salesperson or manager. The manager is also looking to eliminate any "dead wood" in the office—those who make themselves look good through the work of others but don't really produce anything themselves. Only the manager should terminate staff or salespeople.

OFFICE DIRECTION The manager is also responsible for the office direction, philosophy, and culture. If the office is part of a larger company, the manager must be sure that his or her office is in line with the main company's direction, philosophy, and culture. With that said, a manager has a great deal of influence on the office. Aggressive managers will tend to hire aggressive salespeople. Passive managers will tend to hire passive salespeople, and so on, depending upon the manager.

The office will also conform to the manager's beliefs. If the manager believes in community work, so will his or her office. If not, then no money or manpower will be allocated to community work.

COMPENSATION   All managers must be on a salary. They should have no production in real estate sales because of their duties as a manager. It should also be a company policy that managers do not sell (compete) against their salespeople. Allowing your managers to compete can create a tremendous amount of ill will in an office. I once refused to join a real estate company because it was rumored that the manager was taking all the good leads. I don't know if that was true, but I was not willing to take that chance. All of those rumors started because the manager continued to sell real estate after becoming a manager.

The manager's salary must be enough to get by each and every month, but no more. Any other income they make should come from incentives. Real estate is about earning what you are worth. The same should be true for managers. They should get a small salary and then huge bonuses when their office produces profit numbers. I am aware of many companies that pay their managers a huge part of the profits from their individual offices. If the office does not produce a profit, then they receive no bonus—nor do they deserve one. I know of one manager who makes five times his base salary in bonuses.

Salespeople

Salespeople should be the lifeblood of a real estate company, but the wrong salespeople can be the death of the same organization. The only way to prevent the wrong ones from infecting the entire company is to eliminate them, and the only way to be comfortable that you can eliminate the bad ones is to have a continuous recruiting policy. There are several types of salespeople, including the following:

Shooting Stars

A shooting star is the real estate salesperson who just blows the doors off the place. They list everything in sight. They are constantly showing buyers. The star produces more than any other salesperson within his or her first few months. This continues for maybe a year, but then they fade away and are out of the business within two years. What happened? Some people are very good at starting projects but very bad at finishing them. The manager must keep challenging them with new projects and avenues, or the company will lose them.

Other shooting stars are burnout victims. They work so hard that they leave nothing in the gas tank and burn out. The manager must be aware of the potential burnout victim, because burning out can be prevented. Sometimes the manager must force a shooting star to take time off and eventually a vacation. The manager should teach salespeople time management techniques that may free up time for relaxation.

Top Producers

I have seen brokers open a real estate office with three or four top producers, believing that is all they need to dominate a market. Be careful: top producers can be very good to have, but they can also hold you prisoner. They can threaten to leave, and if you don't meet their demands, your office folds. Treat the top producers with respect, but don't let them take control. The maximum proportion of top producers in any office should be 10 to 20 percent; any more than that, and they can take control.

Middle Producers

I love middle producers! They don't become the headaches that top producers can, and they don't need you to hold their hand like new people do. The middle producer will never be a top producer, but he or she will consistently produce respectable numbers in the middle. You make a fair share off of them, and they make a fair share from you. Middle producers should make up 40 to 60 percent of your office.

Bottom Producers

Bottom producers must be on an accountability schedule or be terminated. They are not doing themselves any good, and they certainly are not doing your office any good. As a broker/manager, it is hard to fire a salesperson. You think it seems cruel, and besides, what if you fire them, and they go to another office where they become a top producer? Whatever! Fire them! The rest of the office will take notice that you no longer tolerate bottom producers. I have seen offices made up of 60 percent bottom producers fail and offices with just a few good producers (both middle and top) make a fortune. You should never have an office made up of more than 10 percent bottom producers, and preferably, you will have none.

New Salespeople

An office must have new salespeople or it will eventually die because of attrition. You are losing salespeople. Some brokers don't like to face facts.

Your salespeople are moving away, retiring, or finding what they consider a better deal from your competition. You must bring in new salespeople to survive. New salespeople should make up 20 to 30 percent of your office.

The Perfect Office

The perfect office is one that looks like an overstuffed sandwich with the bread on top being the top producers and the bread on the bottom being the new salespeople and the people in the middle—yes, the middle producers. That is where the meat of any office is located, and it should be thick and hearty!

Searchers

Searchers are real estate salespeople who are never happy with the real estate company at which they are currently working. They are always looking for a bigger, better deal. They spend their time talking about how good *other* real estate offices are to their salespeople. They never blame themselves for their failures. They are called searchers because they transfer their license from broker to broker to find that sanctuary where all is good and money falls from the sky. Of course, they never find that place, but they make everyone miserable while they are around. They will say things like:

> *"If the broker advertised more . . ."*
>
> *"If we had a better looking office . . ."*
>
> *"If we had more help . . ."*

You get the picture. You probably know one. I remember one searcher who literally went to every single office in a small town and still did not find happiness. I once had a real problem with a broker I was working with, so I called my mentor, who was with a different company. I told him my troubles, and he quickly shot back that I could move and then move again because there is no perfect office and until I figured out it was up to *me* I would never make it. Now that is what I call dead-on advice. You see, searchers find fault with everyone but themselves.

Kennel Dogs

Go to any dog kennel and in one of the back cages there is this little mutt that no one adopts, but the kennel keepers cannot get rid of. The dog has no real use or productive value, but there he sits year after year. We have kennel dogs in this business. You can find them in any real estate office. They are the ones that are in the office first to make the coffee. They will answer any question and will probably know the answer because they have been there so long. They always have a kind word and would do anything for you. The problem is, they don't sell any real estate. The manager should fire them, but who could get rid of the kennel dog—he's so nice. As an owner, you should realize that the kennel dog is taking up space a productive agent could use.

Warning! Kennel dogs will gather together. If you are known to keep kennel dogs around, you will get more of them. Do you want an office full of kennel dogs and no producers? If you have the courage to fire the kennel dog, the office will respect the fact you are serious about this business.

Prima Donnas

Prima donnas start out as the "nobody" real estate salespeople that do everything they are supposed to do. Needless to say, by doing all the things they should be doing, they begin to become successful. Now two things can happen: either they respect where they came from and help others who are trying to make it, or they become prima donnas. The prima donna feels that he or she is now better than anyone else (including the owner). Prima donnas will not participate in any office functions because they don't want to be seen with the little people. If any new salesperson starts to out-produce them, the prima donna will sabotage the new salesperson's efforts. In one office I saw a prima donna go after a new salesperson and accuse her of stealing leads just to get rid of her. Nothing was ever proven, but the manager had to get rid of the new salesperson just to make the prima donna happy. The new salesperson went on to become one of the better producers of her next company, and the prima donna went on to destroy her office.

Prima donnas cause the managers many sleepless nights. The manager wants to fire the troublemaker, but the troublemaker is usually the manager's best producer. I once fired my top three producers because they had all three become prima donnas. They would sit around and devise schemes against all the others. I had finally had enough and fired all three. They screamed (and I *mean* screamed) that they would ruin me and went out and formed their own office. My office's profitability went up after they were gone. Why? Because the prima donnas were scaring any other real estate salesperson I had from showing up at the office and taking all the telephone leads. Now the new real estate salespeople received some incoming prospect calls, and they were on a more favorable split with the office. My total production numbers went down without the prima donnas, but my profitability went up. Which would you prefer? Oh, how about this bonus? I got to sleep at night. One further note: their office only held together for three months before they tore each other apart and shut the business down.

Nesters

I mentioned nesters earlier. These are the real estate salespeople who would rather "nest" than find business. As a matter of fact, business could actually get in their way. You can find the nesters in any office. Just walk through and notice the workspace that has a wall full of awards. Then read the dates on those awards. You will find that they are ten to fifteen years old. What have they been doing for the last ten years? Answer: They have been nesting. They sit around and admire their past work instead of finding new work. Nesting is a contagious disease. Correct it or lose your office.

Conclusion

Real estate brokerage staff relations are critical for operating a real estate office. The broker must know how to treat staff and salespeople. The broker should be great at recruiting and retention, and should be able to train new managers. All of these functions must be learned and mastered by the professional real estate broker.

Chapter Eight Review Questions

1. All of the following are requirements to be considered an independent contractor, *except*
   A. must have a written independent contractor agreement.
   B. can be told how to do a task but not what task to do.
   C. must pay own income and social security taxes.
   D. cannot receive any company benefits.

2. What is the easiest way to fill a manager's position?
   A. Hire a headhunter
   B. Run newspaper advertisements
   C. Recruit a manager from your competition
   D. Hire a salesperson from your office

3. Under the "Management Development Program Model," what is not one of the Levels?
   A. Office administrative assistant
   B. Office recruiter and training coordinator
   C. Office manager trainee
   D. Office assistant manager

4. What are the two main qualities of a great real estate manager?
   A. Great communicator and mediator
   B. Great listener and negotiator
   C. Great legal mind and great at working numbers
   D. Great recruiter and great at retaining salespeople

5. What are the duties of a manager?
   A. Coaching
   B. Staff
   C. Office direction
   D. All are duties of a manager

6. What is a "Shooting Star"?
   A. A real estate salesperson that does great, then quits
   B. A group of "Top Producers" that meet to build their business
   C. A listing that sells quickly
   D. A recruiter or broker who is good at recruiting experienced real estate salespeople

7. The perfect office looks like
   A. an inverted pyramid.
   B. a solar system.
   C. an overstuffed sandwich.
   D. a French horn.

8. Searchers
   A. are never happy.
   B. talk about how good other real estate offices are.
   C. transfer license from broker to broker.
   D. all of the above.

9. Kennel dogs
   A. make the coffee.
   B. are unproductive.
   C. are too nice to fire.
   D. all of the above.

Recruiting Real Estate Salespeople

Introduction to Recruiting

Recruiting in the real estate *brokerage* business is the same as prospecting in the real estate *sales* business. Without constant recruiting efforts, a real estate brokerage business is destined to fail because of attrition. Real estate salespeople are always changing. Some leave the business because they are tired of it or make no money at it. Some leave because of a spouse's job transfer. Some leave because of retirement. No matter what the reason, turnover happens. A real estate company that is fully staffed today may be badly behind in a year. I once heard that the agent who will be making you the most money in five years is not even in the business today. I believe that.

The real estate business has changed drastically in the last decade. Current growth plans of companies of all types will ignite the need for sales professionals who can effectively move products and services. This demand will drive up the prices of those experienced salespeople. Because of this demand, the real estate broker should consider hiring and training people with no formal sales experience as well as those with the necessary experience.

The rules of real estate sales have also changed in the last decade. Previously, the real estate salesperson's role was centered on polished canned presentations and the ability to access the Multiple Listing Service. Now the same salesperson must function as a valued and trusted advisor and be a source of a competitive advantage. If the salesperson fails to fill this new position, the consumer will view all real estate services as being equal and will treat real estate people accordingly. The professional real estate salesperson must be able to understand the problems customers face and sort through all the available alternatives.

Selecting Potential Recruits

One of the most important aspects of recruiting is selecting the right talent. This involves the right marketing to get that particular person to be interested. The proper interview process eliminates the undesirable prospect, and the follow-up insures that the prospect stays with your company. Let's look at the types of real estate salespeople that can be recruited.

PRELICENSED PROSPECTS

A prelicensed prospect is a person off the street. He or she may be interested in the real estate profession or may have no interest at all at this time. However, with the right push, these prospects may be the best real estate salespeople.

The recruiting process for these individuals is just like it was in the real estate sales business. We will discuss the actual process of recruiting later.

NEW SALESPEOPLE

New salespeople have just been licensed. They know a great deal about real estate matters that will not make them money. The best thing about new salespeople is that they are trainable. They are excited to be in the real estate business as a career and are willing to do what it takes to become a success. Without proper guidance, these new salespeople will tend to fade into obscurity. With the proper guidance, these new salespeople can go on to become the top producers of the office.

EXPERIENCED SALESPEOPLE

Experienced salespeople are licensed real estate salespeople who have been in the business for at least three years. The experienced people a broker may want recruit are currently with competing real estate offices. Experience does not equate with production. I have seen real estate salespeople who have been in the business for twenty years and still produce on the poverty level. You ask how that can be, and I will tell you: it is because their spouse makes enough money for the both of them.

LICENSE-RETURNED PEOPLE (EXPIRED)

License-returned people have had their license and for some reason have sent it back to the commission. These people no longer practice real estate but could be a huge resource of referral business. If they keep their licenses active and then send you referrals, the brokerage can still pay them for the referrals. If their license expires, they can no longer receive those monies. A brokerage can have several hundred of these "held" licensees and get business from them. The major rule is that these "held" licensees cannot sell; all they can do is refer, no matter how tempting a sale may be.

Top Reasons Salespeople Choose a Broker

The following are a few of the reasons real estate salespeople have chosen their broker:

1. Company reputation

2. Broker reputation

3. Proximity to personal residence

4. Successful office

5. Professional office appearance

6. Education and training

7. Experienced management

8. Skilled and helpful staff

9. Autonomy to do their own business

10. Name recognition

The following are reasons that a salesperson leaves an office:

1. High office expenses
2. Too much bureaucracy and company control
3. Size of commission
4. Too many mandatory meetings
5. Too many fees and charges related to transactions

Notice that the reasons for joining a brokerage all have to do with management and not commissions, yet the reasons for leaving have to do with commissions as well. The underlying factor is the difference between cost and value. If a real estate salesperson recognizes the value your company offers, they will concentrate less on costs. Spend time selling the expertise of your management team and do not compete or adjust a fair compensation structure.

Recruit the Salespeople You Want

Before you begin recruiting salespeople for your office, you should consider what type of salesperson you actually want. As the broker, you can choose the type of salesperson you want (as long as it is not based on certain protected classes). Do you want the aggressive salesperson? Do you want the technology-savvy salesperson? Do you want the fun people? Think about all the things you want in the perfect real estate salesperson and begin to put a list together of the proper characteristics. This list becomes your "Characteristic Profile." Some of the characteristics you may consider important could include following:

Well educated	Financially secure	Full-time
Logical	Psychologically mature	Competitive
Trustworthy	Quick-witted	Experienced in sales
Intense	Aggressive	Technology–savvy
Business-savvy	Team player	Mild-mannered
Family-oriented	Ethical	Honest
Well spoken	Punctual	Humorous
Hungry	Willing to learn	Fun-loving
Professional	Well dressed	Intelligent
Spiritually balanced	Charismatic	Has a great work ethic
Energetic	Talented presenter	Goal oriented
Organized	Emotionally stable	Highly enthusiastic
Self-disciplined	Risk-taking	Persistent
Practical	Decisive	Well adjusted
Optimistic	Energetic	Poised
Socially interactive	Focused	Discerning
Communicates well	Opportunistic	Good problem solver
Great memory	Detail oriented	Patient

You will then need to determine how to measure these characteristics. Can you observe them in an interview, or could you ask certain questions to get the answers? Will the candidate's background reveal the answers? Whatever the method, the characteristics must be measurable or they cannot be used.

Next, you need to pick the top ten measurable characteristics. Limit yourself to only ten, because too many would pressure you to reject a potentially good recruit who met twelve of fifty characteristics, but nowhere near the fifty needed; however, you look at the twelve characteristics that are the most needed, and the recruit should have been hired.

Take the ten characteristics and put them in ranking order from the most important to the least important. The most important should get the highest value and the least important the least value. If there are three very important characteristics, then give them each a value of twenty and put the rest in order. No matter how you determine the points, the values should total 100. Now put these characteristics and point values on paper and use this paper to evaluate the recruit. The value is the total the recruit actually displays. The scale is from one to ten, with ten meaning the recruit is perfect at the characteristic. Multiply the value with the scale to determine the recruits total points. The recruit should attain at least 700 to be hired. Otherwise, the recruit may not fit well into your system. Your Characteristics Profile could look like Table 9.1.

You have a blank "Characteristics Profile" provided for you in the appendix. Notice that this recruit has a score of 814 and with all things considered, should be hired. Using this approach, you should be able to avoid the hassles of recruiting a misfit to your organization.

TABLE 9.1   Characteristics Profile

CHARACTERISTIC PROFILE

CHARACTERISTIC	SOURCE	VALUE	SCALE	TOTAL
1. Integrity	References	20	5	100
2. Enthusiasm	Appearance	20	10	200
3. Persistence	Interview	20	8	160
4. Willingness to learn	Interview	12	10	120
5. Competitiveness	Interview	8	7	56
6. Family oriented	References	5	10	50
7. Communicates well	Interview	5	8	40
8. Psychologically mature	Interview	4	10	40
9. Goal oriented	Interview	4	8	32
10. Well educated	Credentials	2	8	16
TOTAL		100		814

Recruiting Actions

Yes, you must take action to get recruits. Some brokers sit around and wait for recruits to come to them. It will happen, but the broker will never become the success he or she dreams about. Sound familiar? It should be: it is the same speech we give to our salespeople.

The Best Source of Recruiting Leads

The best source of recruiting leads is by far your existing salespeople. They are constantly in contact with other real estate salespeople in an unobtrusive way. They meet other real estate salespeople at events, open houses, or in everyday business. Your salespeople believe in your system and would be active ambassadors for your company if you would simply ask them to do so.

Develop some kind of incentive to encourage your salespeople to recruit. This could be based upon the new salesperson's production. The bonus could be $100 on the first closing and $250 on the second, for a total of $350. You could pay a long-term bonus for recruits, such as 3 percent of the sales of the new recruit for life. However, I suggest waiting until the new recruit actually produces before you pay the bonus.

You should develop a system to contact each and every one of your current salespeople monthly just to persuade them to recruit. The meeting could be short, or it could be a training session for those that who it. If your salespeople feel weird about recruiting for you, get them to give you a list of real estate salespeople for competing firms with whom they would enjoy working, and then you recruit those salespeople. Whatever you do, don't let another month go by without developing the best source of recruiting leads—your current salespeople!

Telemarketing

In the real estate sales business, we train our salespeople to do telemarketing (cold-calling) for buyers and sellers. The same should be said for us in the brokerage business. We can call certain neighborhoods from which we want real estate salespeople. We can call those in our sphere of influence (those that know us and what we do). We can call around a recent listing or sale.

> ### *Be sure to follow the "National Do Not Call" rules.*

Telemarketing (also called *warm calls* and *gold calls*) is the random calling of homeowners to see if there is any interest in selling real estate as a career. This is best type of prospecting for new real estate brokers because of the following factors:

EASY TO FIND

I found through telemarketing that a significant number of people have considered real estate as a career. Calling for real estate sales, it is about one in three hundred, whereas calling for real estate salespeople is about three per hundred calls. You can get more salespeople—all you have to do is make the effort.

MORE CONTACTS WITH LESS TIME

A great deal of effort is spent on recruiting, but the fastest way is simply to call around a neighborhood. There is no set-up time. There is no drive time. There is no planning time. All you have to do is call.

CAN CALL IN ANY WEATHER

If you plan an outdoor event to get recruits and it rains, it could ruin the entire event. The telephones work in any weather; if the weather is so bad that the telephones are out, it may be time for you to seek shelter. This also applies to you. If you are under the weather, you may not feel like meeting people, but you can call from your sick bed and still get recruits.

UNLIMITED MARKET

As I mentioned in earlier, almost everyone is interested in real estate. The hardest part is separating the interested from the curious. The curious tend to flake out before they make you any money. The interested can be ignited with enthusiasm and make you a fortune.

NO COMPETITION FROM OTHER REAL ESTATE BROKERS

I have *never* heard of any other broker calling for real estate salespeople. Are we too good for that? I keep coming back to what we tell our salespeople: *cold-calling works!*

THESE INDIVIDUALS DON'T KNOW YOU ARE NEW

As a new broker, you may be a little apprehensive about recruiting the experienced salesperson. You feel they can tell that you are new. When you call an individual, that person has no clue that you are new to the brokerage business. By the way, for you experienced brokers out there, this is not permission for you *not* to cold call.

PERFECT TO PRACTICE ON

If you are new to the real estate brokerage side of the business, you may need a little help with your telephone techniques and interview techniques. Telemarketing will help you with both.

YOU PROVE THAT YOU CAN ALWAYS GET RECRUITS

I want to be secure that I can always get recruits. If a major defection occurred in one of my offices, I always knew I could get on the telephone and get recruits. Remember, though, a call today may not make you money until a year from now. The recruit has to complete education classes, pass the state exam, prospect, and then close before you see a dime. Don't wait until you need recruits to call—it may be too late.

THE BASIS OF ALL REAL ESTATE BUSINESS

The telephone is the one thing without which the real estate business would be crippled. We use the telephone to transfer information, to verify agreements, to set up appointments, and telephone for thousands of other functions. We *should* use the telephone to prospect for new recruits.

WHEN YOU PERFECT COLD-CALLING, YOU GAIN CONFIDENCE

You look at your real estate office. You opened the doors with only four real estate salespeople and now you have twenty-six. The office is humming with business. And you—you did it! Your efforts in recruiting have made the difference.

Categories of Recruits

There are certain categories of recruits:

Not Interested—No Prospect

Do not follow up with these people. If they are not interested, don't waste your time tracking them. Spend your time calling other people.

Not Interested Now But Maybe in Less Than Two Years—Lead Prospect

You should follow up with these individuals. Two years in the real estate industry is no time at all. You should develop some type of database management system on your computer (like the one you had when you were selling real estate). You can buy elaborate software or use the software that is installed on your computer when you purchased it. With this technique, you are building a pipeline of future recruits.

Interested Soon, But Not Now—Possible Prospect

These prospects could be good, but you will need to create a sense of urgency. Maybe they want to get in the business when their children graduate from high school. They may want to get in real estate after their spouses retire. Whatever the reason to wait, you need to create the urgency, or they will simply wait. The downside of waiting is loss of income. It takes a while to make any significant money in real estate. The prospect needs to understand that if he or she agrees to real estate as a career, it may be a year before they make real money. Don't scare the prospects—they may make some money—but we are talking about full-time employment type of money. The downside for you is that now you have created interest. They can't help talking about the thought of real estate as a future career. Now they are talking with friends who have friends in real estate, and soon you are recruiting for your competition. Offer a bonus on the first closing, offer to pay for real estate education—whatever you need to do to get the prospect to make the jump could be worth it.

Interested Now—Grand Prospect

You have a winner! The prospect starts real estate school right after hanging up with you. He or she is making you money six months later. Be sure to follow up with these recruits weekly to make them feel you care. Don't believe other sneaky brokers are not recruiting your prospect.

Telemarketing Procedure

When prospecting by the telephone, you should call from the office. There are several reasons for this, but the main one is your connection with the business environment. You are near your real estate salespeople, demonstrating how to cold call and proving you will do what you tell them to do. If you call from home, it is too easy to avoid making the calls. Remember, business is business and home is home—do not blend the two.

Here are the actual steps in telemarketing:

Choose an Area You Want Salespeople from, Quickly

Determine the areas around your real estate office. See if there is an area that is in proximity to your office where you have very few sales. You can cross-check the activity through your Multiple Listing Service. Be careful here: don't spend a great deal of time planning to call, spend a great deal of time actually calling.

Call Anytime

Do not be afraid to call because you might be interrupting some family time. With the script below, you do not interrupt because you are not on the telephone long. (Be sure to follow local and national "Do Not Call" laws.)

Call the Individual

Calling is easy enough—until you actually get down to doing it. We will find any number of things we *must* be doing instead of making recruiting calls. None of that matters; you have made the decision to call—now do it!

Look up Addresses and Phone Numbers in the Cross Directory

A cross directory is a directory listed by street, not by names. Do this quickly. Don't be too detailed. This is not rocket science. Just call. You could delegate this task to an assistant.

Be Professional

Sound professional. Do not sound desperate. We are offering an opportunity for a career. If you sound like you are hiring for a job, you will not attract the wealthy housewife whose husband could be a major source of high-dollar leads.

Set up an Interview with the Recruit

Determine the best time for the interview and clear your schedule because you want to give a hundred percent to the interview processes.

Meet the Recruit

The interview should take place in your broker's office. You should be professional but not intimidating. Ask the recruit lots of questions. The actual interview process will be discussed later in the book.

Contact at Least Once a Month

All your efforts are wasted if you do not follow up at *least* once per month. Whether you contact a recruit more than once a month depends on the recruit's motivation. If the recruit has no interest at this point, contacting him or her once per month is plenty. If he or she is close to a decision, you may want to call a couple of times per week. Following up with these recruits is essential. They have many things in their lives pulling them in every direction. Remember, if it was the perfect time for them to work real estate, they would have called you. You are reducing the time for them to make a decision and that can create stress. Give them time, but follow up—otherwise, when they do choose to sell real estate, it might be with your competitor.

FORMS OF CONTACT

You can stay in touch through a variety of methods. Change your contact method each month. You can use mail-outs or e-mails, or you can even knock on their doors. Here are some suggestions:

- Telephone calls
  Just let them know you are there for any questions.

- Monthly mail-out cards
  You can get cards printed to mail out to your prospective recruits. These cards are a great way to disseminate small amounts of information to your recruits.

- Monthly e-mail letters
  E-mail is probably the most effective way to communicate with your recruits if you have their permission (you must follow Anti-Spam laws). E-mail is virtually free. The only cost is the time it takes to write and send an e-mail. E-mail is also less work than regular mail. You can write one letter and e-mail it to all of your recruits. You do not need to take the time to stuff envelopes, write the addresses, place a stamp, and get them all to the post office. And lastly, you are demonstrating that you are technology-savvy and that you stay on the leading edge.

- Knock on their doors
  Don't do this one but maybe once per year. If you are in the area touring property, stop by and invite them to join your group. They probably won't, but they will remember that you thought of them.

TIPS FOR CALLING

Here are some suggestions for speaking with a recruit once you get him or her on the telephone:

STAND   It gives you more energy. Do not get comfortable and relaxed, because that is how you will sound on the telephone. Stand and sound excited, because that is how you would want your recruit to be. Is this an exciting business? Do you have a "once in a lifetime" opportunity to offer? Or is this what you have to do to make it, and you would really rather be playing golf?

SMILE   People can "see" you smile over the telephone. As with standing, you need to show you are having a good time and that you believe in what you are offering. Check yourself by having a mirror in front of you when you make your calls.

ESTABLISH RAPPORT   Make them like you. The best way to accomplish this is to ask them lots of questions. The more questions you ask, the more they believe you really care. You cannot hire new recruits until they believe you care for them.

GIVE A REASON FOR CALLING   You are calling to announce the need for real estate salespeople in their immediate area. This need creates an exciting opportunity, and they now have the fortune to capitalize. The reason is exciting, and you must communicate that excitement.

QUALIFY THEIR INTEREST IN THE REAL ESTATE BUSINESS   This is where you build the sense of urgency. They should not wait until their children graduate from high school. They should not wait until their spouses retire. They should take this opportunity *now* and make their move toward their future.

GAIN THE RECRUIT'S CONFIDENCE   Make them believe in you and what you do. Show your knowledge of the real estate business by indicating how you see them fitting into the opportunity in front of them. Ask them questions to find out what their "hot buttons" are and then use those areas of interest to gain an interview.

CLOSE FOR THE APPOINTMENT   Ask them for a recruit interview. Once you have gained their interest, you must ask for an interview or offer a career night to them. Do not skip this part. All the effort is wasted if you do not close for the appointment.

Telemarketing is a "numbers game": the more you play, the greater is your chance of winning. The more calls you make, the more recruiting appointments you should arrange. You should block out time in your day for prospecting. I used to put an $8^{1}/_{2} \times 11$-inch piece of paper with the symbol "$" on it. If it was hung on my door it meant that I was making money and not to bother me.

Telemarketing Scripts

GENERAL APPROACH

Broker: Hello, is this Mr. or Mrs. _____? *(Pause, wait for answer)* My name is Dan Hamilton with Acme Realty. Have you ever thought about real estate as a career?

Homeowner: **(No)**

Broker: Thanks, bye.

Homeowner: **(Yes)**

Broker: Great! The reason I asked is because we are looking for a real estate professional in your area. Do you have a second to tell me a little about yourself and what interests you about real estate?

SPECIFIC PROPERTY APPROACH

Broker: Hello is this Mrs. _____? *(Pause, wait for answer)* My name is Dan Hamilton, the broker at Acme Realty. I am calling to see if you have considered selling real estate as a career. Have you?

Homeowner: (**No**)

Broker: The reason I ask is, we recently listed/sold a house near yours at _____ and as a result of our extensive advertising, we have generated quite a bit of interest for homes in this area, and we need more salespeople to handle the interest. Do you know anyone that may be interested? How about yourself?

Homeowner: (**Yes**)

Broker: Do you have a second to tell me a little about your situation and maybe when you could begin your career?

Let's review the advantages of each script. The General Approach can be used by anyone. You can call any neighborhood at any time. Here are a couple of quick thoughts. First, notice how fast you get to your main question—the first question. This is important, because people don't want to talk to you any more than you want to talk to salespeople. Don't miss my point: being a broker is proud work. My point is get to the question and get off the telephone. People are not mad if you don't waste their time. The faster you get off the telephone with someone not interested, the faster you can find someone who is interested. If an answering machine picks up, leave a message with the same script given above. Be sure to leave a telephone number where they can reach you.

The question "Do you have a second to tell me a little about yourself and what interests you about real estate?" is a great question for many reasons. When an individual is called from out of the blue and asked if they have ever thought of selling real estate, they are a little skeptical of your motives. You as a real estate broker are a little nervous, talking with a live prospect. The question, "Do you have . . . ?" relieves the tension on their part because they do know about themselves, and they can relax as they tell you in detail about their situation. Since the individual is talking, you now have time to gather yourself and get the interview appointment.

Be consistent in your telemarketing. Don't call all day one day and then do nothing for the rest of the month. Consistent recruiting is always more effective.

Recruiting Door-to-Door

Recruiting door-to-door is also called door-knocking. Recruiting door-to-door puts you face to face with potential recruits. Take a look at all the advantages of telemarketing, and you will see why door-to-door recruiting is not the best way to prospect. With all of the "Do Not Call," "Anti-Spam," and "Do Not Fax" laws passed recently, and more to come in the future, however, door-knocking may become the preferred choice of prospecting.

- *Territory Canvassing*—Getting out in a neighborhood in which you want to recruit salespeople for work and door-knocking for leads.
- *The Warm-Canvass Door*—You have no real reason to be there, but it's a nice area, and you are going to spend a day there to try to discover someone with an interest in selling real estate.

Basics of Recruiting Door-to-Door

1. After you ring the bell, back up a minimum of two feet.
2. Don't stare at the door. Turn up the street and look away.
3. Don't turn towards them until they acknowledge you.
4. Turn with a nice smile. (Be sure to have your real estate name tag on.)
5. Use this phrasing:

> ***Broker:*** Good afternoon. My name is Dan Hamilton, the broker at Acme Realty. There has been a tremendous amount of real estate activity in this area. I was wondering if you'd thought of selling real estate as a career? Do you know of anyone in the neighborhood who might be interested in a new career?

This type of approach can lead to a discussion, during which you will learn more about the community and its residents. Your new acquaintance may know of some neighbor who intends to change careers later on and will tell you about it. If there is no answer at the door, you should leave a door-hanger with information about you and your company.

Agent with Other Company

The "Agent With Other Company" (AWOC) is a salesperson that is currently licensed with a competing real estate company who believes that he or she is happy with his or her current real estate broker. Let's take a look at that logically: who wouldn't want to stay with their current broker if moving to a new company would cost thousands of dollars in expenses and lost income? Our job is to prove our worth.

One important advantage is that the "Agent With Other Company" is obviously interested in selling real estate. AWOCs believe that they can sell real estate effectively with their current real estate company, and if we try to tell them they can't, all we do is irritate them. Most AWOCs over-price their listings, which creates fewer showings and fewer chances to sell. Eventually, they get the idea that they need help with marketing and selling skills. They will then turn to their broker and figure out their broker can't give them good advice or train them in the proper manner to succeed. Now they begin to take notice on the outside. Why are others succeeding and not me? The salespeople that are succeeding may be looking for better office management and support. What we need to do is be there in their thoughts when they decide that they would consider a change.

I have brokers ask me, "Where can I find recruits?" My answer is, "There are always those at your competitors' offices." I know the brokers know that, but they tell me, "I don't want to recruit other real estate salespeople because I wouldn't want them recruiting mine." NEWSFLASH! They are recruiting yours—you just don't want to face it. Remember way back to when you were a salesperson. How many times a week did you get recruited? I know for me it was several times per week.

Keys to Working AWOCs

1. *You must meet these people face to face, or you have nothing.*

Do not believe you have an AWOC recruiting campaign until you have actually met these salespeople face to face. You could meet them for lunch, invite them to a motivational seminar, or meet them at your office (meeting them at your office can be intimidating, so be careful here). Don't fool yourself into believing that sending out mail-outs is a recruiting campaign; it isn't—it's a marketing campaign.

2. *Be a professional, not a broker.*

Sometimes we think of ourselves a little better than the common folk because we have a broker's license and are owners of our own real estate companies. We are not better, and we should not project that. We should act professionally. Do not meet a recruit at a bar—it is not professional. Do not meet a recruit wearing shorts and a T-shirt. All of this is a major turn off to the AWOCs you want to recruit. You are their broker, not their buddy. Do not embarrass a recruit by making a spectacle out of him or her being in your office. All these actions could spell the end of the recruit.

The charisma and appeal of the broker is key to the recruit's decision to join a firm. Would you work for you? You are constantly in the limelight. Accept this—it is what you signed on for. Do you listen well? Can you show empathy for your salespeople's challenges? Determining your weaknesses as well as your strengths is the basis of becoming a powerful broker.

3. *You must be committed to this program for at least twelve months, or don't even start.*

Twelve months? *Are you crazy!!!* No, I am not crazy, but I am correct. If you make a concerted effort to recruit AWOCs for two months and quit, you will see very few results. Remember, these people do not believe they want to leave their current office. What happens is that the broker makes your recruit mad, and then you have them. Question: When does the broker make the salesperson mad? Answer: I don't know, but I do know that it could happen any day, and you want to be the first person that salesperson thinks of during this time of need.

4. *Follow-up.*

Follow-up with these recruits is essential. Very few will switch from their real estate company based on just one meeting. So to actually recruit them, you must keep in touch with them. You can do that through

- Monthly mail-out cards—You can get cards printed to mail-out to your prospective recruits. These cards are a great way to disseminate small amounts of information to your recruits.
- Monthly e-mail letters—E-mail is probably the most effective way to communicate with your recruits if you have their permission (but you must follow Anti-Spam laws).

Furthermore, you must get the meeting honestly. Some real estate brokers will make a big deal of showing the listing of a potential recruit to a "fake buyer" to impress the recruit. The buyer turns out to be a friend of theirs and isn't in the market to buy a house. That is not honest. The only thing we ultimately sell is our selves. If we don't believe in ourselves, how can others believe in us?

AWOC Action Plan

1. Call the AWOC.

Call the AWOC's cellular telephone, not his or her real estate office phone number. If you do not have his or her cell number, call the office and ask for it. You can call AWOCs at home, but talk with them at their office only as a last resort.

2. Set up an interview with the recruit.

Determine the best time for the interview. You need to realize their time is their money, yet you do not want to look like you have nothing going on. You may want to agree to a time and indicate that you will rearrange your schedule to accommodate them because they are that important. Make sure you are not interrupted during the meeting because you want to give a hundred percent to the interview processes.

3. Meet the recruit.

The interview should take place in your broker's office. You should be professional but not intimidating. If the AWOC is apprehensive about meeting at your office, meet him or her at a nice restaurant (but not during the lunch rush). Also, do not meet for dinner—it could be misunderstood. During the meeting, ask the AWOC lots of questions. The actual interview process will be discussed later in the book.

4. Contact at least once a month.

All your efforts are wasted if you do not follow up at *least* once per month. Whether you contact an AWOC more than once a month depends on the recruit's motivation. If he or she has no interest at this point, contact once per month is plenty. If the AWOC is close to a decision, you may want to call a couple of times per week.

5. Follow up for twelve months.

Calling on an AWOC

    Broker: I am calling for Bob Vinson.
    Salesperson: This is Bob.
    Broker: Bob, my name is Dan Hamilton, and I am the broker at
                     Acme Realty. I have been tracking your performance,

	and I was wondering if you have thought about looking into the advantages of working with our company.
Salesperson:	No, I am happy where I am at but thanks for calling.
Broker:	I am glad to hear that. One more thing: our company is offering an invitation-only real estate seminar on the morning of the sixteenth describing how to increase your real estate business, and I was wondering if you would be my guest to that event.

Let's analyze this script. With the first things you say, you are asking the AWOC to switch companies. Is this too early? No. We teach our salespeople that they must ask for business, so we had better do the same. We then ask again, but this time disguise it by offering a seminar. If AWOCs are really that happy, they will say "no" to my offer of education, but if they not getting the education they feel they need, they will say "yes."

Now, about that seminar: you should be offering real estate training classes in your office at least once per week. If you are not, remember other brokers are reading this book, and they will be recruiting your salespeople. You are simply asking the AWOCs to attend your training session. Once there, they will see that you provide services to your salespeople that their current broker does not. After the seminar, ask them to take a look at your office. Plan to have the tour end at your office door and then ask them to take a seat. Now follow the interview process and end the interview with a "close" to get them to work with you.

If they give you resistance try this:

Broker: Is it the interruption of your business that is keeping you from simply talking with me about your future?

If they respond "no," probe further; if they respond "yes," continue:

Broker: Well, would you mind if I sent some information that might help you build your real estate business?

Whatever the answer:

Broker: I'm sure you have thoughts about your future; before you make any changes, will you at least talk with me?

This script is designed to get an interview and build good will. Remember, this is only the first step in the recruiting process.

Alternate Response:

Broker: I believe in the real estate business, and I believe we should all work together. When you get a new listing, please fax over an information graphic sheet to me, and I will distribute it to my salespeople to help you get your listings sold.

If the AWOC responds:

AWOC: I am on a high split that you couldn't match.

Broker: Great, that must mean you are a top producer. When would you like to sit down and discuss how we can make you even more money?

AWOC: Not right now, maybe by the end of the year.

Whatever time frame they give you, call back every month and verify that their situation has not changed. Remember, AWOCs can get mad at a moment's notice. You might be the only real estate broker that has kept up with them and cared about their situation, so they might end up joining you.

Once you have the AWOC interview should send them a card reminding them of the appointment.

AWOC "Fair Deal"

The dialogue with the AWOC is one of a "Fair Deal." As the words "fair deal" indicate, it is a deal of valuable items. What the real estate broker wants is a recruiting interview. What the AWOC might need is any number of services, and the broker has to find which service will trigger the AWOC to act. The services the broker has to offer include

- Table funding
- National company
- Production awards
- Professional ad writing

- Administrative help
- Great location
- Marketing assistance
- Advantageous compensation
- Management expertise
- Family culture
- Team atmosphere
- Private office
- Unparalleled training
- Noncompetitive managers
- Top-block service
- Relocation business
- Career planning
- Social events
- Ancillary business
- Management advancement
- Accounting functions
- Community service

. . . and any number of other services you offer on a daily basis. Of course, these are examples; if your company does not offer some of these services, you should delete them and add your advantages. What you offer as a "fair deal" is extremely important. This is the beginning of your value package.

Each time you call an AWOC, begin with some small talk like, "How is your business going?" or "Did you have a successful weekend?" The AWOC's responses to these types of questions are always the same: they did great, even if nothing really happened. The AWOCs respond that way because they still believe they don't need you. Don't take this to heart; we know they will need us, maybe not just yet. After the small talk, you need to offer a "fair deal."

Additional Items You Could Offer

Sometimes you must offer the top producers just a little more to help convince them to make the move. These items range from simple gifts to monetary contributions to their bottom line; of course, you would only offer them if you actually provided the service or gift:

- Offer to have the company pay for the first set of personal marketing materials.
- Offer to have the company pay for announcements sent to their service area and clients.
- Send flowers, books, gift certificates, or dinner certificates.
- Send a letter of appreciation as soon as the interview is over.
- Offer the recruit a private office if you have one to give.
- Offer a recruiting bonus for any real estate salesperson the recruits bring with them.
- If your company has several different real estate offices and a corporate headquarters, arrange to have the recruit visit and get a tour of the place.
- Offer to pay for an advertising page for the new salesperson.

Watch for Events

Events taking place in your competitors' real estate offices are some of the best leads to find possible recruits. Every dispute, policy alteration, promotion, demotion, arrival, and departure—that is, every change—can develop into an opportunity.

Additional Ways to Improve Your Recruiting Efforts

Here are some more tips for recruiting:

Terminate Unproductive Salespeople

Terminating unproductive salespeople will not only give the office a lift but may help in recruiting additional salespeople. No professional real estate salesperson wants to work with those who are not serious. Give competitors your problems. Attract their solutions. Immediately target offices that hire your garbage.

Respond When Competition Offers Your Salespeople a Great Package

When competitors are recruiting one of your salespeople, see how what they offer is different from what they offer their existing salespeople. If you find out they are offering a special package not offered to their own salespeople, call and ask them what's going on—especially if the competitor's salespeople don't know this is happening. The only way to find this information out is through open communication with your salespeople.

Alter Current Compensation to Keep Salespeople

Many companies will arbitrarily raise a salesperson's commission to keep him or her. Inform the other salespeople of the office who had earned more and are now on a lower split. Call and congratulate them on the "new commission plan!"

Respond When Competitors Send Letters to Your Salespeople

Use this as an opportunity to praise. Tell your salespeople that they must be doing a good job, and that you appreciate them being with you. Have your salespeople take the letters to listing appointments. Have them use the following script:

> *Salesperson:* Mr. and Mrs. Seller, I appreciate the fact that you are going to interview with Acme Real Estate Company, and as a matter of fact, I have been offered work with them (show letter). Instead, I have chosen to work with the best company, my company—shouldn't you?

Respond When One of Your Salespeople Is Recruited

Send a thank-you note addressing the fact that they want *your* salespeople, obviously because your people are good. This will tend to stop further recruitment because they know you are aware of what is happening. Respond if a competitor's salesperson appears in the newspaper.

Send flowers and a note to the salesperson at the office saying, "Congratulations!" Then call a few days later. Their current broker probably did not say a thing to them.

Advertising for Recruits

The easiest and most frequently used form of recruiting is through print advertising. Many brokers have enjoyed success with the use of simple classified ads. The ads are designed to make the telephone ring with inquiries of interest. The ads should be aimed toward new licensees; very few experienced real estate licensees will answer an advertisement.

Recruiting ads do not need to be wordy. They need to catch the eye of the reader, create enough interest to cause the reader to take a desired action, and direct the action. Before preparing the ad copy, analyze the type of prospects you want in your office and identify their traits and characteristics. Decide who your target recruit might be.

In addition to your personal appeal, which is critical to the success of your ad, every classified ad should carry the reader through four selling steps. These steps are Attention, Interest, Desire, and Action, or AIDA, as they are known through the advertising community.

Attract Attention

You need to catch the prospects' attention with the first few words of your ad, or you will lose them forever. A catchy headline may do the trick. In fact, the headline is probably the most important part of your ad. Other tips for attracting attention include

- Using sincerity, not clichés.

- Describe the ability to control your own time. Real estate salespeople can make their own schedules and work when they choose, and this also gives them the freedom to respond at any time. People want to control their own time. However, if you feel this type of ad will get a lot of lazy people calling, try running the ad without using it. Always document your results to determine the best use of your money.

- Using a lot of white space (that is, space where nothing is written). White space in print advertising attracts attention to your ad.

- Occasionally asking questions in your ad. People have a natural tendency to be attracted to questions.

Arouse Interest

Once you've got a reader's attention, use the interest stage to pull him or her in for further reading. Otherwise, the prospect will stop reading and move on to the next ad. Create interest and desire with the features your company offers to real estate salespeople and the benefits those features deliver.

Create Desire

This stage creates desire: the desire to be part of your company. Writing skill is necessary here to create the right atmosphere for the prospect. If space is available, list the company's most desirable features so that the prospects will able to see themselves selling real estate with your office. Anything less, and you will not receive a phone call.

Call for Action

To get the interview, you must ask for the interview. In ad writing, you must ask for the call. Research has found that

- You will receive a greater response if you close the ad with a request to call, using your full name. Be active. Tell your readers to "Call now!"
- Using the word "please" softens the close, and greater response occurs. So *please* call for action in your ads.

If your ad copy tells all the essential facts clearly, holds the reader's attention from start to finish, and makes a specific call to action, it will be successful. The following is a checklist for writing the ad:

1. Organize all the facts from the reader's viewpoint, not your own. Potential real estate salespeople are looking for a company they feel meets all the needs they have.

2. Appeal to emotions, such as love of success, status, and family responsibility, and so forth.

3. Keep It Simple and Short (KISS). Avoid long-winded sentences; however, do not abbreviate or use real estate jargon. If it is important enough to put in an ad, it is important enough to spell out. Sometimes we get too close to real estate and forget what it is like to be a newcomer to the business, so write the ad looking at the real estate business from the neophyte's perspective.

4. Use meaningful words that stir emotion. Make the readers "feel" the money pouring in. Make them imagine touching the cash and making deposits into their bank accounts.

5. Inspire confidence. Don't use exaggerated descriptions that are not believable.

6. Differentiate your marketing. Advertise in different types of print media.

Ads have the potential to yield large numbers of telephone inquiries. It is important for the broker/recruiter to have a system in place in the company to handle these inquiries, and to consider the following tips:

- The broker and recruiter should NEVER take these incoming calls directly. You should want to control the conversation. The receptionist should be trained to field these calls and solicit the information you need for an appropriate callback. This allows you greater control of your time and positions you to structure the phone conversation.

- Individuals calling into the office should be invited to a "Career Event" held on a regular basis in the conference room at the real estate office. Avoid the temptation to "sell" over the phone. Recruiting is a process. Answering this call is only a part of the process. It is the first step.

Examples of Advertisements

The following are examples of advertisements that could be run to get real estate recruits call your company:

NEED A JOB?

Then don't call me. I am looking for the person who is pursuing a career. I can offer you the opportunity to make a living and a life for yourself. Call today for a career event date.
Dan Hamilton 817-555-1212.

DON'T QUIT JUST YET!!!

Before you leave your present job, let us show
you how you can increase your income.
No experience necessary. We will train you.
Once trained, you can quit your job
and pursue a rewarding career in real
estate. For the next career event
date call
Dan Hamilton 817-555-1212.

JOB SECURITY!!!

A career in real estate offers you job security.
Never worry about layoffs or terminations.
Once you learn the real estate business,
you can control your destiny. We will train you.
All you have to do is have the willingness to
work, to be trained, to work flexible hours.
For more information on the next career
event call
Dan Hamilton 817-555-1212.

YOU DETERMINE YOUR WAGES!!!

You work and you earn. No one can stop you
except yourself. Call today and learn when
the next real estate career event is to be
held in your area.
Dan Hamilton 817-555-1212.

Message for Voice Mail:

Thank you for calling Acme Real Estate Company. Your call is very important and answering your questions about a career in real estate is our greatest priority. If you will leave your name and a number where you can be reached between four o'clock and six o'clock this afternoon, our Career Development Director will contact you. Again, thank you for calling, and we look forward to our discussion later today.

Recruiter call back script

Recruiter: Hello. May I speak with Mr. Smith?

Mr. Smith: This is Mr. Smith.

Recruiter: This is Dan Hamilton, the Career Development Director from Acme Real Estate Company, returning a career inquiry call from you. How long have you thought about real estate as a possible career?

Mr. Smith: Well, I haven't really. Your ad just sparked my interest.

Recruiter: Great. What I would like to offer you is a career event where I discuss all the information necessary for you to make an intelligent decision if real estate is right for you. Could I register you for an upcoming career event?

Mr. Smith: Sure.

Recruiter: Great, I look forward to meeting you.

Once you have set an appointment with a recruit, you must send a reminder card to be sure he or she will show up. You can add any additional information on the reminder card that you would like.

Conclusion

Once you have set an appointment with a recruit, the next phase in the recruiting effort is the actual recruiting interview. The interview will be explained in detail in the next chapter. Remember, though: you can be the best at interviewing and not recruit any salespeople because you have not completed the actions to set appointments. Do not pass this chapter over and concentrate on interviewing. Take recruiting actions and then you will have plenty of interviews.

Chapter Nine Review Questions

1. Recruiting in the real estate brokerage business is the same as
   A. prospecting in the real estate sales business.
   B. stealing in the criminal world.
   C. misappropriation in the corporate business.
   D. research in the academic world.

2. What are some of the top reasons that real estate salespeople choose a broker?
   A. Education and training
   B. Name recognition
   C. Paid salary
   D. Proximity to personal residence

3. Which of the following is the best source of salesperson leads?
   A. Knocking on doors
   B. Courting existing salespeople
   C. Fourth of July floats
   D. Advertising

4. Which of the following is not a good reason for telemarketing for recruits for a real estate office?
   A. To gain confidence as a broker.
   B. It's good practice.
   C. There is an unlimited market of potential recruits.
   D. It's the most expensive type of recruiting.

5. What should you do once you have a possible recruit on the telephone?
   A. Stand
   B. Smile
   C. Apologize for taking up their time
   D. Establish rapport

6. Which of the following in no way violates the "Do Not Call," "Anti-Spam," or "Do Not Fax" regulations?
   A. Unsolicited telephone calls
   B. Door knocking

C. Mass e-mails

D. Faxing a new listing

7. If a broker chooses to go after AWOCs (Agents With Other Companies), how many months minimum are necessary to see any results?

A. 3

B. 6

C. 12

D. 24

8. Which of the following is part of an AWOC (Agent With Other Company) Action Plan?

A. Find an area to call quickly

B. Call the individual

C. Ask for an interview

D. All of the above

9. All of the following could be offered to entice AWOCs (Agent With Other Company), *except*

A. paying for the first set of personal marketing materials.

B. paying for announcements sent to their service area and clients.

C. offering a recruiting bonus for any real estate salesperson the recruit brings with them.

D. offer a higher commission split than current salespeople receive.

10. Which of the following events at a competitor's firm would require immediate recruiting action?

A. Mergers

B. Reorganizations

C. Major policy changes

D. All of the above

11. What is the easiest and most frequently used form of recruiting for real estate brokerages?

A. Billboard advertising

B. Print advertising

C. Door knocking

D. Event sponsorships

12. What is *not* one of the four selling steps in writing a classified advertisement?

A. Awareness

B. Interest

C. Desire

D. Action

13. When writing an advertisement for real estate, all of the following should be done, *except*

A. use clever clichés.

B. use lots of white space.

C. use the word "please."

D. ask for action.

14. When writing an advertisement for real estate, all of the following should be done, *except*

A. organize all the facts from the viewpoint of the broker.

B. appeal to emotions.

C. keep it simple and short.

D. differentiate your advertising.

10 Recruiting Interview

Recruit Interview

You have accomplished a worthwhile goal—getting an interview with a real estate recruit. That success will quickly be dashed if you stink at interviewing. The new recruit and the AWOC must be treated differently. The first thing you should do is introduce the new recruit to real estate as a business.

Recruiting Introduction Discussion

When recruiting a person considering a career in real estate, the broker should make the person aware that real estate sales is a unique business for the following reasons:

1. Real estate sales involve complex and intense transactions, including written contracts, spaced negotiations (buyer and seller do not negotiate directly), marketing, and finances.

2. From the first meeting with a client to the actual closing, real estate business can take a great deal of time, many things can go wrong, and tempers can flare. The recruit also needs to understand that the money is not received until the property is closed.

3. There are numerous laws and regulations that the real estate salesperson must follow.

4. Real estate is usually the largest single purchase a buyer will ever make and the largest sale the seller will ever make.

5. Residential real estate is a relationship business. The more people like and trust you, the greater success you will achieve.

Recruiting Interview Hints

When an individual agrees to meet with you and let you present the advantages of real estate and working with your company, you should do the following:

- As soon as you hang up with the recruit on the telephone, you should put a note in the mail reminding him or her of the date of the interview and a business card.

- Clear your schedule and tell your assistant to hold your calls. Give this recruit the respect he or she deserves. I think too many brokers have been in the business so long that talking with a recruit is "ho-hum." Don't let this happen to you. Get back that enthusiasm that you had when you first began.

- During the interview, write down anything the recruit says. If it is important enough for the recruit to say, it is important enough to write down.

- Prepare in advance for surprises during the interview. Flexibility is the key.

- We cannot use the same presentation with proven producers that is used with new licensees.

- The interview should be held in a conference room, not in the broker's office. A broker's office is too much of a power place for a recruit. If the conference room is too open, choose a more secluded room. Remember, you should never be alone with a member of the opposite sex, for obvious reasons. Offer the recruit a soft drink, a notepad, and a writing instrument.

- The first "interview" is really a planned involvement presentation.

- You should create visual aids that address the wants and needs of the real estate salesperson. This is the time to show off the company web site.

- You should list the features of your office, and then emphasize the benefits of using those systems. Be sure you differentiate yourself from your competition. If you know your competition cannot offer something that you can, ask the recruit: "Have you ever seen anything like that before? Can you see how we can help you build your business better than any other brokerage company?"

- When finished with the interview, show the recruit through your office and introduce him or her to your real estate salespeople

INTERVIEW OBJECTIVES

We must have a preplanned series of objectives for the interview. Here are a few objectives you should incorporate into your interview:

BUILD RAPPORT   You and the prospect should get to know each other. Concentrate on them and their lives, not just real estate. No one will work with you unless they like and trust you.

ASK QUESTIONS   Spend most of your time asking questions. Questions allow you to control the interview process and gain information. Another benefit to asking questions is that it shows concern for your prospect.

ELIMINATE THE COMPETITION   You must eliminate your competition. You have competition from the recruit's current employer and any other brokerages out there. Do not disparage your competition, but do know what services they offer and design ways of using this information to your advantage.

DO A "WANTS AND NEEDS" ANALYSIS   You should conduct a "Wants and Needs" analysis during the interview to find out what motivates the recruit and how your company can aid him or her in fulfilling that motivation. A "Wants and Needs" analysis is explained next.

> *"Top Producer Recruiting Rule—Prospects will always want the best packed proposal, with **all** of the benefits included, from the most reliable company, at the higher commission split, that the most unreliable company with the least amount of benefits is offering!"*
>
> *—Jim Gilreath, national recruiting and retention expert and speaker*

Questioning Techniques

When interviewing recruits to work with your real estate company, you must use lots of questions. Questioning is by far the best way to communicate. We should ask questions to achieve the following goals:

- To gain control
- To isolate areas of interest
- To get minor agreements
- To arouse emotions
- To show we care
- To isolate objections
- To answer objections

Questions can be placed in two major categories: the open-ended question and the closed-ended question.

The open-ended question solicits a discussion on the part of the recruit. The recruit can talk forever because of your question. The best open-ended questions paint a picture, and the recruit finishes that picture for you.

Some examples follow.

Broker: Without limitations, how much would you like to earn in the real estate business and what would you do with that money?

Broker: What are your concerns about changing real estate companies?

Broker: Describe your ideal work environment.

The closed-ended question is meant to solicit a "yes" or "no" answer. It is used to direct the recruit, preventing the recruit from expanding on an answer. Some examples of closed-ended questions include:

Broker: Do you want this room as your personal office space?

Broker: Can you make a decision today?

There's another reason to discipline ourselves to ask questions instead of immediately responding with our own answers: a question engages the other person and helps create a more meaningful exchange and a better relationship. It shows we are interested in what that person has to say. You can't move forward in real estate recruiting with a reluctant prospect unless and until you manage to create a climate in which that person is talking with you, not just listening to you.

"Wants and Needs" Analysis

A "Wants and Needs" analysis helps identify a potential recruit's real estate brokerage wants and needs and helps you to match recruit's and broker's wants, needs, and motives to the specific services available for the real estate salesperson.

The "Wants and Needs" analysis will give you an opportunity to "read" your recruits better and paint a picture of their wants and needs. The most effective way to "read" your recruit is to listen. Spend more time listening and less time talking. When you do speak, the best way is through probing questions or questions that have purpose.

In a wants and needs analysis, the rapport-building step should take place in the first few minutes of each new, important contact with a person. From a psychological viewpoint, rapport-building is extremely vital to the outcome of the communications process. The significance of the rapport-building step becomes apparent when we analyze it from a behavioral viewpoint. When individuals place trust in each other or feel comfortable with each other, they lower their defense mechanisms and become more open and agreeable to listening to ideas. The intensity of the defense barriers will vary with each individual and the specific situation.

It is your responsibility as a professional real estate broker to take action to reduce these defense barriers and relieve the tension that exists in all communication situations in the initial stages. It is important to recognize that this defensive reaction on the part of the other person is not a reaction to you personally. It is a reaction to the situation and is normal and natural. The specific techniques you utilize to lower defense barriers will vary depending upon your natural behavior and personality. The important point is that you should recognize that defense barriers do exist and develop your own techniques to lower them and establish rapport.

However, a recruit's decision to choose a particular real estate office to join is often more emotional than practical. Getting a sense of his or her lifestyle gives you better insight into their emotional needs. Ask questions like:

- Who else will your decision affect?
- Do you need a private office?
- Do you have any special needs that are a concern?

- How soon would you consider joining our company?
- Must you settle any matters before making the decision?
- Do you currently have any listings? Pendings? If so, when will they close?
- Are you familiar with the procedures for changing real estate companies?
- Have you interviewed any other offices that you liked?
- Did you make any written agreements?
- Are there any other real estate agents who may want to move?
- Why are you thinking of moving?
- What do you like best about your present company?
- What do you like least about your present company?
- Do you have any special interests or hobbies?

If you have to interview your recruits more than three times, perhaps you should sit down and reevaluate their wants and needs.

Additional Recruiting Interview Questions

The main thing a broker should concentrate upon is asking the recruit meaningful questions. Questions allow you to control the interview as well as show concern for the recruit. Here are a few questions you could ask:

GENERAL INTEREST QUESTIONS

- "What do you (think you will) like most about being in real estate?"
- "Do you (think you will) prefer listings or buyers? Why is that?"
- "Where do you see yourself in five years? Ten?"
- "How do you feel about the market?"
- "What is your most successful marketing idea?" or "How do you plan on marketing yourself?"
- "What's most important to you in a real estate company?"

OFFICE/MANAGER QUESTIONS FOR THE AWOC

- "May I ask why you joined 'Competitor Realty'?"
- "Have the reasons why you chose the company then and the reasons why you are with them today changed at all?"

- "What do you think of the company's overall office policies?"
- "Would you like to see any of those polices changed or improved?"

Discover what the recruit likes most/least about the owner, manager, company, and other salespeople in the office. Anything he or she likes, you had better be able to duplicate. Anything he or she dislikes that also characterizes your company, you should be able to correct.

The broker now has an idea of the recruit's wants and needs. The next step is to show the recruit how the company meets those wants and needs. The best way to handle the presentation part of the interview is to use a presentation manual.

Recruit Presentation Manual

A recruit presentation manual, also called a *marketing book,* is a manual showing the recruiting candidate the broker's value package for the real estate salesperson. This manual sends a consistent message over and over again. Because it is consistent, the manual keeps you from straying to areas that might be construed as violations of the federal, state, and local employment laws. (Hopefully, this is not a problem to begin with, but the manual helps prevent any errors.) The presentation manual serves two main purposes:

1. Provides a visual presentation of the services offered. A majority of people are visual in nature. This means recruits may gain a greater understanding of the company by seeing it all laid out before them rather than just being told about it. The presentation manual accomplishes this goal.

2. Provides a track for the real estate broker to follow. One of the biggest fears of a new real estate broker is the recruiting appointment. The broker just does not know what to do and what to say. The presentation manual overcomes this dilemma.

Main Topics of a Recruiting Presentation

The following is a list of topics that should be covered in a recruiting interview and the order in which they should be presented:

Rapport-building

"Wants and Needs" analysis

Broker's duties

Company value package

Compensation structure

Asking to join

Recruiting Packet

A recruiting packet includes of all the documents needed to place a property on the market. Most real estate companies will make up listing packets for their salespeople. If the company does not do this, the real estate salesperson must. A complete listing packet should at least include all of the following items:

- Independent Contractor Agreement
- Company Office Policy Manual or Supplement
- Advertisement Request Form
- Compensation Agreement
- Company Agency Manual with Authorization
- Yard Sign Installation Form
- Suggestion-for-Training Form
- Office Repair Form
- Commission Disbursement Authorization
- Any additional forms required by law or the broker

Keep several of these packets in your briefcase and in your automobile. You never know when you might need a recruiting packet.

Costs of Recruiting

In setting up a recruiting campaign, you must know the costs. The following lists several items that could cost you money:

- Recruiting print advertisements
- Design, printing, and postage for recruiting brochures
- Cost of exterior lighted signs and/or yard signs
- Salary and benefits or fees for a staff recruiter

- Career nights

    Advertising

    Printing

    Time

    Signs

    Room rental

    Refreshments

- Recruiting Contests
- Bonuses for salespeople or managers who bring in new salespeople
- Branch managers' time spent recruiting (calculated using a percentage of salary and benefits)
- Interview time
- New salesperson's aptitude or other profiling assessments
- Company-paid costs associated with licensing
- Cost of trainers, office space rental, and training materials
- Start-up supplies such as signs, stationery, and business cards
- Administrative time for processing new salespeople

First, add up all of the previous costs that you have for a given year and divide by that number of new salespeople who've joined your company in the last twelve months. You'll get the cost for recruiting each new salesperson.

Second, calculate the other costs of operating your office, excluding sales commissions, off-the-top franchise and referral fees, MLS and NAR® costs reimbursed by salespeople, and management commission overrides, but including all other fixed expenses.

Divide total fixed expenses by the number of full-time salespeople you have. That's your cost of retaining salespeople.

Add the cost of recruiting to that of retention, and you'll have a sense of what you're spending to acquire a new salesperson and support that person's share of your overhead.

You may also want to factor in how long it'll take new salespeople to generate enough dollars to offset recruiting and start-up costs.

Objection Handling Techniques

When you practice the art of recruiting real estate salespeople, you will find that some of them will have concerns that they believe will hinder them from joining your real estate company. We call these *objections,* and we want to discover how to handle those. Here are some suggestions to help you:

- Develop powerful, preplanned responses for each objection to be successful at recruiting the best. List the most common objections you hear. Then create a list of compensating benefits. Get your salespeople's input about what they like about your company.
- The objections you'll hear will change, depending on the type of salesperson and company you'll be recruiting from. Make sure you customize your responses.
- Best way to prevent objections—Be prepared!
- Keep your responses short.
- Practice—Drill—Rehearse.

Objection versus Rejection

It is important not to read the resistance in an objection as a personal rejection. All of us fear rejection to varying degrees, and it is important to recognize that we may have a tendency to take an objection personally, especially if we've had a tough day. Begin thinking of objections as questions with emotional content. This will help you deal in a more positive way with the substance of the objection and the person objecting.

Whatever the case, don't worry. Most objections are not as serious or formidable as they seem. Often what appears to be an objection is merely a request for more information.

Objections can help you if they mean that your listener

- Is interested in what you are saying
- Is listening attentively enough to have objections
- Is thinking through your solution
- Is trying to resolve foreseeable difficulties
- Wants more information about your proposed solution

Remember, too, that the absence of objections can be a warning that your recruit may not be interested, or is not listening.

Objection versus Question

The main distinction between an objection and a question is that a question requires only information. An objection has some emotional content and often indicates resistance to your offer. In the latter case, you have to provide reassurance as well as information.

Open-Ended versus Closed-Ended Questions

Open-ended questions are the ones that can have the recruit talking for hours. Closed-ended questions only have a "Yes" or "No" response. You want to ask open-ended questions when you want to gather information. You would want to ask closed-ended questions when you want to severely direct the conversation. Both can be used effectively. The best way to handle a stall is to ask questions. These questions should be very directive and should be closed-ended.

Tips for Addressing Objections

Here are some tips for addressing objections:

1. Agree with the recruit.
2. Direct the recruit to his or her final objection by asking minor questions.
3. Now you know the recruit's final objection and should be able to handle a true objection. (True objections will be discussed later.)

The usual final objection from an experienced real estate person is commission splits or office fees, whereas the usual final objection from a new real estate salesperson is training and broker support. Direct them to those areas by using closed-ended questions. For example:

Recruit: I would like to think it over first.
Broker: I understand that this is a difficult decision. Let me ask, are you thinking about the size of our office?
Recruit: No, the size is fine.
Broker: Is it the area where the office is located?
Recruit: No, I like the area.
Broker: Is it me, do you like and trust me?
Recruit: Of course, I like you.

Big pause, then slowly . . .

Broker: Is it your proposed commission split with us?

Recruit: Well, you know, it is less than I was hoping for.

Broker: I remember, but let me ask you, if we could agree upon a commission split, would you join my company today?

Recruit: Yes . . . yes, I would.

Notice the way the broker moved through a series of questions towards the final objection and then closed on that objection.

Handle Objections by Asking Questions

To handle objections, you must ask lots of questions. Sound familiar? It should. It is the same thing I said about handling stalls. When you become great at asking questions, you will be great at handling objections. Your questions must have a purpose (we call these *probing* questions).

Here are seven steps for handling objections or addressing concerns that almost always work in your favor. These steps also work well in defusing tense situations.

STEP 1: HEAR THEM OUT

When someone trusts you enough to tell you what's bothering him or her, be courteous and listen. Don't be quick to address every phrase uttered. Give the person time; encourage the person to tell you the whole story behind their concern. If you don't get the whole story, you won't know what to do or say to change his or her feelings. Don't interrupt, either, because you may jump in and address the wrong concern. Important point here: While listening to your recruits, you should take notes on everything they say. Doing so allows you time to analyze what they are saying so that you have notes to reflect upon at a later time. But most importantly, it shows you care about them.

STEP 2: FEED IT BACK

By rephrasing their concerns, you're in effect asking for even more information. Be certain the recruits have aired it all so no other concerns crop up after you've handled this one. In doing this, you're asking them to trust you. Clarify the concern by probing to learn why they feel that way. People sometimes need help expressing their feelings. This approach helps all parties understand the true nature of the concern. Begin your probing questions as follows:

Broker: If I understand . . .
Broker: Are you saying . . . ?
Broker: Will you tell me more . . . ?
Broker: Will you explain further . . . ?
Broker: What you are saying is . . .

When the concern is clear, move on to the next step.

STEP 3: QUESTION IT

This step is where subtlety and tact come into play. If the recruit objects to not having a private office, don't say, "What's wrong with that?" Instead, gently ask, "A shared office makes you uncomfortable?" If it does, the recruit will tell you why. Maybe he or she doesn't want privacy. Maybe it feels like a demotion. Now you can move forward and handle the objection.

STEP 4: DIGNIFY IT

Dignify the concern by voicing genuine understanding of how the other person might feel the way he or she is feeling. Noting that many other people in the same situation have felt the same way warms the other person to your response.

Broker: I can appreciate that. Other candidates for our company have felt the same way.
Broker: I understand how you feel.
Broker: That's a reasonable point of view.
Broker: That's a good question.

STEP 5: DISCUSS IT

Once you're confident that you have the whole story behind a concern, you can discuss it by providing information that explains the advantages of your perspective and reassures the other party.

Broker: We have a large number of salespeople that take advantage of our . . .
Broker: Market data shows we are selling our inventory in ninety days or fewer . . .
Broker: I could help you with . . .

STEP 6: CONFIRM YOUR ANSWER

Once you've answered the objection, it's important that you confirm that your recruit heard and accepted your answer. If you don't complete this step, the recruit is very likely to raise the same objection again. If he or she agrees that your comment addressed the concern, then you're one step closer to persuading the recruit. If he or she is not satisfied with your answer, now is the time to know—not later, when you're trying to get the recruit's final approval to go ahead. Confirm that the concern has been successfully addressed. Ask the recruit if he or she believes the information you have just presented could make a difference in the situation at hand. Ask if he or she sees the benefits. (Make sure it is no longer a concern.)

> *Broker:* Will that be okay?
> *Broker:* Does that sound like a service you could use?
> *Broker:* Do you see the benefit of . . . ?

STEP 7: LEAD ON

Lead on to the next section. Don't just keep talking. Take a conscious, purposeful step back into your presentation. If it's appropriate, turn the page in your presentation binder or booklet. Point to something other than whatever generated the objection. Take some sort of action that signals to the other person that you're forging ahead.

These seven steps, if you learn them and apply them properly, will take you a long way toward achieving your goal of selling others, even when they raise objections or concerns.

Objection Handling Worksheets

Objection handling worksheets are used to prepare for all anticipated objections during an interview session. Realize that while all objections cannot be overcome, good interviews help recruits move closer to a decision to join your company. The main key to handling objections successfully is identifying the specific nature of the objection, which can only be given by the recruit. Remember that any time an objection is resolved, the opportunity exists to move the recruit closer to making a change.

Here are the basic steps in writing an objection handling worksheet:

1. List all potential objections you can anticipate against someone joining your company.

2. List all the potential causes of those objections.

3. List potential questions to identify the cause for the individual's objection. You will need more than one question to match the style of the interaction. Phrase these in actual question format.

4. List objection handling techniques for each cause. Phrase these using your actual wording.

If you complete these objection handling worksheets, you will find that you are prepared to handle almost any objection. Note the objections you struggle with on a worksheet.

Closing Techniques

When I meet a person, my first goal is to get him or her to like me and trust me. If you tell me something, I have a tendency to doubt you. Work on asking rather than telling. The following are techniques used either by you or on you. Some of them are manipulative. To be manipulative, the technique would benefit only you, not your recruit. Be sure your interest is always directed toward your recruit. If you choose not to use them, at least you will recognize them when they are used on you. These techniques are in no specific order.

Trial Close

The trial close is used to take the temperature of the recruit. A trial close asks a question and if the recruit agrees, he or she is interested. If the answer is negative, the recruit is not ready to make a decision. The best trial closes are "tie-downs" and "if-then" closes.

The following is an example of a trial close: "When do you want to take possession of your office?" If the recruit likes the house, he or she will answer. If not, he or she will protest. Now you know whether or not to move to the final close.

The Tie-Down Close

A tie-down is a question at the end of a sentence that demands a "yes" response. It is used to affirm a positive the recruit shows an interest in. If the recruit responds with a "yes," he or she might be interested. If the recruit is apathetic to your "tie-down," then this is not right for the recruit, and you must change direction. Here are some examples of tie-downs:

Broker: A reputation for professionalism is important, isn't it?
Broker: It would be convenient to move as soon as possible, wouldn't it?

> *Broker:* The services we offer could make you money, don't you agree?
>
> *Broker:* In a well-recognized office in this area, you could serve your clients better, couldn't you?
>
> *Broker:* You are interested in your listings having complete exposure, aren't you?

The question is not necessarily used to get an answer; just a nod of the head will do. Use the tie-down in the beginning of the sentence and in the middle if you so desire. Here are further examples:

> *Broker:* Wouldn't you agree that this an enjoyable working environment?
>
> *Broker:* Isn't it exciting the activities that can be accomplished with a large advertising budget?

Like all the techniques, this one can be overused, so be careful.

Alternate of Choice Close

An alternate of choice is a question with only two answers. Both are minor agreements leading toward major decisions. For example:

> *Broker:* I have an opening now for an interview, or would later today be more convenient?
>
> *Broker:* I can be available at 2:00 p.m. or 4:00 p.m. Which time would better suit your schedule?
>
> *Broker:* I can clear my schedule for you on Saturday or Sunday. Which would you prefer?
>
> *Broker:* If everything goes according to your plan, about how soon would you like to move, sixty or ninety days?

Assumptive Close

An *assumptive close* is a question that assumes the recruit agrees with your proposal or statement; if not, they must stop you. For example:

> *Broker:* Mary, what is your license number for the transfer papers for the real estate commission?
>
> *Broker:* We have our office meeting on Friday, do you want me to introduce you at that time, or shall I wait another week?

Feedback Question Close

The feedback question close is taking a minor objection and warmly feeding it back in the form of a question. For example:

Recruit: I don't want to jeopardize my current pendings.

Broker: You don't want to lose your pendings? Will you elaborate on that?

Recruit: I don't want to make anyone mad at me.

Broker: Oh, you don't want to make your previous broker angry? What makes you think he (or she) won't understand?

Recruit: Can you guarantee me that I will make more money than I am now?

Broker: Can I guarantee you more money? Does your current broker guarantee you money?

Recruit: Will you put a notice of my changing companies in the local newspaper?

Broker: Do you want me to run a notice of you changing companies in the local newspaper?

Recruit: Will you advertise my listings without my approval?

Broker: Would you prefer that we call before we advertise any of your listings?

Similar Situation Close

A *similar situation close* involves relating a (true) story about someone else who was in the same situation that your recruit is in now. For example:

Broker: He was so hesitant; then he went ahead with the change-over, and today he has moved and is a top producer.

Recruit: I think it would be best to move at the end of the year.

Broker: That certainly is true. The best time of the year to transfer real estate companies is at the end of a year; however, it's a proven fact that few recruits are willing to wait to the end of a year to take advantage of the income potential of working with our company. In fact, it's possible that any positive that you would achieve would be offset by the loss in income you would see if you did wait. Have you ever changed real estate companies before? It can be a rude awakening. In fact, a while back I had a real estate recruit who was determined to wait to the end of the year to make a change.

Unfortunately, by waiting he lost thousands of dollars in increased commission income that he would have received by making the change early. He said that after he analyzed the differences, he decided he never should have waited. This is the type of thing that bothers me about waiting to make the change, and I would hate to see the same situation happen to you.

Reduce to the Ridiculous Close

There are all kinds of ways of describing the cost of something. If you went to the Boeing Aircraft Company and asked them what it costs to fly a 747 from coast to coast, nobody would tell you it is $50,000. They would tell you it is eleven cents per passenger mile.

You are working with a recruit who truly wants to change real estate companies but doesn't want to pay the costs of making a move. Consider using the following script:

Broker: How much do you think it will cost you to make the move?

Recruit: Well, once you consider that I will have to produce new personal brochures, business cards, and marketing materials, probably $5,000.

Broker: I know $5,000 seems like a lot of money, but tell me, how long do you plan on selling real estate?

Recruit: The rest of my life.

Broker: Well I appreciate that, but let's say you only sell real estate for another twenty years. If you break down that $5,000 per year, you're only looking at [punch your calculator, since you carry one with you] $250 a year. If you look at the big picture, you get the advantages of dealing with our company, including the additional advertising we do, for the price of a nice hotel room for one night!

Broker: Let's see what that works out to be [punch the calculator] per month. Twenty dollars, hmm. What does it cost for you and your spouse to go to the movies?

Recruit: Well, I guess about eight dollars a person.

Broker: Add popcorn and a drink, and you are well over the twenty dollars. And for that twenty dollars, you can get your own private office and access to a shared secretary!

Broker: I wonder what that is per day? [Punch the calculator.] Sixty-six cents per day! That is less than you would pay for a cup of coffee, and I am not talking designer coffee.

Broker: Let's get serious, you want to make the change. We are sure the costs will be outweighed by the increased services you will receive. As a matter of fact [rummage through your pocket for three dimes and toss them on the table], let me pay for your first day. All I need you to do is authorize this paperwork, and I will do my best to get your transfer through within the week. [Hand the recruit your pen.]

Some explanation is necessary. First, not all techniques work all the time, but all of them work some of the time. Also, note that the recruit wants to make a change. If you are pushing the recruit into a decision just to get another recruit, you are being manipulative. We are professionals, not high-pressure salespeople. To use this technique properly, start big at an annual figure and work your way down to the daily amount.

I used this technique on an accountant once. After I finished, the accountant said, "Your numbers are all wrong. Financing $5,000 is a lot different, plus there are tax consequences and the time value of money to consider. But I do want to join your company, so I will pay the $5,000." Now, I am not sure what happened, but the recruit joined my company. Sometimes the recruit just needs a moment to reflect.

Puppy Dog Close

This close is just like it sounds, and it came from pet shop owners. A family might walk into the pet shop and look at a cute puppy dog. The kids and the wife fall in love with the puppy. The husband also falls in love with the puppy but is hesitant to buy the puppy. The pet shop owner says, "It's Friday, take the puppy home with you over the weekend and, if on Monday you don't want it, just bring it on back." What happens? Of course, the family never brings the puppy back.

This is a favorite technique of auto dealers. They offer to let you take the car for a test drive, hoping you will fall in love with it and won't be able to give it up. So how can we use this in real estate recruiting?

Have the recruit use a spare desk with a telephone, or better yet have his or her space already prepared. Offer the recruit the use of the desk while you do some quick paperwork of your own. While using the desk, the recruit begins to feel part of your office.

Good Guy/Bad Guy Close

The famous police interrogation: One bad cop beats up and threatens a "perp" until it gets out of hand, and the good cop steps in and removes the bad cop: "Come on Joe, go get yourself some coffee." Joe, the bad cop, steps out saying, "Okay, but I am not done with you yet!" The good cop says, "Man, you had better tell me what I want to hear before Joe gets back, 'cause I have never seen him that mad."

I have never attempted this close, but it is easy to see how it could work. One person is the "heavy" and tells the recruit what would be expected if he or she joined your company. They act somewhat harsh and demanding. The other person is the "mediator" and tells the recruit all of the benefits the recruit should expect from the brokerage firm. By working both sides, you give the recruit a complete view of the organization.

The team should realize that some recruits need the real aggressive push, while others prefer a softer approach. This team could literally cover all territory.

Take-Away Close

The *take-away close* is most famously used by car salespeople. They ask you for your best offer and whatever you say, they reply, "What? I can't do that; I guess you will have to find another, less expensive car. Could I show you the . . . ?" But no other car will do for you, so you pay the greater amount.

You can use this technique in real estate, but be very careful. This one is very touchy. Recruits can and will feel you are manipulating them if you use this technique more than once.

Appeal to the Higher Authority

When a real estate broker is asked to do something that he or she does not want to do, he or she is tempted to blame it on someone or something else. For example, a recruit asks us to raise our commission splits and the standard reply is, "That is against the company policy." Don't you hate somebody telling you, "I'm sorry we cannot do that because it is against company policy"? That is an example of appealing to the higher authority. The real estate broker must be thought of as the higher authority in a transaction. As the broker, you should be able to negotiate with the recruit for the best of both parties. No matter what, do not appeal to the higher authority.

If–Then

The *if–then* close is one of my favorites. It is the perfect trial close. For example:

Recruit: Will I get relocation business?

Most real estate brokers respond with:

Broker: If we have some, you will be put on a rotation basis.

Or

Broker: Sure.

There just isn't anything there. No talent, no skill. The recruit is clearly interested because he or she asked a question about the income he or she could make *only* if he or she joined your company. Let me rephrase the recruit's question:

Recruit: I really want to join your company. I want to change today if you can close me. If not, I will join another real estate company. Oh, by the way, if you offer relocation business, that would be great!

Does that phrasing help? In my book, that is what the recruit is saying. If recruits want the house that badly, I am going to get it for them. If I were to close them right here, I would see how motivated they really were.

Broker: Mr./Mrs. Recruit, if I can guarantee you relocation business, then would you agree to join our company?

However the recruit responds, I now know a whole lot more than I did ten seconds before I asked the question. Don't miss the opportunity to use a great close if it is handed to you. This is the difference between a professional real estate broker and "just another" broker. As with all techniques, don't overuse this one.

Conclusion

For many real estate companies, determining which real estate salespeople will do well is simply a guess. They hire everyone and the ones that succeed, succeed, and those that don't will leave. Just keep hiring—that's the ole "Hire 'em if they can fog a mirror!" attitude.

In today's real estate marketplace, the broker may want to be more careful. The courts are now recognizing the relationship between a broker and their salespeople and are finding fault with brokers because of their salesperson's actions. Another concern is whether the new salesperson will fit into the culture of that particular real estate office. The wrong salesperson could harm office camaraderie and negatively impact overall productivity.

Chapter Ten Review Questions

1. An objection is a question that should be answered.
   A. True
   B. False

2. In what type of close do you ask, "When do you want to make the announcement that you have changed offices?"
   A. "If–then"
   B. "Questioning"
   C. "Trial"
   D. "Puppy Dog"

3. What must a broker do to handle an objection?
   A. Give lots of reasons.
   B. Ask a lot of questions.
   C. Ignore all the objections.
   D. Take a lot of notes.

4. A "benefit" to a recruit always answers what question?
   A. Will I make more money?
   B. Will it sell faster?
   C. So what?
   D. Will it be more convenient?

5. While listening to your recruits, what is the most important thing for you to be doing?
   A. Smoking a cigarette
   B. Thinking of how to close them
   C. Watching their body language
   D. Taking notes on everything they say

6. All of the following are objectives of a recruit interview, *except*
   A. building rapport.
   B. eliminating the competition.
   C. promising anything.
   D. doing a "Wants and Needs" analysis.

7. A "Wants and Needs" analysis accomplishes all of the following, *except*
   A. identifies a recruit's likes and separates those from the recruit's must-haves.
   B. matches the recruit to the services you offer.
   C. creates an effective way to "read" a recruit.
   D. provides a sure way to determine the success of a recruit.

8. What are the main purposes of using a recruiting presentation manual?
   A. To keep the broker on track
   B. Visual presentation
   C. Both A and B
   D. Neither A nor B

9. Which of the following is not a step in the recruiting interview?
   A. Determination of the race of the recruit
   B. Rapport-building
   C. Conducting a "Wants and Needs" analysis
   D. Discussing the company value package

10. All of the following should be included in the recruiting packet, *except*
   A. the Independent Contractor Agreement.
   B. the Company Office Policy Manual or Supplement.
   C. the Compensation Agreement.
   D. all should be included.

11. What is the difference between "Features" and "Benefits"?
   A. Features are what the recruit expects, and Benefits are those beyond expectations.
   B. Features are earned only by independent contractors, and Benefits are earned only by employees.
   C. Features are the aspects of the service, and Benefits fulfill a need or satisfy a preference.
   D. Features are on birds, and Benefits are small outbursts.

12. If a recruit *cannot* say "yes" to joining your company, that is called
    A. a condition.
    B. a stall.
    C. an objection.
    D. a rejection.

13. What type of question solicits only a "yes" or "no" response?
    A. Probe questioning
    B. Closed-ended
    C. Controlled questioning
    D. Open-ended

14. All of the following are steps in the handling of objections, *except*
    A. anticipate it.
    B. feed it back.
    C. question it.
    D. dignify it.

15. "A reputation for professionalism is important, isn't it?" is an example of what close?
    A. Anticipation close
    B. Tie-down close
    C. Assumption close
    D. Questioning close

16. If you are the broker and a recruit asks you, "Will I get relocation business?" the best response would be
    A. "sure."
    B. "you will be put on a rotation basis."
    C. "if I can guarantee you relocation business, then would you agree to join our company?"
    D. "I don't know, but I can find out for you."

Retention of Real Estate Salespeople

Introduction to Retention

Brokers should work hard to recruit new real estate salespeople, but they should not neglect their current sales staff. Retention is the second most important step in making a brokerage profitable. Here are some words a broker should live by:

> *Recruit the right talent*
>
> *Hire the right talent*
>
> *Develop the right talent*
>
> *Retain the right talent*

Call Nights

Brokers design call nights for prospecting so that salespeople can obtain buyers and sellers. Call nights are great for the brokerage because the more listings a company has, the more money that brokerage will make. It also has the benefit of "retention." Most real estate salespeople like to gather together; they are a sociable bunch. You as a broker should have events at least once a month to keep your "family" together. Now, what kind of event would you like to hold: an event at a bar, where attendees drink until they can't stand up and then have to drive home, or a call night, where pizza and soft drinks are served and telemarketing calls are made to generate business?

The key to making a call night successful is, first, to call it a "call night." We don't want to misinform anyone about our intentions. We want telemarketing calls made. You should make a general announcement to everyone so that you don't exclude anyone, but you may also want to send a few personalized invitations to the core group that listens to what you say and follows your lead. Once these people tell others of the fun and business they are getting from a call night, more will begin to join.

The event should start with a snack or dinner so those that are late won't miss out. Call nights provide time for bonding, so allow about a half hour to eat and talk. The next thing on the agenda is to have about thirty minutes of introduction and training. During this time, welcome any new members and go over some of the highlights of the event from the past.

Next, train salespeople using the latest prospecting scripts and telephone techniques, and explain any new regulations that apply. Have new information each time so your veterans can look forward to learning something. Provide handouts about what you teach so they'll have something to take with them. You do not have to teach everything at once; this should be a recurring event, so you will have plenty of time to teach about telephone prospecting. Demonstrate the actual script for prospecting several times to make the salespeople feel comfortable with the routine. Then put them on the telephone so they can call. Assign them to telephones and give them lists of numbers to call (follow the National Do Not Call regulations), tracking paper to monitor their calls, and the script they should use.

Your job now is to monitor and coach them as they call. Record any things that happen from which others can learn. Walk around from person to person. Lead them in cheering for successes, and coach in private. After about forty-five minutes to an hour, call them back to the training room.

Once everyone is back in the training room, have a summary session to recap the things that occurred while prospect calling. Make sure to address any negative feelings, but concentrate on and celebrate the successes. This is where you teach the entire group, using examples of situations you observed, offering better ways to handle those situations. Match each person with an accountability partner. The two partners should continue prospecting during the next four weeks. Each should call the other and make them accountable for prospecting.

You should end with some simple game to play together to build unity. After the game, give everyone an assignment page (continue prospecting or any other specific assignment you deem necessary) and tell each person individually that you appreciate him or her.

The event should be fun and exciting. The event is even better if you can design it around some kind of theme. No one should be calling from behind a closed door. When someone gets a prospect, everyone cheers! You can only get this excitement by having interaction between salespeople. You, the broker, lead those cheers because without your leadership, no one will know what to do.

Company Events

At least twice a year you should invite the entire company to participate in some type of event. The event should be big but not necessarily expensive. For example, you could hold a "family day" picnic where salespeople and their families bring a covered dish and some meat to grill. The company provides the drinks and condiments. Have some type of game or sporting event, or simply enjoy each other's conversation.

Other events could include:

- Chili cook-off
- Day at the movies
- Night at the opera
- Sporting events
- Community work
- Fund-raising for a charity
- Easter egg hunt
- Christmas party
- Thanksgiving feast
- Awards rally

The type of events should be geared toward to the main populace of the company. If the group wants to go play bingo, arrange an event night complete with a bag of goodies and bingo markers. If the group is into athletics, sponsor a company softball tournament with a trophy for the winners and fun for all.

AWARDS RALLY

Holding a companywide awards rally is so important that it deserves its own section. I believe every real estate sales company should have a year-end awards rally for its office to reward those who have made the company a success. Don't underestimate the power of awards. I have known top real estate salespeople who have left one real estate company for another simply because they felt unappreciated.

The awards can be simple or elaborate, depending upon the type of award given. Award criteria should be posted throughout the year so that your salespeople will know what it takes to get one. Do not give an award for mediocre production; make your people strive to get one. Giving an award to everyone so no one feels left out is just rewarding poor production and diminishing the value to the genuine producers.

Some real estate companies hold this awards rally at hotel convention rooms where everyone dresses formally for dinner. Others have a breakfast ceremony, and still others have this event at their own office. No matter the size or spectacle, it still must be held. Major awards that should be given include

- Top producer in sales volume
- Top producer in dollars earned
- Top listing agent (total number)
- Top sales agent (total number)

You have an unlimited ability to reward behaviors you want repeated. If you want your office to concentrate on listings, you should develop more listing awards, such as

- Most listings from For Sale By Owners
- Most listings from Expireds
- Most listings from Sphere of Influence
- Top number of listings in any month

The kinds of awards you can give are limitless. Just be cautious not to give an award away to anyone who did not really work to achieve it. If you give away the award for "top number of listings in any month" and one of your salespeople lists fifty lots that belong to "her daddy" at $2,500 each, you may be awarding someone who does not deserve it. You should have minimum requirements for the awards; listings must be at $50,000 or greater for at least six months to be eligible for awards. Only ten percent of the listings can come from any one source. These requirements will allow you to reward the behavior you want to see again.

Training

Training is one of the most important services a broker/owner can offer a real estate salesperson. Proper training will help the most experienced salesperson make more sales and the least experienced to get a good start on his or her new career, and will save any real estate salesperson from some of the education that is obtained through the "School of Hard Knocks."

Larger firms usually offer more extensive programs than smaller firms. Most universities, colleges, and junior colleges offer courses in real estate. At some learning institutions, a student can earn an associate's or bachelor's degree with a major in real estate, or even advanced degrees concentrating on the real estate industry. Many local real estate associations sponsor courses covering the real estate fundamentals, risk reduction, and legal aspects of the field. Advanced courses in mortgage financing, property exchanges, investment, and other subjects are offered infrequently.

Covering the Costs of Training

Should a broker/owner of a real estate office charge for training? There are many aspects that should be considered.

THE COST TO THE REAL ESTATE COMPANY   No matter what type of training is offered, there will be costs associated with it, such as the printing or purchasing of materials, the facility to hold the training, and the talent fee for an instructor. Presentation equipment may need to be purchased. All of these items add to the broker's costs.

Smaller brokers usually do all the training in-house, and the broker instructs the classes, which are provided, at no charge to the salespeople, to make them better at the real estate business. Larger brokers provide training in-house but also frequently hire trainers from outside their offices to do specialty training at extremely high costs. As a broker, do not get caught up in the line, "If I can get your real estate salespeople to sell just one more house, this training will more than pay for itself." That is a standard promise, and you could spend a fortune on real estate courses when you would have received those extra sales if you had motivated and monitored your salespeople better. Never pay for a course you could provide yourself.

SALESPEOPLE'S EXPECTATIONS   A real estate salesperson expects his or her broker to provide certain types of training classes, such as new agent training to get the newly hired salespeople started, risk reduction training to keep salespeople safe, and current topics training to keep them up-to-date. Veteran salespeople expect too much from new salespeople. They seem to forget what it was like to be new. If a new salesperson makes a mistake or costs a veteran salesperson some extra time, the veterans will blame the lack of training as the culprit.

TRAINING OFFERED BY THE COMPETITION   A broker/owner will need to monitor what the competition is offering to their salespeople. If one company offers training as a benefit free of charge to their salespeople whereas you charge a fee, will you lose salespeople? If you don't charge a fee, will you lose too much money because of the cost of the training? Salespeople will leave one company for another because of "lack of training." Sometimes you will find out that the training was actually being held, but the salesperson never attended. Don't get frustrated, as I did as a trainer. I felt that I provided the best training available, but in the end I got complaints because I did not provide better training.

OTHER BENEFITS OF TRAINING   In one real estate office where I was the training director, we had our own real estate school approved by the state's real estate commission to offer certified prelicense and continuing education, meaning we could hold certified training classes for our salespeople. For example, we offered a marketing class for free to the salespeople, but if they wanted the credit hours for their license renewal, they had to pay a fee. We had the right to publish that we offered FREE marketing classes to our salespeople, and we also offered to get their education requirements met while in class. Everybody loved the idea and paid the fee. A loss center became a profit center overnight.

JUST-IN-TIME TRAINING

Just-in-time (JIT) training is the training provided right before a sales event occurs. Suppose a new real estate licensee wants to hold an open house but does not know how. The real estate trainer would teach the licensee the basics of holding an open house at that time. A real estate salesperson cannot know everything about the real estate business, especially if he or she is relatively new to the business. Just-in-time training does not replace weekly training, but it does add to it. Just-in-time training allows the salesperson to move ahead with the belief that if he or she needs training, it will be provided just-in-time.

The broker or training director should be available to train just-in-time classes when the need arises. Nothing is more frustrating to a salesperson than needing training and being unable to get it. If you find yourself doing too many JIT training situations, it may indicate that actual classes in classrooms are necessary.

FIELD TRAINING

Field training is offered to new real estate salespeople to help them on their first one or two listing appointments. The trainer, broker, or manager will attend new salespeople's appointments to help win listings for the salespeople and the company. The trainer should not "do" the listing but be there to help. The salesperson must be the presenter. If the trainer does the presenting, two unwanted results may follow: first, the seller might bond with the trainer rather than the salesperson, and second, the salesperson might come rely on the trainer to *always* attend the presentations. Instead, the salesperson should feel the action and understand the dynamics. The salesperson should be the focal point. The trainer is there to help if a problem arises and to review the presentation with the salesperson after the appointment. The salesperson should begin to believe that he or she could present independently.

Right after the presentation, the trainer should go to a local fast-food restaurant and review the events that occurred during the presentation. The trainer should make notes during the presentation so as not to forget what to cover during the review. Each negative should be offset by one or two positives. The feedback should be honest but not cruel, and it should be immediate because any time lost means the feedback will rapidly lose its impact.

OFFICE MEETINGS

A broker/manager should offer salespeople specialized training at every office meeting. The training should be short and concise. Topics could include

- Contracts update
- Telephone techniques
- Fair housing review
- Agency law review
- Listing new construction

- HUD 1 (closing document itemizing all costs and charges) discussion
- Latest technology
- Legal case studies
- Figuring seller net sheets
- Best practices
- Prospecting quick hits
- Marketing ideas
- Business planning
- Tax implications
- Staging property
- Working with referrals

The training should be diversified, timely, interesting, and exciting. Do not let your salespeople dread the training. Instead, give them a reason to show up.

NEW SALESPERSON TRAINING

New salesperson training should be offered weekly, depending on the number of new salespeople the office has. This training should be for twelve weeks or until the new salesperson can operate independently, and it should cover basic prospecting, basic career planning, and seller and buyer presentations.

Instructors should be rotated as often as possible so that the new salespeople will get differing insights to the real estate business and be exposed to a variety of moneymaking ideas. The more marketing and prospecting ideas the new real estate salesperson learns, the better.

To further the new salesperson training, the trainer should make the students accountable for completing an assignment before each class. The assignments could have a wide range. The broker could ask the students to talk with loan officers about mortgage services, to call on a particular group of individuals for business, to design a real estate business plan for themselves. The broker could require the students to have the assignments checked off as they complete them. By being accountable for their assignments, the students prove they have been paying attention, and the training will result in greater real estate production. Don't let the salespeople become full-time students and part-time salespeople.

Here is a list of classes that should be offered at regular intervals; select courses according to your office's needs:

- Real Estate Professionalism
- Ethics in the Real Estate Business
- Characteristics of Successful Real Estate Salespeople
- Technology Uses in the Real Estate Industry
- Time Management and Planning
- Psychology of Marketing, Promotion, and Advertising
- Real Estate Law of Agency
- Alternative Representative Agreements
- Prospecting for Seller Appointments
- Seller Listing Procedures
- Prospecting for Buyer Appointments
- Buyer Listing Procedures
- Objection Handling Techniques
- Client Follow-up
- Referrals in the Real Estate Business
- Real Estate Contract Writing
- Real Estate Negotiation
- Activities After Contract Acceptance
- The Closing and Funding Process
- Real Estate Financing

Provide these courses on a rotating basis. The training should be offered every so often for the sake of your newest sales associates.

EXPERIENCED SALESPERSON TRAINING

Experienced salesperson training is for those salespeople who have been in the real estate business for long enough that they know the basics of the real estate business. The training should cover new types of prospecting, new technology, and using a personal assistant.

Every brokerage company should devise ways to help the experienced salesperson attain top producer status. These classes would be designed to teach the experienced salesperson and then make him or her accountable for putting the learned techniques into production. Monitor what you teach, because if you don't, it will be a waste.

TOP PRODUCER TRAINING

Top producer training is for salespeople who fall within the upper 5 percent of production. This type of training should focus on developing the real estate person's character and on topics such as conflict management, retirement planning, and personal marketing.

Business planning is a must for the top producers, who do not need prospecting techniques because what they are doing is obviously correct. The broker should coach each top producer individually. This accomplishes two major objectives. First, it builds the top producers' business by making them accountable directly to the broker, and second, it gives them specific times to spend with the broker, making them feel important.

SPECIAL SITUATION AND LEGAL TRAINING

During the course of a year, national training experts hold seminars in the local area, and the broker/manager should be aware of these events. These events generate a great deal of excitement and motivation. Don't miss these opportunities to get your salespeople involved.

All the salespeople should be aware of all the new laws and any changes to existing laws. Your salespeople may act as if this training is a drag, but in the end they appreciate it, especially if the training is enlightening and may have saved them from some legal battle.

Mentoring/Teams

A mentoring program is one in which a veteran real estate salesperson is paired up with a rookie salesperson. The veteran is to take the rookie out and show him or her the real estate business firsthand. Training occurs by observation and explanation. Be careful, though: sometimes the veteran will use the rookie to do all the dirty work and not actually teach him or her anything. Some real estate companies charge a fee or a "percentage of sale" for this mentoring.

Most real estate companies allow real estate teams to be formed. A real estate team is where two or more real estate salespeople get together and work as a team. All the production goes to the team and all the expenses and profit is allocated to each member. Again, be careful: do not allow teams to be formed in your office unless everyone gains. Real estate business tends to be an individual business, and teams can be difficult. If members are not truly out for the best for the team, the individuals will tend to scrap.

Office Policies and Procedures Manual

Every professional real estate office should have an office policies and procedures manual. As the broker, you will need to be sure your salespeople are trained in referencing the manual for any questions and their personal performance. A manual without training on its use and effectiveness is worse than worthless.

An office policies and procedures manual can be great recruiting tool because it gives a potential recruit an insight into what is expected of them and your company's professionalism. Most brokers never show a recruit their office policy and procedures manual until they have agreed to work with their company. I know of no brokers that use their manual as a recruiting tool. If the recruit is from one of your competitors, you will impress him or her because the competitor's office doesn't even have a policy and procedures manual.

Imagine that two associates in your office just found out they've both been working with the same buyers. How would you, the broker/owner, handle such a situation? Your best option is to check your office policy and procedures manual. The manual should explain the procedure to handle such a challenge. You might not make everyone happy, but you'll have a clearly outlined, fair plan.

From handling for-sale-by-owners (FSBOs) to settling commission issues, a well-designed policy and procedures manual for the real estate office is a must because it avoids a lot of unnecessary confusion and disputes among the salespeople as well as outlines the rules and regulations of the real estate commission.

The policy manual should be given to each real estate salesperson, and everyone should read it. We all know that a salesperson might not read every page, so a good practice is to have all salespeople sign a notice that indicates that they have read and understood the policy manual.

When writing a policy manual, you should include the following:

- Commission splits
- Bonuses

- E&O (Errors and Omissions) insurance
- Administrative fees
- Training
- Production expectations
- Office support
- Independent contractor agreement
- Agency rules
- Dress code
- Termination
- Assistants
- Corporate structure
- Ethics
- Contract writing
- Membership in associations
- Office hours
- Office appearance
- Office functions
- Office maintenance and cleaning
- Lockup and security
- Personnel records
- Sales documentation
- Front desk
- Sexual harassment
- Advertising
- Telephone operations
- Office equipment
- Postal services
- Office files
- Personal items

- Food in the office
- Confidentiality
- Conflicts of interest
- Property signs
- Printed material
- Smoking
- Types of listings
- Offers
- Disclosures
- Referrals
- Sales meetings
- Performance review
- Awards program

Once you have written your office manual, you should get a second opinion from an attorney on certain sections, such as settlement regulatory compliance and the process for terminations. The manual should be a fluid, responsive document, yet once issued, the document cannot change unless the changes are thoroughly thought out. If you have to make a change, you should distribute it to all salespeople and get their signatures to prove that they understand the changes. You could have a consultant write an office manual for you, but the cost is typically prohibitive.

Ancillary Businesses

Agents appreciate a broker that can offer their clients the benefits of ancillary businesses. Ancillary businesses have grown out of the need and demand by the consumer to have a "one-stop-shop" set of services from a real estate company. Consumers want to trust their real estate professional to aid in services such as mortgage, title, inspections, and appraisal all the way to telephone service and discounts on travel. The more of these "concierge" services a real estate company provides, the more valuable that company is to the consumer. In some real estate offices, the ancillary business is a huge revenue source. Real estate companies charge a fee to an ancillary business to get recommendations from the salespeople. Be careful here and consult an attorney, because participating in this type of cooperative business practice could violate the Real Estate Settlement Act or state regulations if not handled properly.

Conclusion

Retention is an important function of a real estate broker, second only to recruitment. Retention mostly revolves around the broker's ability to show genuine interest to each and every one of his or her real estate salespeople. Certain programs should be implemented to insure that communication is available and used throughout the organization. Good brokers will not neglect their current salespeople but will nurture them and support them.

Chapter Eleven Review Questions

1. What do we call an event designed for prospecting so that salespeople can obtain buyers and sellers?
   A. Career nights
   B. Call nights
   C. Opportunity time
   D. Sales rally

2. Which of the following is not recommended for a company event?
   A. Chili cook-off with prizes given for best entry
   B. Christmas party with open bar
   C. Fund-raising for a charity
   D. Sporting event

3. Which of the following award should not be given at an awards event?
   A. Top producer in sales volume
   B. Top producer in dollars earned
   C. Top nester for the company
   D. Top listing agent

4. What is one of the most important services a broker/owner could offer a real estate salesperson?
   A. A more conducive compensation structure
   B. An in-depth marketing campaign for leads
   C. The best Internet and Web presence available
   D. Comprehensive and detailed sales and legal training

5. What should a broker/owner consider when deciding whether to charge for training?
   A. What is the cost to the real estate company?
   B. What does the salesperson expect?
   C. What does the competition offer?
   D. All of the above.

6. What type of training is offered to the new real estate salespeople to help them on their first one or two listing appointments?
   A. Just-in-time training
   B. Listing training
   C. Field training
   D. Probationary period training

7. What type of training should be offered at real estate office meetings?
   A. Contracts update
   B. Telephone techniques
   C. Best practices
   D. I-win-you-lose philosophy

8. What type of training should be offered to new real estate salespeople?
   A. Real Estate Professionalism
   B. Ethics in the Real Estate Business
   C. Characteristics of Successful Real Estate Salespeople
   D. All of the above

9. What other type of training should be offered to new real estate salespeople?
   A. Technology Uses in the Real Estate Industry
   B. Time Management and Planning
   C. Psychology of Marketing, Promotion, and Advertising
   D. All of the above

10. What other type of training should be offered to new real estate salespeople?
   A. Real Estate Law of Agency
   B. Alternative Representative Agreements

C. Prospecting for Seller Appointments

D. All of the above

11. What type of training should be offered to new real estate salespeople?

A. Seller Listing Procedures

B. Prospecting for Buyer Appointments

C. Buyer Listing Procedures

D. All of the above

12. What type of training should be offered to new real estate salespeople?

A. Objection Handling Techniques

B. Client Follow-up

C. Referrals in the Real Estate Business

D. All of the above

13. What type of training should be offered to new real estate salespeople?

A. Real Estate Contract Writing

B. Real Estate Negotiating

C. Activities After Contract Acceptance

D. All of the above

14. What type of training should be offered to the top producing real estate salespeople?

A. Conflict management

B. Retirement planning

C. Personal marketing

D. All of the above

15. In which program is a veteran real estate salesperson is paired up with a rookie salesperson?

A. New agent assignment program

B. Dependent contractor program

C. Mentoring program

D. Liaison program

16. All of the following should be addressed in a real estate office policy manual, *except*

A. the company-offered commission splits.

B. the E&O insurance policy and premiums.

C. the preferred office religion.

D. the training the company provides.

17. All of the following should be addressed in a real estate office policy manual, *except*

A. production expectations.

B. the class of people hired.

C. the support the office provides.

D. independent contractor agreement.

18. All of the following should be addressed in a real estate office policy manual, *except*

A. agency rules that apply to the office.

B. the office dress code.

C. the office termination policy.

D. the office required sexual preference.

19. All of the following should be addressed in a real estate office policy manual, *except*

A. the office corporate structure.

B. association memberships that are required.

C. the required marital status of each employee.

D. the office hours and required work hours.

20. All of the following should be addressed in a real estate office policy manual, *except*

A. the office policy forbidding the addition of any new children to management staff.

B. the office functions.

C. the office policy on personnel records.

D. the office policy on sexual harassment.

12 Real Estate Business Development

Introduction

The business development/relocation business is an incredible source of business revenue for the real estate brokerage office. However, in the day-to-day operation of a real estate business, brokers tend to overlook the relocation business. Relocation business ranges from a sole transferee to the relocation of an entire organization. The larger the move, the more detailed and technical the move becomes, and the more additional personnel are needed.

In many markets, bottom-line revenue from relocation activities may be as high as a fourth of the office's total income. Corporate relocation business exists in good times and bad. When the economy is good, corporations tend to expand. When the economy is bad, corporations downsize or transfer employees to other areas of service. Mergers and acquisitions frequently take place, resulting in the movement of personnel.

Transferees have a high degree of motivation. The increasing practice is for corporations to offer "bonuses" for employees who sell their home themselves. This often eliminates the necessity of the company purchasing the home, which means corporate dollars may be saved. Transferees are under a time crunch, since living expenses in the new location may only be paid by the company for a limited time. For many transferees, the move to the new location is not optional.

Corporate clients are unique opportunities for repeat business as well as referrals to other companies. Corporate clients and relocation management companies do not have time to train sales associates about every transaction and will continue to utilize the services of well-trained relocation professionals who understand their expectations and manage their costs.

Setting up a Relocation Mind-Set

Before you go after the relocation business, you need to figure out the personality of your office and what you can sell to relocation directors. (I will use the term *relocation director* or *director* to name the person you talk to, regardless of whether that is the actual title.) You need to determine whether you will be the lead for your company and perhaps the only person going after relocation business or whether you will develop a new department in your current organization. If you already have a business development department in your company, how can you and your team get more relocation business?

First, you need to determine how you are going to position your company. Positioning determines your marketing message. Your positioning should convey a unique and strong selling proposition that decidedly sets you apart from the competition. Ask yourself these questions first:

- Who is our target market and what do they really want from us?
- What is our business promising to fulfill?
- What are our strengths and weaknesses?
- Who are our competitors and what are their strengths and weaknesses?
- What are our values?
- What are the trends and gaps in the current marketplace, and what is the best way to capitalize on them?

Finding Relocation Business

Before the real estate professional can make any money in the relocation business, he or she must find potential clients. This business will mirror the prospecting the real estate salesperson conducts to find individual sellers, but on a larger, corporate scale. The following sections give some ideas on where corporate relocation can be found.

Corporate Calling

The best and most efficient way to find corporate relocation business is to design a system for corporate calling. Corporate calling involves finding the correct people to call. Make a list of companies in your market, along with any state or federal agencies, universities, hospitals, community colleges, and school districts. Check with the local chamber of commerce, search online, do research at the library, visit the economic development council and planning committees, and try to come with names, addresses, phone numbers, and e-mail addresses of the people that handle personnel for these companies. Once you locate the correct people, you should call them.

There are two types of calls. The corporate fact-finding call is simply to find out information. You want to find out whom to call and whether they have any plans for relocation. The more information you obtain, the more versed you will be when it comes time to ask for business. The second type of call actually asks for the business or at least sets up an appointment to discuss the possibility of relocation business. The latter would be used when dealing with smaller operations.

Use the following script for use with either type of call:

FACT-FINDING CORPORATE CALL:

Broker: "Good morning, my name is Dan Hamilton with Acme Real Estate Company, and I was wondering if you could spare a couple of minutes and help me answer a few questions?"

Receptionist: "Sure."

Broker: "What is the main function of your organization?"
"How long have you been at your present location?"
"Who handles any corporate moves?"
"Have you seen any indication you may need to expand?"
"Thank you for your time; do you think I could call you again if I had any further questions?"

Receptionist: "Sure."

Broker: "Thanks again. Bye."

PROSPECT-GENERATING CORPORATE CALL:

Broker: "I was calling for the person that handles any relocation or corporate moves."

Receptionist: "I don't know who that would be."

Broker: "Could I speak with someone in the personnel department?"

Receptionist:	"We don't have a personnel department."
Broker:	"Could I speak with the owner or manager?"
Receptionist:	"I am the owner."
Broker:	"Great, my name is Dan Hamilton with Acme Real Estate, and I was wondering if you ever relocate anyone associated with your company?"
Receptionist:	"Well no, we are not that big, but I am thinking about selling my house and then moving closer to my office."

Too bad you didn't get any relocation business. But because you made the call, you will get a listing and a sale. Not bad for a few calls. Activity breeds activity. If you say you are going to corporate call and never do, then how could you get these types of leads? You never know how a call will turn out, but I do know what happens if you never make the call. If your brokerage doesn't list or sell actual real estate (i.e., is a non-compete brokerage), refer this lead to someone in your office who needs motivation, and make him or her pay you a referral fee.

Here are some variations on the Prospect-Generating Corporate Call:

Broker:	"I was calling for the person who handles any relocation or corporate moves."
Receptionist:	"That is Rhonda. Please hold, and I will transfer you."
Broker:	"Thank you."
Director:	"This is Rhonda."
Broker:	"Hi, Rhonda, my name is Dan Hamilton with Acme Real Estate, and I was wondering who handles your relocation business."
Director:	"We don't transfer a lot of people each year, but we use a real estate person here locally."
Broker:	"I am also here locally. Would you consider using my company and me for the next relocation?"
Director:	"Well, I don't know."
Broker:	"Tell you what I can do for you: I could stop by and demonstrate the advantages of dealing with professionals in the relocation industry, that is, advantages to you *and* your employee. I am available today, or would Thursday be better?"

*****

> *Director:* "We have a contract with a relocation management firm for all our relocation needs."
>
> *Broker:* "I am glad to hear you are taken care of. Can I ask what company you are currently dealing with?" (Your office may be on the approved list for that relocation management company. If not, look into the application process for that relocation management company.)
>
> *Broker:* "Does your company offer relocation benefits to new hires?"

Often, new hires are not eligible for benefits but still need real estate assistance upon arrival. The contact person may be able to route these employees to you. Also, if you make a great impression and do well with new hires, the contact person may be in a position to recommend you to the relocation company or to someone in a department higher up in the company who may have the ability to require their relocation provider to use you.

Now, the director may not jump at the chance of meeting with you, but you are a paid real estate professional and your job is to stay in touch with him or her without being pesky. If you would like more information on following up with corporate clients, just keep reading!

Next time you are driving around town (and we do this a lot), begin making a list of the small to medium companies in your area. Be sure to read all the publications that print information about businesses relocating to or from your area. Watch for companies that are expanding or laying people off. Investigate further any company that is leasing additional space. You will find that the smaller the company, the more centralized the contact will be; in the smaller companies, the contact is usually the owner. The larger corporations have contracts with relocation management companies or handle relocation matters through an in-house program. These larger companies may be harder to get inside, but with persistence it can be done.

FINAL TIPS ON CORPORATE CALLING

1. Set a target date for getting started, and then do it.

2. Start with a few smaller companies. These companies are rarely solicited and are easy to approach. Perfect your presentation and proposals with them. Move on to bigger companies as you gain confidence and experience.

3. Coordinate every corporate-calling opportunity at a management level within your firm. To have everyone in the office calling on the same companies would not be productive.

4. Develop a basic list of services you offer; this is referred to as your *Value Package*. As you interview companies and learn their specific needs, you can customize your basic proposal and Value Package.

5. Keep a written record of your corporate calling efforts: the number of calls you made, the date and time of the phone calls, the number of proposals sent, the number of presentations made, and when to conduct follow-up calls.

6. It is best to target a specific number of companies, perhaps up to ten. Then keep up with them monthly. Once you master these, you can always add more.

7. Keep your contact at the company informed when you are working with one of the employees.

8. Dress appropriately. If you do not know what this means, there are numerous books that can help you.

9. Always ask for the business.

10. Stress the benefits of working with your company, both for the employee and for his or her company.

11. Be sure to highlight your strengths in technology.

Additional Ways to Find Relocation Business

PAST CLIENTS, CUSTOMERS AND REAL ESTATE SALESPEOPLE

These are people you have conducted real estate business with. With any luck, they were pleased with how you helped them, and now they will want to help you. If the transaction did not go as well as you would have liked, you should call them and be ready to apologize and build that relationship again. All of the people you have had business with work somewhere. That is the business you want. Businesses are always transferring employees into and out of the area. Establish lines of contact with other agents in your office as to whom they know at local small to medium companies for relocation business. These past clients and associates may

(1) introduce you to the human resource department staff and/or the personnel director and possibly help set up an appointment for you, or

(2) allow you to use their names as references and/or include testimonials from them with your proposal.

THE MILITARY

The military (all branches) transfers and relocates personnel all over, all the time. If there is a military base in your area, call or visit it. If you do not work near a base, visit recruiting stations. You might first talk with the commander, who may lead you elsewhere. If the base is large enough, it probably has a personnel director. Generally, people in the military are highly professional and structured, but they will allow time to speak with the local business people. Some bases only do transferees through third-party companies (discussed later), but you and your office may still might get a couple of leads about those relocating that year, and that is better than nothing. Also, by making this connection you may reach the local military person who wants to live off base and/or simply move to another residence, neither of which would go through the third-party company.

COMMERCIAL BROKERS

Commercial brokers usually help businesses buy or lease space for their companies but rarely want to help them find a place of residence. Become acquainted with these brokers. They may have the first contact with a new company relocating to the area.

THIRD-PARTY RELOCATION COMPANIES

Large companies with lots of relocations might choose a third-party relocation company, such as Cendant Mobility or Prudential Relocation, to arrange the transfers of their employees. These companies handle the entire relocation move for a company. It is very expensive but worth it compared to handling the move without them. You can contact these companies and ask to submit a proposal to be one of the designated brokers in an area for them. If successful, you will be required to meet their requirements for the relocation business.

COMMUNITY INVOLVEMENT

Become active in your local community. The leaders of a community enjoy giving back by joining civic and charitable organizations. You should not join these organizations to get business; you should join them because you want to help. However, if business results, it becomes a double bonus. People in the civic and charitable arenas are less defensive and will bond with you more quickly at a community event than they will if you approach them while they are at work. These people will grow to like you and trust you more at these functions than any other time and place.

COMPANY INVOLVEMENT

Your entire staff, including managers, sales associates, and support staff, must be kept aware of the importance of relocation opportunities and of the myriad of programs and new referral lead sources. Make sure the relocation department is properly introduced to the whole staff. Explain to all managers and sales associates how the relocation department fits into the company's overall business plan and goals.

You or your relocation director must be current on trends in the relocation industry and provide ongoing training for your "corporate team" of sales associates. Being on this relocation team should be an achievement, not an automatic right. These team members should be full-time and detail-oriented, and they should understand the paperwork necessary for the job and always be professionally dressed. They need to be knowledgeable about the area they serve. They should understand the disclosure and buyer/seller representation laws for your state, the minimum knowledge required to answer questions from a relocating buyer/seller intelligently. Establish criteria for sales associates who will be handling these referrals. Encourage continuing education and seminars for all staff.

BUSINESS "FARMING"

This category of "farming" (cultivating business until it starts to produce money) is effective, but it is time consuming. Unlike S.O.I. (Sphere Of Influence) and geographical farming, business farming cultivates relationships with "business" people whom you do not necessarily know but who work in an area about which you and your office have expertise. As an expert, you should know as much about that area as you can. Business farming can be successful because most people, both men and women, work during the day. When a bank robber was asked why he robbed banks he simply replied, "That is where the money is." That is why we want to farm for prospects where prospects are—at their place of business.

When approaching businesses, do not wear a name tag or any career apparel, and do not carry a briefcase or large notepads. You do not want to look like a salesperson. You are not there to solicit sales; you are there only to introduce yourself and your company. The only thing you should have is a small notepad and pen (a PDA is great!) that you keep hidden in your pocket. Walk into the office (if in a business complex) and introduce yourself and your company to the receptionist. The receptionist is the person you want because he or she will know everything about the company. The owner or manager will be too "busy" to talk with you. Do not hand the receptionist a card. Use the following script:

Broker:	"Cindy?" (If you see her name on her name plate; if not just say "Good morning.")
Receptionist:	"Yes."
Broker:	"My name is Dan Hamilton with Acme Realty. I am going to be in the area working and just wanted to stop by and introduce myself to you."
Receptionist:	"Okay."

Depending upon the receptionist's mood, you can continue with small talk, or excuse yourself and leave.

Broker:	"I see that you are busy; it was nice meeting you."

Either ask for her name or ask to take a business card if one is displayed. Do not ask for any business; it is not the time yet. When you step out of the door, you should record her name, the business's name, the address, and any other information you gathered by talking with her on the notepad in your pocket. Move on to the next business. Repeat this process for ten to twelve businesses; this now constitutes your business farm area. As when geographically farming, do not overextend yourself; start small and grow as your systems get better.

After you have been through your business farm once, you should return each month on the same day and time (for example, first Tuesday at 9:15 a.m.) so everyone knows your schedule. Each time, try to find out more information. Do not expect the receptionist to remember your name. Do not offer any services or ask for business. Continue this for about six months, and then bring in a gift. I would usually bring a box of a dozen glazed donuts. My business card (made into a sticker) went on the outside of the box and on the inside (when the box is opened). Walk in and leave the donuts. Do not worry about feeding the masses: it is fine if a dozen is not enough for everyone because you are simply prospecting the receptionist. After a while, you will find that on your day to bring donuts some employees will be hanging around up front for you and your donuts. And, by the way, if you negotiate with the donut shop, you can probably cut yourself a deal.

Eventually, the receptionist may start to give you information; she may say that she is not sure that she should tell you this, but they are transferring Bob in accounting to Seattle, and he will need to sell his house and buy another one. You have now started the harvest of this business. Be sure to update the receptionist on the referral and bring her a gift after closing. Just imagine if the company needs to relocate its entire operation—you might get the entire move of multiple executives.

I have found that as long as you keep your visits brief and you do not try to sell anything, no one gets mad. I also found out that it would take at least six months for the receptionist to know your name and what you do. This should be a "part" of your business, and it is kind of fun.

Meeting with Personnel Directors and Others

When you have an appointment set with a personnel director or other decision maker, follow these steps:

A. Take someone from your business development/relocation department with you. The large real estate companies have entire departments dedicated to this function. They have the scripts and material to make things happen. Their job is to help you get the business, so let them do their job. If you have this advantage—USE IT! If you don't, you will need to do it yourself, so continue on.

B. Keep your appointments, arrive a few minutes early, dress in a business suit, and stay only a few minutes, because these are busy professionals. Leave your proposal and briefly review your services with them. Explain how your program will save them time and money and make their job easier. Ask for one opportunity to prove your worth. Close them if you feel it is appropriate. Then, thank them for their time.

C. Send them a thank-you note as soon as you get back to your office. Remind them that your services are at no cost and explain again how you may benefit their company. Also, if they requested additional material, be sure to get that to them in a timely manner.

D. Follow up every thirty days with a postcard about a new service or a program only available through your office that would benefit them. You could mention an alliance with an apartment locator or a discount on car rentals, hotels, and so on. You could send a relocation article you have read that would be relevant to their business. Be sure to send a birthday card once you find out their birthday. It is not important what is in the mail-out, as long as you remain on their minds.

E. Periodically, telephone and ask if they are interviewing companies and if so, if they would give you the opportunity to prove the quality and benefit of your services.

F. When they use you for the first time, you had better respond. Give more than you promised and make them feel special. However, do not compromise your integrity. Sometimes we want so badly to make an impression that we do things we would not ordinarily do. Once I was working with a group to relocate each one on their executives to a new area. I was to get 18 listings to sell that averaged $350,000, or about $6 million in sales. Not bad for one relocation. The first one I was given demanded that I list his house 20 percent over market, even though the area would only support activity in the 4–6 percent range. I would have never taken that listing except that I wanted all the other business. Needless to say, that house never sold. Later, I found out that was my test case. The owner of the company knew that this partic-ular seller would be difficult, and if I could handle him and get his house sold, I could have everyone else. I could not do it, so I got nothing. I compromised my integrity and lessened my standards and got what I deserved—nothing. I should have done what I normally do, and that is to refuse to list his property. I might not have made that sale, but I would have gotten the rest.

A Letter of Introduction and First Contact

Some companies will not grant you a personal appointment right away but will agree to review a letter and/or proposal of your services first. Be sure to address the letter to the decision maker and describe the benefits of working with your firm. Have several of your colleagues review your letter for comprehension and content.

You should call the person to whom you sent the letter within the next week. When you call you should use one of the following scripts:

GENERIC

Broker: "Hello, Mr./Ms. Jones, this is Dan Hamilton from Acme Real Estate Company. I sent you a letter last week introduc-ing our company and my services. Did you receive it? I am very excited to talk with you because we believe we can save you time and money, and make your job easier. We are a full-service company, very experienced in relocation, and would appreciate an opportunity to explain some of our programs and how they can benefit you and your organization. They come without cost or obligation. Now, I am available on Tuesday, or would later in the week be better for you?"

SPECIFIC—ADD TO GENERIC

Broker: "As a matter of fact, we are currently working with ABC Company here in the area with their relocation employees. Their business is similar to yours and we have tailored our program to be an integral part of their recruiting process. Now, I am available on Tuesday, or would later in the week be better for you?"

If a real experience or business relationship can be used, it will provide credibility and may cause the contact person to seek a recommendation from this other company or convince them to give you a chance. Be sure your contact at the other company knows that ABC Company may be calling them and make certain you have their permission to do this.

OBJECTION-HANDLING SCRIPTS

If they respond negatively to the above scripts, you might want to respond in the following fashion:

Director: "We are currently working with another relocation company and are happy with their work."

IF THE DIRECTOR SEEMS ADAMANT:

Broker: "Understood. The next time you look to make a change would you consider us?"

IF THE DIRECTOR SEEMS OPEN:

Broker: "I am glad to hear you are taken care of. By the way, it doesn't hurt to have a back up just in case something goes askew. I would love the opportunity to be that back-up person. The only way you could trust me as your back up is if you knew I could handle the business. I can demonstrate that ability if you would let me meet with you only for a few minutes. Now, I could make arrangements for later today, or would tomorrow be better?"

Director: "Thank you, we are not interested."

Broker: "I appreciate your time on the phone and should something change in your company or you need real estate assistance in any way, please call. Thank you again."

(Use the follow-up program described later in this chapter.)

ALTERNATE OBJECTION

Director: "We don't want to give all of our relocation business to only one company."

Broker: "Interesting. What is the reason for that?"

Director: "We don't want to be tied to any one company."

Broker: "Would you consider us for that position if we could prove we can save you time and money for both you and your relocation employees?"

The First Corporate Presentation

The reason I say the "First" is because you need to be prepared for multiple presentations to get the business, but it will be worth it. Once you have set your first appointment, you will need to learn as much as you can about their operations, locations, products manufactured, services offered, and anything else, whether you feel it is important or not.

The presentation should be multimedia and include any marketing material your company has that is appropriate. Always bring everything you *could* need, and then if you don't need it, you don't have to use it. Here are some suggestions for presentation tools:

(1) An agenda of the presentation

(2) An area map showing the location of your office(s) and total service area

(3) An original copy of your proposal and extra copies for everyone attending the presentation

(4) An example of a Newcomer's Packet (the Newcomer's Packet will be discussed later)

(5) A few graphics of your better listings

(6) Any of your company brochures that are professionally printed (not photocopied)

(7) A PowerPoint presentation of your proposal. If you need a laptop computer—get one. Borrow one if you have to, and the same goes with a data projector. Professionals expect multimedia presentations, so you had better give them one. If you don't know how to use PowerPoint, learn. On the other hand, be prepared to do your presentation without any visual aids. Who knows when something will go wrong? You forget the projector. The room won't facilitate a projector, or whatever. Never rely on audio-visuals.

(8) You! You are the main part of the presentation because if they do not believe you, they will never buy what you are selling. Dress professionally, but do not look like a salesperson. Be discreet: if a company is relocating, they may not have told their employees yet, and you don't want to start such rumors.

PRE-PRESENTATION   Be sure to find out how many players are on their team and try to bring the same number with you. You do not want to be the only person and have five players against you, because that can be very intimidating. The opposite is also true. You don't want five people with you if only the personnel director shows up, because he or she may be threatened and reject you before you start.

A week before the presentation, hold an initial meeting with your presentation team to discuss strategies and to anticipate any problems that may arise. Review the proposal and presentation. You should bookmark the important pages so you can refer to them quickly.

On the day of the presentation, arrive a little before the meeting time so you can set up. If it is a conference room, make sure the room is arranged so that there is no "head" of the table. You want a discussion, not a battle for power. Once the players enter the room and sit down, be sure each has an agenda and a copy of the first proposal. If you are in an office, you may have to project the data on the office wall, use the computer screen itself, or not use the PowerPoint presentation at all. Begin with ice-breaking comments, such as

> *Broker:* "Thanks for meeting with me (or us). First, let's look at the agenda. We will cover the following topics. . . . Do you have anything else you want to be sure is covered?"

ASK QUESTIONS   To begin the presentation, you should conduct some small talk. Once seated at the conference table, you want to ask a member of their team for a glass of water. The hospitable thing for the "home team" to do is offer you something to drink. You are allowing them to be hospitable to you. Only take water, ice water if you prefer. Anything else may get complicated, so only ask for water. After a very short period of time (these are business people, so respect their time), begin casually with the following questions:

(1) How many people do you transfer to or away from this location within a year?

(2) How are you currently assisting an employee relocation situation?

(3) Do you have branch offices? How do they handle relocation decisions?

(4) How is your relocation department set up? Is it independent or part of another department?

(5) What does your company provide in the way of home finding assistance?

(6) What assistance is offered if the transferee needs to rent?

(7) Who else are you talking with about the relocation of your employees?

(8) What is more important to you and your company in using us as your relocation company, the amount of money you could save, the time you could save, or the convenience of not having to worry about the relocation of employees?

(9) What would it take for you to allow us to be your relocation specialists?

These questions should be asked exactly as written and in the order they appear above. The specific wording and order make a difference. The questions put the relocation director through a process of evaluating the relocation of their employees.

By asking questions, you will find out more information, including the information you will need to close them. Ask questions, then *listen*. Ask "add-on" questions depending upon their answers. Exude confidence. Always talk in a low but strong, well-modulated voice. Don't rush. Show interest. Write down everything they say, no matter how you feel about what was said. By writing everything down, you will have the best records possible while at the same time making your client feel important.

THE ACTUAL PRESENTATION   Once you have the additional information the questions provide, you will begin the actual presentation. You will need to present your services and programs in a manner that will demonstrate how you will save them time and money, and make their job easier. This is where you begin your PowerPoint presentation. Be open to questions, yet lead on through the presentation. Don't allow the presentation to get bogged down. Tell them exactly what the transferee may expect when working with you. The presentation should cover the following points:

A. About your company

B. About you personally

C. About the home buying and selling process

D. Close for the business

Always present the features of working with your company; then be sure to give them a benefit from that feature. The three benefits of working with you are that doing so will save them time and money, and make their job easier. Remember that one of the major benefits is most important to this particular director. Concentrate on satisfying that need.

Discuss Company Results   In this section of the presentation, you should discuss the positive activities of your company. You should be using your PowerPoint presentation or a relocation presentation manual at this point to keep you on track. You should discuss any successes, the number of sales, and any recognition and awards. You should list a select group of addresses and the length of time it took your company to sell them. The time should be sixty days or less. Use only the street name, not the street number. You do not want to give directions; all you want to do is impress the director with the number of houses your company has sold within sixty days.

During this time, you should describe the team you have formed. This team should include you, all the real estate salespeople in your office, and any affiliates such as appraisers, inspectors, mortgage officers, title officers, and structural engineers, to name a few. Now would be a good time to promote anything your company does that the competition may not do. Think outside the box to develop this section to its fullest. Ask your staff and other salespeople in the office for their ideas.

At this moment, you should be asking a series of questions to get your point across. I hate the word *presentation* because it means "I talk and you listen." We need to get the clients involved because we need their input, and they feel better about us if we are concerned about their opinions. It is a much different effect when you ask, "What is most important to you?" instead of "This is the most important thing you should be concerned about."

An involvement technique you should develop is to let the director finish your sentences for you. Do not labor at this. It should be very natural. You have a sentence that has an easily recognizable finish and instead of finishing you pause slightly and allow the director to finish for you. If they do what they are supposed to do and finish your sentence, you congratulate them with, "right" or "exactly," and they will continue to do it.

Once you have completed with the company results discussion, you must "close" this section out with the director. You must make sure to "close" every section because that way you eliminate the possibility that the director will come up with an objection later on that should have been addressed at this point. When I was a rookie real estate broker I was afraid of objections. What if I could not handle the objection? How silly would I look? Because of my fear and lack of presentation skills I received tons of objections and was always stressed. I began "closing" each section as they came up and I found out I rarely received any objections. Say the following:

Broker: "Mr./Mrs. Director, do you have any questions about my company?"

Director: "No."

Broker: "Do you believe my company can help you and your company with your relocation needs?"

Director: "Yes."

The key point here is that they must give you a "yes." Do not accept the answer of, "Well, I guess." You must drive the point home by asking again.

Discuss Personal Results   During this discussion you should describe your personal results. You should include the way you have led your office to the position it is in today and the number of sales you have had in the last year. You should talk about the clients you have helped to achieve their goals. You should show them letters of recommendation. (If you don't have letters of recommendation, GET THEM!) You should discuss your personal successes, including all your real estate awards. Remember to "close" this section out.

Discuss the Home Buying and Selling Process   A professional real estate business development broker should have two presentations. The first one should be a standard presentation that can be used in any situation.

The second type presentation should gear specifically to the current potential client.

The standard type presentation and the specific type both follow the same format. Each should spell out the step-by-step process to sell a transferee's property or to find a transferee his or her next home. It should include each activity and when it is to be completed. EACH STEP should be included. This is a time some relocation specialists fail. They do not mention the little things. You should include the following information:

FOR SELLING A PROPERTY

- Entry into the MLS
- Presentation to the office salespeople
- Office tour and their response
- Advertising campaign
- Marketing flyers
- "For sale" sign installation
- Lock box installation
- Presentation at the local ASSOCIATION OF REALTORS®

FOR BUYING A PROPERTY

- MLS property search
- Property viewing
- Property valuation
- Property inspection
- Closing

Once this is completed, it should be updated as time progresses and sent to the relocation director so that he or she knows you are working. Last but not least, "close" this section out.

Close   To finalize the presentation process, you need to close them for the business. You need to ask to work with one transferee to test the value of your service. If the above doesn't work, promote the fact that your services are free and that home finding can be fun with the right assistance but very stressful for someone not familiar with an area. Without additional cost to the company, you will be able to handle the needs of their transferees.

FOLLOW-UP No matter what happens at the presentation, you must follow up with the corporations you have called. This may be done with letters, phone calls, postcards, e-greetings, copies of relocation articles that may relate to an important issue for their business, any company brochures, and announcements of any new programs that may save them money. You should be in communication with them at least once per month, weekly if they are ready to make a move.

RELOCATION NEWSLETTER

A great way to follow up with your relocation prospects is to develop a relocation newsletter. In it you include any current relevant information in the relocation business. These should be condensed versions of major stories, not longer than one page, front and back. Do not make these too complicated. You can find stories on the Internet and copy them and paste them into your newsletter. Be sure that you give the author credit and that you have the right to reproduce the article (usually you can if you give them credit). If you want to write your own newsletter you can, but do not let it take up too much of your time; it won't bring in money. Some companies will produce these and send them for you. Just be careful about the price.

RELOCATION PRESENTATION MANUAL

This is a three-ring binder with all of the information you included in your presentation. There are two reasons to create such a binder: first, it can serve as a back up if your audio-visual equipment fails during a presentation, and second, it can be used at any time and place, especially when a PowerPoint presentation is not appropriate.

The sections in your manual should mirror your actual presentation:

1. About your company
2. About you personally
3. About the home buying and selling process
4. Close for the business

Be sure this is a very high-quality marketing piece. It should be on the best card stock with multicolor typeset and pictures. The entire manual should be bound in leather with raised lettering.

The Proposal

Components of a Proposal

Writing your proposal to receive the relocation business from a company is the most important step in showing your potential client your professionalism. The proposal should read like a business plan with the following components:

A. Information including to whom the proposal is addressed, from whom the proposal originated, and the team you have formed for the relocation process

B. The reason for the proposal

C. An overview of the entire proposal

D. An explanation of why the company and transferee would benefit from using your services

E. A brief overview of experience and training relative to relocation

F. A list of services you will provide for sellers and/or buyers

G. A detailed description of the anticipated impact of your activities

H. Highlights of your company's cost-saving services

I. Your competition's list of services compared to yours, showing how your services are superior

J. A performance evaluation after each relocation opportunity

K. A list of references, including other corporations or relocation management companies you have assisted

L. A few testimonial letters, if appropriate

Guidelines for Writing a Proposal

A. Be specific about what services you offer. Your proposal should tell a story about you, your company's services, your professionalism and integrity, your knowledge of the relocation industry, and how you can address the needs of the company and transferee.

To be effective, it must

1. Be meaningful to the corporate contact and their superiors
2. Be simple and easily understood but not demeaning

3. Use correct grammar and spelling

4. Answer the question "What's in it for me and my company if we choose you and yours?"

B. Confirm in writing all the little details with which you will assist.

C. Give a brief history of your company and your accomplishments relative to relocation services.

D. Concentrate on the issues you have discovered to be important to *them*.

E. Read it once, then read it again and again. Experienced professionals know that several readings of a proposal are necessary to be sure that you are communicating the information you want to communicate. Check the entire proposal for the following: technical consistency; spelling; page numbering; section/subsection numbering or lettering; and consistency of appearance of headings, subheadings, font types, and font sizes.

F. Make sure you leave plenty of time for copying, binding, and delivering the proposal. Remember, the copy machine senses when an important document is being copied, so it will break, jam, or smudge. Have a back-up plan that includes having extra paper and toner on hand and sending the proposal out to be copied. Before and after copying your proposals, check to see that each copy contains all pages and that they are in the proper order.

G. Use tables, charts, and graphics to summarize information and break up your narrative.

H. Bind the proposal in a professional cover.

Relocation Services Offered

Here is a list of some of the services you could offer as a relocation specialist:

- As a recruiting partner for the company, you will promote the new location to the spouse while the company will promote the job opening to the employee.

- You can provide a Newcomer's Packet with vital information on schools, housing, taxes, houses of worship, childcare, and much more.

- You can offer individual and family relocation counseling.

- You can offer assistance with mortgage pre-qualification through a preferred mortgage company.
- If the relocation person needs to rent before buying, you can provide rental assistance.
- You can help with job search for the spouse.
- You can provide national and international assistance for all transferees.
- You can provide basic real estate services, as a professional and competent real estate professional should, such as assistance with selling and buying, management and coordination of a number of related details, and maintenance of open communication channels.
- You can provide information about relocation management company operations (which you should know thoroughly).
- You can offer agency representation to their transferees.
- You can provide discounts for their transferees on loans, temporary living, car rental, and hotels.
- You will be (and should be) easy to communicate with and accessible by phone, fax, and e-mail.
- Your company can and should have the financial ability to pay vendors up front on corporate listings.
- You possess real estate expertise of geographic area.
- You can offer a home purchase program if the house doesn't sell in a given time frame.
- You can help the transferee with the movement of household goods.
- You can offer temporary living for those that have found a home but cannot move at this time.
- You can provide home-finding trips or destination assistance.
- You can and should present advice on tax implications of buying or selling real property.

There should be minimum qualifications for all of the involved real estate salespeople; they must be full-time with at least three to five years of experience, have previous relocation experience, be available at reasonable times, be successful at assessing buyer's needs, and be detail-oriented and professional in appearance and conduct.

Creating a Company Relocation Packet/Brochure

A Relocation Packet is used in advance of a presentation. It is a "silent salesperson" giving the director the feeling they are dealing with a professional person with relocation systems in place. In creating a Relocation Packet for your company, you should answer the following questions:

- What can you do for the corporation and their transferring employees?
- What special skills and knowledge do you bring to the transaction?
- What distinguishes you from the competition?
- What does your relocation and real estate track record look like?

First of all, you should create a company brochure to be placed in your packet. In creating your brochure, follow these guidelines:

1. Create a perception of competence, value, and success.
2. Devote one part to the services you provide. It works best to use bullet points as much as possible.
3. Use front and back pages or panels.
   a. Keep the front page or panel attractive, but simple. Motivate the reader to pick it up and read it. Include your company name, logo, and a brief tag line or slogan.
   b. On the back page or panel, include a three- to four-paragraph corporate biography that instills confidence in your prospects that you possess the abilities and expertise to perform as promised.
      (1) Tell the reader what motivated you to start the business and why you are the ideal person to be doing this.
      (2) Highlight your education, credentials, and accomplishments.
      (3) List professional affiliations, human-interest items about the company, and any other pertinent information you may want to add.
      (4) List contact information: phone, address, fax, e-mail, and Web site.

The packet should contain the following information and materials in addition to the brochure:

1. Your personal profile. Specifics you may choose to include:
   a. A fact sheet about your company

  b. A brief summary or résumé about your broker, management teams, and the business development director

  c. A list of all of your relocation services, such as

   (1) Departure services, including premarketing, third-party relocation buyouts, asset management, and REO (Real Estate Owned—bank owned) services

   (2) Destination services, including buyer brokerage, area tours, comprehensive Newcomer's Packet, rental assistance, and so on

   (3) Property management

   (4) Commercial and investment services

  d. Press clippings of group-move assistance, charity fund-raising, or anything else that is newsworthy.

  e. Photographs of the office and the relocation team

  f. Letters of recommendation from past clients

  g. List of current clients, group-moves handled, and any current corporate inventory if permission is given to use their names

  h. List of professional associations in which you have a membership

  i. Lists or certificates of awards you have earned

2. Endorsements and testimonials

Creating a Newcomer's Packet

A Newcomer's Packet is simply a group of documents and printed materials that will help a transferee with the possibility of a corporate move. The following should be included in a Newcomer's Packet:

1. Information about the area to which they will be moving

2. Information about brokerage services

3. Information about your company

4. Information about the relocation services offered

5. Information about whom to contact for more information or property viewings

6. Information about ancillary services, such as mortgages, inspection, and utilities

7. Information about possible discounts on services, such as cable television, moving services, and telephone installation

Relocation services and corporate calling are among the most over-looked aspects of the real estate industry. This business is very lucrative and will reproduce itself once the proper contacts have been made. Spend some time developing this business, and you will be happy you did!

Land Development

A real estate broker might choose to add land development to his or her reper-toire of services offered to the public. Land development is the taking of "raw" land and converting it into higher-priced land with roads, sewage, water, and utilities to suit the needs of builders. The broker-developer may construct dwellings or commercial buildings on the subdivided land or even develop an entire community. Once these buildings have been completed, the broker/developer may then proceed to market them through other real estate salespeople or through the broker's own organization. For this specialization in real estate, the broker must have a suitable contractor's license or work with or for a licensed contractor and comply with subdivision laws.

Notary Functions

A broker could offer notary services as a convenience to clients and as a service intended for the general public. A notary must keep a sequential journal of notary acts and be certain that the person whose signature on a document is to be acknowledged personally appears before the notary and provides acceptable forms of identification. The question is whether the broker should charge for this service. Most brokers do not offer this service because title companies often have a notary on staff.

Property Insurance

Most property insurance is sold through insurance companies. It is com-mon, nevertheless, for the larger real estate brokerage offices to offer in-surance polices. Generally, these real estate companies represent insur-ance companies, but some actually purchase the insurance company and roll the company under their real estate umbrella of services. Insurance is a natural feeder business and an extra source of income for the real estate broker who already has real estate sales transactions originating in the broker's office.

A real estate broker who also acts in the capacity of an insurance sales-person is acting as the agent of the insurance underwriter and is governed by the carrier's instructions. A real estate broker could suggest their insurance, but of course the client should always have the opportunity to select his or her own source of insurance.

Conclusion

A broker should always be aware of ways to add business to the bottom line. Too many brokers look only to residential real estate for their income. Smart brokers know that a residential real estate sale opens the doors to many other avenues to make a profit. Do not miss the opportunities available. I once was told that anything listed on a closing statement could be a source of revenue for a broker; I believe that that is true, assuming that the revenue is attained legally and with the proper documentation and disclosures.

Chapter Twelve Review Questions

1. In positioning your marketing message for your company's relocation business, all of the following questions should be asked *except*
   A. what is our business promising to fulfill?
   B. what are our strengths and weaknesses?
   C. what are our values?
   D. all are important questions to be asked.

2. What is the best and most efficient way of finding corporate relocation business?
   A. Corporate calling
   B. Advertising
   C. Knocking on corporate doors
   D. None of the above is effective

3. You should start your corporate calling campaign on smaller companies. Why?
   A. Because they have the largest number of transferees.
   B. Because they have a smaller service area.
   C. Because they have larger relocation budgets.
   D. Because they are rarely solicited and are easy to approach.

4. All of the following are good sources of relocation business, *except*
- A. past clients, customers, and real estate salespeople.
- B. the military.
- C. inmate #0227 at the State Penitentiary.
- D. commercial brokers.

5. Once you have a presentation set for relocation business, you should do all of the following, *except*
- A. notify your state real estate commission.
- B. prepare an agenda of the presentation.
- C. have an original copy of your proposal and extra copies for all that will be attending the presentation.
- D. have an example of a Newcomer's Packet.

6. During the actual presentation to a relocation director, you should ask which of the following questions?
- A. How many people do you transfer to or away from this location within a year?
- B. How are you currently assisting an employee relocation situation?
- C. Who else are you talking with about the relocation of your employees?
- D. All of the above questions should be asked.

7. The presentation should follow which of the following steps and in what order?
- I. About your company
- II. About the home buying and selling process
- III. About the weaknesses in the company's overall management philosophy
- IV. Close for the business
- V. Disparagement of your competition
- VI. About you personally
    - A. I–II–VI–III–V
    - B. I–VI–II–IV
    - C. VI–I–II–III–IV
    - D. II–VI–I–III–IV

8. Which of the following are reasons for having a Relocation Presentation Manual?
   A. Electronic audio-visuals can fail.
   B. They are extremely cheap to make.
   C. They are best for groups of fifteen or more.
   D. All the above are valid reasons for having a Relocation Presentation Manual.

9. All of the following are essential components of a Relocation Proposal, *except*
   A. information stating to whom the proposal is addressed.
   B. the reason for the proposal.
   C. an overview of the entire proposal.
   D. all of the above.

10. All of the following are guidelines for effective writing of a Relocation Proposal, *except*
   A. be exacting, lengthy, and detailed.
   B. answer the question "What's in it for me and my company if you choose us."
   C. give a brief history of your company and your accomplishments relative to relocation services.
   D. all of the above.

11. If you lose a presentation to another relocation company, you should
   A. file a complaint with an arbitrator.
   B. send derogatory letters about the behavior of the relocation director to the owner of the company.
   C. call the director to arrange an in-person or telephone debriefing to find out the reasons for your loss.
   D. initiate a federal investigation of the competitor.

12. What are some possible reasons for failure of a relocation proposal?
   A. Failure to understand the needs of the company
   B. Failure to include confidential information about your company
   C. Improper proposal format
   D. All of the above are possible reasons

13. All of the following are reasons to create a Company Relocation Brochure, *except*

A. it demonstrates your company's value.

B. it creates a perception of competence.

C. it is your relocation proposal in a handout form.

D. it expresses the successes your company has attained.

14. What should be included in a Newcomer's Packet?

A. Information about the area they will be moving to

B. Information about your company

C. Information about ancillary services, such as mortgages, inspections, and utilities

D. All of above

15. What are some other business development aspects a broker could add to make additional income?

A. Land developing

B. Insurance

C. Notary functions

D. All of the above could be added

13 Real Estate Business Planning

Introduction

Any business that has a chance to survive begins with business planning. A good owner plans the business, then executes that plan. Planning may be avoided for any number of reasons, including lack of knowledge, fear, and too much enthusiasm, which can blind reason. This chapter will teach the reader how to begin to plan to run a real estate brokerage business. Any business that fails to plan is bound to fail.

Writing a Business Plan

Writing a business plan is one of the most important aspects of starting a real estate business in today's changing environment. Starting a real estate brokerage is a challenge in itself. So many people looking for a change are jumping into the real estate brokerage business without first planning their new venture. The importance of planning your business venture cannot be over-emphasized.

Your business plan should convey your business's overall goals. It should also entail the core values of this business. It should be written in a way to help your business succeed today, tomorrow, and far into the future.

By taking an unbiased look at your business, you can identify areas of weakness and strength that you might otherwise overlook. Planning can mean the difference between success and failure.

The idea of a plan is to help keep you mentally focused. In a sense, it is sort of like setting a goal; you write it down, follow it, and make changes and updates as needed. Doing so will help you keep everything in proper perspective, because without a step-by-step business plan, there is no way you can keep your real estate brokerage business running successfully.

Writing a business plan is simply the process you'll use to organize your business goals and strategies. It is a written expression of your business ideas, and it also provides information needed for others to evaluate your business. A thorough business plan will show any investors that you are prepared for the real estate business.

When it comes to preparing your business plan, you are going to organize it to fit your particular circumstances. A business plan should be one of the first things a new real estate broker should implement before getting too involved in the real estate brokerage business. It is best to plan a business before you start it.

Cover Page

The cover page tells what business is being planned and how to reach the writer. Your cover page should read "Business Plan" and should include your

- Personal name
- Business name
- Business logo
- Business trademark
- Business charter
- Address
- Telephone number
- Fax number
- E-mail address
- Broker license number

The date should also be included on you cover page.

Table of Contents

The table of contents should be one page and should give details of the content of your business plan. Your table of contents indicates how well you have organized the entire plan and should make it easy to navigate through your plan.

The table of contents provides a quick and easy way to find particular sections of the plan. All pages of your business plan should be numbered, and the table of contents should include page numbers. After you assemble your plan and number your pages, go back to the table of contents and insert page numbers. Be sure to list headings for major sections, as well as for important subsections.

Executive Summary

The executive summary is a brief statement or account summing up the purpose of the business and covering the substance or main points of your business; it determines what kind of first impression you make on your readers. The executive summary should answer the following questions:

- What is your distinct service?
- What are your personal goals?
- What are your personal objectives?
- What is your business or previous job history?

While your executive summary is the first part of your plan, write it last. As you create the other sections of your plan, designate sentences or sections for inclusion in your summary. Your executive summary should be between one and three pages long and should include your business concept, financial features, financial requirements, the current state of your business, the date when the business was formed, the principal owners and key personnel of the business, and its major achievements. Use industry association statistics, market research from other sources, and other documenting information to back up statements you make.

Keep your executive summary short, interesting, and polished. Have several people read it—both those who know your business and those who do not—to check for clarity and presentation.

Mission Statement

The discussion of your business should begin with your mission statement, one or two sentences describing the purpose of your business and to whom your real estate services are targeted. Not being clear in your mission statement indicates that you are not clear about the purpose of your business.

Vision Statement

Too many real estate brokers make the mistake of operating without a vision, a situation that hampers their business's ability to grow and prosper. A real estate broker without a vision will have difficulty describing his or her business. A concise, easy-to-understand description of your business will not only help you write your business plan but will also benefit you in any number of other day-to-day situations.

> *The vision has about it the suggestion of prophecy and the tacit implication that it will be acted upon. A vision must not be wasted. The vision quest is in some sense a covenant between the seeker and the sought. The seeker does not necessarily know what it is that he seeks, but he knows that it is a relation that will change his life and give it strength, direction, purpose, and meaning.*
>
> *—N. Scott Momaday*

A real estate company should write a vision statement for the company to follow. The vision statement should follow these guidelines:

- A vision statement must be based in reality to be meaningful.

- To be relevant, a vision statement must be believable to the entire company, including the salespeople. It should inspire everyone associated with the organization.

- A vision statement must be inclusive and make people want to be part of the future of the company. It should allow people to feel like they are part of a greater whole and to see how their work contributes to the welfare of the entire company.

- A vision statement focuses on the future. A good vision should orient the company toward the future.

- A vision statement should help in the development of strategies that will lead to future success.

- A vision statement should make it easier for everyone to make the right decisions the very first time.

- A vision statement should point out any unproductive behavior patterns that are not aligned with the vision statement.

- A vision statement should be modifiable as the culture and environment changes.

Strategy

The strategy is developed as an integral part of a comprehensive framework that encompasses the vision, the execution, and achieving the desired results. A company strategy is designed to thoroughly plan out the ways to achieve the corporate goals. The strategy should motivate the people of the organization to carry out the strategy. Personal issues are fully taken into account, deadlines are easily identified, and solutions developed.

One specific type of strategy is an exit strategy. An exit strategy is a plan to sell the real estate business even before operations have begun. Planning for the exit of the current ownership assures that the company is heading in the right direction. Some owners believe it is kind of creepy thinking of selling at such an early stage in business, but waiting will create even more issues and problems.

Continuous Improvement

A broker should believe in the theory of "continuous improvement" of the company's services and business operation. Continuous improvement is the belief that effort should be spent to look at all the services and business operations of a real estate company and begin to make small changes to improve them. Continuous improvement involves

- Planning and implementing process-based improvements

- Gaining enthusiastic support of all real estate salespeople and staff

- Systematically aligning the whole organization behind your program

- Systematically identifying activities with the highest impact on your organization's well being

- Institutionalizing a culture of continuous improvement

- Attacking the activities that are the easiest, quickest to implement, most significant, and most (for parallel structure) highly visible

Defining Your Customers

It is important to be thorough and specific when creating a description of the target customer for your real estate services. This description defines the characteristics of the people you want to sell to and should indicate, among other things, whether your customers are cost- or quality-conscious, under what circumstances they buy or sell, and what types of concerns they have. If you have an existing business, list your current customers and the trend in your sales to them.

To create a customer definition, describe your target customers in terms of common identifiable characteristics. For example, you could target professional couples in the metro Dallas area who need to move out of the city. Or you could target people relocated by their company to your area.

Narrow the field by briefly describing customers you don't want to reach. You may want to decline working with consumers that believe in "I win, you lose" or "I know more than you" types that will go for your commission as soon as they get a chance, or with first-time home buyers who will take up more of your time than you are willing to give.

A common mistake is to describe customers in general terms, such as "all people who want to buy a house" or "anyone who needs a real estate professional." To avoid this stumbling block, make a list of the characteristics of the people or companies that will be interested in your real estate services. Be sure to include details of what geographic region you plan to sell to. Is your market national, regional, international, or local?

This section defines the total market size as well as the slice of the market your business will target. Use numbers as well as trend information to make a case for a viable current market and its growth potential.

The Market

This is one of the most important parts of the plan, taking into account current market size and trends, and may require extensive research. Many of the sections that follow—from prospecting to marketing to the amount of money you need—will be based on the sales estimates you create here.

When writing about the real estate market, be sure to talk about factors affecting market growth: industry trends, socioeconomic trends, government policy, and population shifts. Show how these trends will have a positive or negative impact on your specific business.

Always cite all sources for your data and state the credentials of the people providing this data.

Sales and Marketing

This section of your business plan describes both the strategy and tactics you will use to get customers to use your real estate services. Sales and marketing is the weak link in many business plans. A strong sales and marketing section can serve as a map for you, and you will have a workable plan and the resources for promoting and selling your services.

SALES AND MARKETING STRATEGY

Important elements for a sales and marketing strategy include whom you are targeting with your initial push and what customers you have designated for follow-up phases. Other elements of a sales and marketing strategy include

- How you will find your prospects and, once you find them, how you plan to educate them about your real estate services
- What features of your service you emphasize to get customers to notice you
- Any sort of innovative marketing or sales techniques you will employ
- Whether you will focus your efforts locally, regionally, nationally, or internationally, and whether (and if so, why) you plan to extend your efforts beyond your initial region

MARKETING PLAN

Your marketing plan explains

- How your business will differ from that of your competitors
- Who your customers are
- Who your market is
- How long this market will need your service
- The characteristics of your average customer
- The environmental factors of your business
- Who your competition is
- What competitive advantage you have over your competitors
- The best way to sell your real estate service
- How you will promote and market your service

SERVICE

Describe each of the services your business supplies to customers, with a particular focus on how it will help the client achieve his or her goal. Go into as much detail as necessary. What are the applications for buyers and sellers? Underscore the specific features or variations that your services have.

Emphasize the activity that sets your service apart from your competition. Why will your services be successful in the marketplace? If there is a chance your competition will begin offering services that also have your unique features, then you devise new ways to offer something valuable and special.

Be specific in describing your competitive edge. Don't just say something like "we intend to provide better service." Explain how you will do so, and why that sets you apart from your competitors.

POSITIONING

Position is your identity in the marketplace: how you want the market and your competitors to perceive your service. Your positioning is based on your customers and competition. You position your real estate business as having the shortest marketing time, being the most dependable, having the best rates, or providing the best service. You can emphasize cost, convenience, flexible services, unique services, or some combination of these. You may be positioned as a boutique, traditional, or aggressive real estate office. Positioning is based on image. Develop your position by answering the following questions with brief, direct statements:

- What is unique about your service?
- How do you want people to view your services?
- How do your competitors position themselves?

Information About Your Business

This is general information about your business formation, including

- Your form (sole proprietorship, partnership, limited liability business, or corporation)
- A statement of all of your business licenses
- A statement of your business insurance requirements
- A description of any other laws and regulations that affect your business

Business Description

You must be able to present a clear portrait of what your business does. Your business description furthers your corporate vision and includes: who you are, what you will offer, what market needs you will address, and why your business idea is viable.

A typical business description section includes

- An overview of the real estate industry
- A discussion of your particular real estate business
- Description of your real estate services
- Your position in the real estate industry

Begin your business description with a brief overview of the real estate industry. Ultimately, you want to demonstrate that real estate is a great industry with an excellent long-term outlook. You're also setting the stage for your business description by showing where you fit in the marketplace.

Discuss both the present situation in real estate, as well as future possibilities. You should also provide information about the various market segments within the industry, with a particular focus on their potential impact on your business. Be sure to include any new services or other developments that will benefit or possibly hurt your business. Are there new markets and/or customers for your business/companies such as yours? What about national trends or economic trends and factors that will impact your venture?

Describe your industry like you're telling a story. Grab attention with strong, exciting language that will get readers interested in your industry and your business. Answering "why" makes any description stronger. Saying "the market will grow at 9 percent annually" may sound impressive, but what caused that rate of growth? Adding ". . . because a growing number of baby boomers are now in the real estate market either moving up or down in the cycle" makes it stand out.

This is not a discussion of your competition. That information will come later in the competitive analysis portion. Instead, you are providing an overview of the industry in which you will compete with other companies.

Many business plans make the mistake of basing their market observations on their beliefs. Instead, you will want to research your industry and back up your observations with facts. Be sure to note all sources.

Trade associations are excellent sources of information about trends in your industry. The main trade association for real estate is the NATIONAL

ASSOCIATION OF REALTORS®. For additional information, consult the *Gale Encyclopedia of Business and Professional Associations.*

General business newspapers and magazines (like *The Wall Street Journal* or *BusinessWeek*) and trade newspapers and magazines (those covering real estate) often report industry-wide trends as well. Many research and university libraries carry various trade publications and newsletters.

Don't be afraid to include negative information about your industry. Discussing the possible roadblocks your business might face shows you have a realistic view of the market.

You also want to include the more technical aspects of the real estate business. Remember that you're telling your business's story, so even though there are specific areas you will need to cover, you will want to keep it lively and interesting. Some questions you should answer include

- When was the business founded?
- When did you get your license?
- What is your business legal structure? Sole proprietorship? Corporation? Partnership?
- Who are the business's principals and what pertinent experience do they bring?
- What market needs will you meet? Whom will you sell to? How will your service(s) be sold?
- What support systems will be utilized? Customer service? Advertising? Promotion?

Your business focus often depends on your market. A small-town real estate brokerage can sell residential, commercial, and farm/ranch properties because they may be the only real estate company that sells those properties in the area. A larger market would require greater specialization to set itself apart from the competition.

Operations

The operations section explains how you plan to actually run the day-to-day operations, bills, and customer service of your business. In this section, you should answer the following questions:

- Who are your the employees?
- What are their credentials?

- How does the business make money?
- How do you price your service?
- What office supplies does your business use? (List your supplies and supplier.)
- How easy or difficult is it to obtain supplies?
- Are their prices steady and dependable?

Service Fees

Discuss what you will charge for your service and how you derived the cost. Once you have briefly explained your service fee and rationale, discuss where this cost strategy places you in the spectrum of the other providers of real estate services. Next, explain how your fee will attract customers, maintain and hopefully increase your market share in the face of competition, and produce profits.

Costs tend to be underestimated. If you start out with low costs and low fees, you leave yourself with little room to maneuver, and fee hikes will be difficult to implement. If you charge more than existing, competitive services, you will need to justify the higher fee on the basis of quality, timeliness, and/or services offered.

If a fee will be lower than that of an existing, competing real estate service, explain how you will maintain profitability. This may happen through more efficient marketing and promotions, lower labor costs, lower overhead, or lower supplies costs.

Personnel Development

In this section, you will describe the current state of your service and your plan for completing its development. This section must include details of personnel development and training costs, location, and labor requirements.

Present and discuss a design and personnel development budget. This budget should include the cost of all education, seminars, and consultants. Be sure to include labor, materials, consulting fees, and the cost of professionals such as attorneys.

Development Status

Describe the current status of your real estate services and what remains to be done to make your services ready to be marketed. Include a schedule detailing when this work will be completed. Even though your business plan is for a service business, there is still a strong need for a development status section. Service companies have to set up offices, make plans for fielding calls, get stationery and business cards, conduct market research, gather references, and do a sample mailing of sales pieces, among other things.

Service Process

Describe the process of delivering the service, from the first marketing step to the last step at closing. Include such things as

Marketing—Describe the marketing efforts you will engage in to discover those that want to buy or sell real estate. Explain the process; do not make this a specific marketing campaign because there is an entire section for that. Give an overview of the company's goals and desires, and how marketing will help achieve those goals.

Prospecting—Similar to marketing, except that in this section you describe the process of prospecting, which is actually going out and getting the business through your direct efforts. Marketing, on the other hand, is making the effort to be known so the clients contact you. Prospecting should be part of everyone's daily business. The real estate salespeople should be prospecting for those that want to buy or sell real estate. All staff and managers should be constantly prospecting for new recruits into the real estate profession.

Listing—Explain the process of listing. Explain the listing appointment and the sales and negotiation efforts that must be undertaken before the listing is taken. Don't miss a step here or overlook any small detail. Listings are the name of the game, so make sure that anyone reading your business plan could recognize that by the amount of time you spend detailing listings.

Staging—Walk through the process of staging a house for sale. Staging is the moving of furniture, cleaning, and decorating a property for the most effective showings possible. Staging a property makes it appear to be the best to any consumer during a showing.

Servicing—Completely describe the process of getting a property sold. Determine the actions that will be taken and explain why these efforts are important. Servicing includes all the marketing actions taken, as well as communication with the client.

Showing—Portray the process of showing a property to a buyer. Detail the wants and needs analysis that must be completed with the buyer. Include the actual property selection process.

Selling—Describe the actual selling of the property to the buyer. Include the sales techniques used and the time it takes. Describe any incentives that your company will use.

Evaluating—Illustrate the process of evaluating a property to determine a fair market value. Completely describe the steps taken in the appraising process. Using the "sales comparison" approach to value, demonstrate how subject properties are chosen and then evaluated. Complete the process by describing the reconciliation procedure.

Financing—Depict the process of obtaining financing for property and the processing of the loan. Discuss the possible financing types a potential buyer could choose.

Inspecting—Show the inspection process and the benefits for all parties in the transaction. Determine how an inspector is chosen and who should pay the costs involved.

Negotiating—Discuss the nuances of negotiating in the real estate business. Include negotiations between the salespeople and their clients, as well as negotiations between the clients. Negotiations generally involve contracts, so be sure to analyze those negotiations carefully.

Accounting—A real estate broker must account for the client's funds involved in a real estate transaction. The broker must account for the earnest money and make sure it gets into the correct hands. He or she must review the "closing statement" to be sure all the items on the statement are correct and complete.

Contracting—Contracts are legal documents where two parties agree to do or not to do certain things. Contracts that are typically used are the "independent contractor" agreement between the broker and the salesperson. The listing agreement is between the broker and the seller. The buyer-broker agreement is between the broker and the buyer. The purchase agreement is between the buyer and the seller. With all these legal documents in place, you need to describe how your office will deal with them.

Closing—The "closing" is the time that all the paperwork is signed and the funds are transferred. Describe the procedures used during a closing. Talk about how your salespeople should behave and document that behavior. The "closing" should be a good time. The seller gets the opportunity to move on with his or her life and the buyer gets into the home of his or her dreams. However, it is also a time of tension. When there is tension, you need to have policies and procedures in place to handle any situation.

Tracking—Your office should have procedures in place to track and follow up on all of your clients and salespeople. These people need contact with you, or they will forget you. It is difficult to get new business, so be sure not to lose your current business through lack of communication.

Outsourcing Marketing

This section should point out why and how the decision of whether to develop a marketing campaign or to outsource it was made. The strategy focuses on whether you will create a marketing campaign for the distribution of your marketing pieces or purchase a service that will do all of that for you. This is a complicated and costly decision, so spend extra time and effort explaining this in the business plan. Consider the following questions:

- Does your office have the capability to do a professional marketing campaign?

- How much would it cost to purchase the equipment to do the marketing campaign you have envisioned?

- How long would it take to recoup the capital cost of the equipment?

- What would it cost to maintain the equipment and purchase raw materials per year?

- What would it cost in man-hours to do the marketing campaign in-house per year?

- What would it cost to outsource the marketing campaign (be sure to include any additional set-up charges)?

- In the long run, would developing or outsourcing the marketing campaign be more efficient?

Location

Discuss geographic location for your brokerage firm. In real estate, location can be a huge bonus to the production numbers if your office has walk-up business. Choosing a location was discussed previously in this book, so use that information in this section. Justify the location decision by talking about greater traffic flow, proximity to available staffing, or other factors important to your business.

Method of Sales

Describe available distribution channels and how you plan to use them. In this section, you demonstrate the ability and knowledge to get your real estate services into the hands of your target customers.

Don't make the mistake of confusing sales with marketing. Sales focuses on how you get your services into the hands of your customers. Marketing is concerned with how you educate your potential customers about your service.

Many real estate brokers that form real estate brokerages assume that a sales team can be set up with minimal time, effort, and expense. This is not the case. It can take as long as a year for a salesperson to become acquainted with the real estate industry. Even if you use salespeople who are intimately familiar with a territory and market, expect there to be ramp-up time.

Advertising and Promotion

Your advertising and promotion campaign is how you communicate information about your service. This section should include a description of all advertising vehicles you plan to use—newspapers, magazines, radio and television, telephone directory, and so on—as well as your public relations program, sales/promotional materials (such as brochures and listing sheets), trade show efforts, and the like. If you're using an advertising and/or public relations agency, be sure to discuss the talents of its staff and what efforts it is contracted to make on your behalf.

If you have a public relations plan in place, include a copy of your press kit and a list of targeted media in your business plan. This will further demonstrate that you know exactly how you plan to reach your target audience.

If trade shows will be an integral part of your recruiting strategy, be sure to include a trade show schedule outlining at which expos you'll be exhibiting. And don't forget to explain why you've chosen those shows.

If advertising or promotion is a critical expense, you should include a budget showing how and when these costs will be incurred.

Management Description

Use this section to describe business management, including the responsibilities and expertise of each person. If you are a one-person operation, detail the fact that you have the expertise to function in each of the needed management areas. This may be difficult, but with a small operation it can be successfully done. Also detail future plans to hire additional management help as needed. Anticipate which positions will need to be filled, when you anticipate they will need to be filled, and why they will need to be filled.

If your operation is larger and you need positions you have yet to fill, detail that you will need to hire to achieve the goals set out in the service development schedule. Describe the talents each person needs to possess and how the addition of the person will help the business meet its objectives.

Be sure to have major categories of business management covered, such as marketing, sales (including customer relations and service) and quality assurance, accounting, and administration. You do not have to have personnel devoted to each of these areas, but you should have people who will be able to assume these responsibilities as needed.

Include relevant details in your management description, but save complete résumés as attachments to your plan. Emphasize people who have already committed to working with your business.

Ownership

A short section on who owns and controls your business will help provide a better understanding of who will be making decisions. Discuss the involvement of owner. Will the owner(s) be an integral part of the business or be silent owner(s) and let the management team operate the business? You should include the owners' résumés in the appendix.

Board of Advisors

You should form a Board of Advisors. A Board of Advisors is a group of non-salaried business talent that is available to you for business advice. This talent includes attorneys, appraisers, inspectors, accountants, advertising professionals, as well as other real estate brokers, mortgage brokers, and title officers. The presence of such people on your Board of Advisors indicates your ability to attract talent to your business. In your description of each support service, describe what strengths the individual possesses, as well as what experience or contacts he or she brings to your business. Outline his or her employment, training, education, and expertise. Highlight each board member's experiences and how he or she will help your business thrive. Ask industry peers for the name of the best advisors for your industry. Include résumés for each of your Board of Advisors in the appendix of the business plan. If the board members have industry connections, good reputations, or potential to raise capital for your business, you should be sure to include these facts. A strong Board of Advisors is an asset to a business. It can add credibility to your management team and increase your likelihood of success.

Create a board that complements existing management. Create a chart to determine the kind of talent needed to move your business ahead. List the skills your management possesses. You can then make a list of the skills you need to acquire and the people who possess those skills.

Competition

The business plan must include a section that analyzes the competition. This section should contain evidence of research and be quite lengthy. Each competitor in the real estate industry should be investigated and then detailed in this section. In a geographic area with multiple competitors you should investigate a variety of competitors, but it may not be feasible to investigate them all. If possible, include their annual sales and their market share. Each assessment should include why these real estate companies do or do not meet their customers' needs. You should then explain why you think you can capture a share of their business.

Strengths and weaknesses can fall into a number of different categories. Market dominance, quality of service, service fees, marketing and advertising capability, image, size of company, company philosophy, and breadth of services are all ways real estate companies differentiate one company from another. Ask yourself: Who is the cost leader? Who is the quality leader? Who has the largest market share? Why have certain brokerages recently entered or withdrawn from the market? These factors are critical to a successful competitive analysis.

The investigation should include

- Production numbers
- Number of associates
- Years in business
- Number of locations
- Business structure
- Commission structure
- Advertising strategy

- Services offered
- Areas served
- Franchise/independent

The competition section should also include any other information the broker deems necessary to make the best decisions. Finding the information may be tricky, but the effort should be made. You could research your competitors by shopping their stores or calling them to see what they offer and what they charge for it. To create a list of your competitors' strengths and weaknesses, look at areas such as pricing, value, service, and timeliness. Your market research should look at commissions, add-on services, and reputation in the marketplace.

The competition section indicates where your real estate services fit in the competitive environment. It should demonstrate that you are prepared to cope with the barriers to your business's success. Many business plans fail to give a realistic view of their true competitive universe by defining the competitive field too narrowly. Think as broadly as possible when devising a list of competitors by characterizing competitors as any business customers may patronize for similar services.

To determine your competitors' strengths and weaknesses, evaluate why customers buy from them. Is it cost? Value? Service? Convenience? Reputation? Very often, it's "perceived" strengths rather than "actual" strengths that you will be evaluating.

Consider describing those who are not your competitors. For example, people may think that an attorney competes with you. You will want to stress that attorneys provide legal documents but rarely ever sell real estate and do not understand the market the way you do.

Financials

This section deals with the development and implementation of a plan for the achievement of one's overall financial objective. It also describes how and where you plan to get money to get your business started and running, and should answer the following questions:

- How will you finance your business?
- How will you manage your finances?
- What needs to be financed?
- Where will your finances come from?

Financials are used to document, justify, and convince. This is the section in which you make your case in words and back up what you say with financial statements and forms that document the viability of your business and its soundness as an investment. It's also where you indicate that you have evaluated the risks associated with your venture.

Risks

No business is without risks. Your ability to identify and discuss them demonstrates your skills as a broker. You will show that you've taken the initiative to confront these issues and are capable of handling them. The following list of problems is by no means complete, but it should give you an idea of some possibilities:

- Your competitors cut their prices (commissions).
- A key customer (such as a builder) cancels a contract.
- The industry's growth rate drops.
- Service costs exceed your projections.
- Your sales projections are not achieved.
- An important ad campaign flounders.
- Important ancillary businesses (such as lenders) fail to keep their promises.
- Your competitors release a new, better service.
- Public opinion of your service changes.
- You can't find trained salespeople or staff.

Evaluate your risks honestly. To generate a complete list of risks, examine all of your assumptions about how your business will develop. The flipside of many of them may be risks.

Financial Statement

This is a financial report that includes:

- A balance sheet
- An income statement
- Accounts Receivable

- Accounts Payable
- A debt schedule
- Reconciliation of net worth

This should be included for new and existing businesses; project the following financial statements for the next three years (monthly for the first year, annually for second and third).

Estimated Sales

Estimated sales for your real estate business are based on your assessment of the advantages of your service, your customers, the size of your market, and your competition. This should include sales in housing units and dollars for the next three years, with the first year broken down by quarter. These numbers will be crucial to other financial documents you present later in the plan.

Use a one-paragraph summary to justify your projections. Be sure to use a concise statement of what sets your service apart from other real estate brokerages in the marketplace. Also state why you see your customer base growing, and indicate how you will go after this business.

Do not make outlandish projections. They will ruin your credibility as a reputable businessperson. A common mistake is assuming your business will have a few modest years and then a dramatic increase in sales when "the market takes off." Use "best case," "worst case," and "likely" scenarios to create a spectrum of sales projections.

Operating Expenses

By creating a financial form called "Operating Expenses," you pull together the expenses incurred in running your business. Expense categories include: marketing, sales, and overhead. Overhead includes fixed expenses such as administrative costs and other expenses that remain constant regardless of how much business your business does. Overhead also includes variable expenses, such as travel, equipment leases, and supplies.

A complete and thorough examination of every detail of every operating expense, both fixed and variable, should be conducted and included in this section. Start by asking the following questions:

- Is this expense necessary?
- Could this expense be eliminated or reduced?

- Could some of these expenses be combined?
- Could these expense items be purchased in bulk to take advantage of economies of scale?
- Could the lease of the space be negotiated or reworked?
- Could any loans be negotiated or reworked?
- Could reducing the costs of utilities in any way attain savings?
- Could you outsource any marketing/advertising campaign at reduced cost?
- Could you outsource your accounting/payroll functions at reduced cost?
- Can you implement any polices or procedures that could reduce or eliminate employee theft of services and supplies?

Any and all of these suggestions could help you reduce your expenses. Any reduction of expenses is a direct bonus to the bottom line of the financial statement.

Capital Requirements

This form details the amount of money you will need to procure the equipment used to start up and continue operations of your business. Capital equipment can be leased or purchased. For this section of the business plan, refer to capital equipment, those things which you buy. A complete analysis of lease versus buy on all the capital equipment your real estate office will need should be completed and included in the business plan. Leasing of equipment will be covered in the operating expense section. Capital requirements also include depreciation details of all purchased equipment. To determine your capital requirements, think about anything in your business that will require capital. For real estate sales, this might be a moving van, fax machine, desktop and laptop computers, telephone system, and yard signs.

Cost of Services

For a real estate sales business, the cost of services is the cost incurred in the execution of the service. To generate a cost of services chart, you need to know the total number of housing units you will sell for a year and the cost to produce each sale.

The cost of services chart allows you to see how much money it takes per closing. It also allows you to determine the money you have left over after a sale to use in your budget planning.

Income Statement

The income statement is where you prove your business can and will generate cash. This document is where you record revenue, expenses, capital, and cost of services. The outcome of the combination of these elements demonstrates how much money your business made or will make, or lost or will lose, during the year. An income statement and a cash flow statement differ in that an income statement does not include details of when revenue was collected or expenses paid.

An income statement for a business plan should be broken down by month the first year. The second year can be broken down quarterly, and each year after can be broken down annually. Analyze the results of the income statement briefly and include this analysis in your business plan. If your business already exists, include income statements for previous years.

Avoid insufficiently documented assumptions about your business growth. In other words, if you say you expect your firm to grow by 30 percent in the first year and 50 percent in the second, you need to document why those numbers are attainable. It can be because similar real estate brokerages have had this growth path; because the industry is growing at this rate (cite the source for this data); or because of projections from a specific market researcher, industry association, or other source.

Cash Flow Statement

A cash flow statement shows readers of your business plan how much money you will need, when you will need it, and where the money will come from. In general terms, the cash flow statement looks at cash and sources of revenue minus expenses and capital requirements to derive a net cash flow figure. A cash flow statement provides a glimpse of how much money a business has at any given time and when it is likely to need more cash. The cash flow statement is critical for budgeting purposes. Analyze the results of the cash flow statement briefly and include this analysis in your business plan. As with all financial documents, have your cash flow statement prepared or at least reviewed by a reputable accountant.

Do not fall in to the common trap of underestimating cash flow needs. This can lead to undercapitalization, which means your funds will prove inadequate for meeting your obligations.

Balance Sheet

Unlike other financial statements, a balance sheet is created only once a year to calculate the net worth of a business. If your business plan is for a new real estate business, you will need to include a personal balance sheet summarizing your personal assets and liabilities. If your business exists already, include the past years' balance sheets up to the balance sheet from your last reporting period. Analyze the results of the balance sheet briefly and include this analysis in your business plan.

Conclusion

Completing a business plan for your real estate brokerage firm does not mean it will succeed, but it does mean you have taken the time to analyze your future, and with the best estimates you can make your company is or will become a thriving enterprise. Having a business plan is essential for obtaining funds from lending institutions. Writing a business plan creates a roadmap for your company to follow down the road of financial freedom.

Chapter Thirteen Review Questions

1. What is one of the most important aspects of starting a real estate business in today's changing environment?
   A. Writing a business plan
   B. Finding the right location
   C. Hiring the right salespeople
   D. Having the best marketing

2. A business plan should convey
   A. the goals of the business.
   B. the core values of the business.
   C. the methods to help the business succeed today, tomorrow, and far into the future.
   D. all of the above.

3. The cover page should include which of the following?
   A. Personal name
   B. Business name

    C. Business logo

    D. All of the above

4. The cover page should include which of the following?

    A. Business trademark

    B. Business charter

    C. Business address

    D. All of the above

5. The cover page should include which of the following?

    A. Business telephone number

    B. Business fax number

    C. Business e-mail address

    D. All of the above

6. The executive summary should include which of the following?

    A. A description of your distinct service

    B. A statement your personal goals

    C. A statement of your personal objectives

    D. All of the above

7. The mission statement is *not*

    A. a description of the purpose of your business.

    B. best copied exactly from other real estate brokerages' mission statements.

    C. only one or two sentences long.

    D. all of the above.

8. In writing a vision statement, a person should follow which of these guidelines?

    A. A vision statement must be based in reality to be meaningful.

    B. A vision statement must be believable to the entire company, including the salespeople, to be relevant. It should inspire everyone associated with the organization.

    C. A vision statement must be inclusive and make people want to be part of the future of this company. It allows people to feel like they are part of a greater whole and see how they contribute to the welfare of the entire company.

    D. All of the above.

9. In writing a vision statement, a person should follow which of these guidelines?

   A. A vision statement focuses on the future. A good vision should orient the company toward the future.

   B. A vision statement should help in the development of strategies that will lead to future success.

   C. A vision statement should make it easier for everyone to make the right decisions the very first time.

   D. All of the above.

10. When writing on the real estate market, be sure to talk about which of the following factors affecting market growth?

   A. Industry trends

   B. Population shifts

   C. Government policy

   D. All of the above

11. What are some of the elements of a sales and marketing strategy?

   A. Locating prospects

   B. Features of your service

   C. Marketing and sales techniques

   D. All of the above

12. The marketing plan should answer all of the following questions *except*

   A. how will your business differ from its competitors?

   B. what are the advantages of the compensation structure for your salespeople?

   C. who are your customers?

   D. who is your market?

13. The marketing plan should answer all of the following questions *except*

   A. what sales contests should you initiate?

   B. what are the characteristics of your average customer?

   C. what are the environmental factors of your business?

   D. how will you promote and market your service?

14. All of the following describe "Position in Marketing," *except*

   A. your ranking in total dollar sales in any given year.

   B. your type of real estate office.

    C. your identity in the marketplace.

    D. how you want the market and your competitors to perceive your service.

15. A typical business description section includes

    A. an overview of the real estate industry.

    B. a discussion of your particular real estate business.

    C. a description of your real estate services.

    D. all of the above.

16. What is a legal document where two parties agree to do or not to do certain things?

    A. An independent contractor agreement

    B. A listing agreement

    C. A contract

    D. All of the above

17. The financial section of your business plan should answer which of the following questions?

    A. How will you finance your business?

    B. How will you manage your finances?

    C. Where will your finances come from?

    D. All of the above.

18. You business plan should discuss which of the following risks?

    A. Your competitors cut their prices.

    B. The industry's growth rate drops.

    C. Service costs exceed your projections.

    D. All of the above.

19. You business plan should discuss which of the following risks?

    A. Your sales projections are not achieved.

    B. An important ad campaign flounders.

    C. Your competitors release a new, better service.

    D. All of the above.

20. The financial statement should include all of the following, *except*

    A. a balance sheet.

    B. an income statement.

C. a debt schedule.

D. a marketing statement.

21. Your expense analysis should answer all the following questions, *except*

A. is this expense necessary?

B. could the lease of the space be negotiated or reworked?

C. could reducing the costs of utilities in any way attain savings?

D. all of the above.

22. Which of the following is not a variable expense?

A. Travel

B. Equipment leases

C. Office supplies

D. Office furniture

14 Financing a Real Estate Business

One of the most critical areas of concern for a real estate brokerage is finances. A majority of real estate brokerages start out without the proper capital to effectively operate. Once the company realizes its dilemma, it is usually too late for financial bailout.

Borrowing money to begin operations as a real estate brokerage is difficult because the lending institution does not see the asset versus liability of a real estate company as viable. What kinds of things constitute the assets of a real estate company? The only tangible assets are some office equipment and supplies. The main assets are the salespeople, and the company does not "own" them; but do not feel too bad, because this is the troubled path of almost all service industries.

Applying for a Business Loan

Borrowing money is one of the most common sources of funding for a small real estate business, but obtaining a loan isn't always easy. Before you approach a lender for a loan, it is a good idea to understand as much as you can about the factors the lender will evaluate when it considers making you a loan. If you choose to apply for a business loan, you should be aware of several factors the lending institutions will be concerned with, including those discussed here.

Ability to Repay

The ability to repay must be proven in your loan package. Lenders want to know you will have the cash flow from the business to meet debt payments. In order to analyze the cash flow of the business, the lender will review the past financial statements. Lenders feel better with businesses that have been in existence for a number of years because they have a financial track record. If the business has consistently made a profit and that profit can cover the payment of additional debt, then it is likely that the loan will be approved. It is much more difficult to obtain a loan if the business has been operating marginally or if the business is a start-up.

Collateral

Collateral is anything of value that a lender could take to replace the loss of money in case of a default on a loan. The lender could attach a certificate of deposit (CD) held in a bank or take a lien against real or personal property. The lender is looking to reduce its risk in making the loan.

Collateral can be defined as those personal and business assets that can be sold to pay back the loan. Every loan program requires at least some collateral to secure a loan. If a potential borrower has no collateral to secure a loan, he or she will need a cosigner who has collateral to pledge. Otherwise, the borrower may have difficulty obtaining a loan. The value of collateral is not based on the market value, but rather is discounted to take into account the value that would be lost if the assets had to be liquidated.

Some say that lenders will only lend to those who don't need the money. Can you blame them? If you have plenty of money, that means that if I loan you some, you would have enough to pay me back. If you don't have any money and I loan you some, or if something went wrong, how would you pay me back? The key here is that as a lender, I make money on each loan. Wouldn't you want to loan money where there is less risk? Taking this further, you need your loan package to be sound enough to make the lender feel less at risk.

Credit Rating

Credit rating is the overall credit score that you personally have obtained. Your credit rating is based upon your past history of credit and your ability to pay that credit back. The better your score, the better credit you have demonstrated and the less risk the lender feels it is undertaking.

You should have your credit checked out at least once per year. The credit bureaus must give you a credit report yearly if requested. You need to check if there are any reports of negative credit. This can happen very easily, so don't wait until you actually need the credit to check it because clearing it up (even if it is a mistake) may take over a year. You do not need to hire any credit reporting company to obtain the report or to challenge any discrepancies. All you have to do is file a report with the credit bureau, and they must investigate. If the entity that filed the report does not respond, the credit bureau must eliminate the information from your record. Again, this seems easy, but it will not happen overnight, so be patient. If the entity responds and confirms the credit problem, you now must take that up with the entity that filed. This will run into more time and hassle but remain persistent and you will finally have your credit back in line. You want to make sure that, when the lender pulls your credit report, all the errors have been corrected and your history is up-to-date.

Once you receive the credit report, be sure to check your name, social security number, and address at the top of the page. Make sure these are correct. There are people who have found that they have credit information from another person because of mistakes in their identification information.

On the rest of your credit report, you will see a list of all the credit you have obtained in the past—credit cards, mortgages, student loans, and so on. Each credit will be listed individually, with information on how you paid that credit. Any credit where you have had a problem in paying will be listed towards the top of the list. These are the credits that may affect your ability to obtain a loan.

If you have been late by a month on an occasional payment, this probably will not adversely affect your credit. However, if you are continuously late in paying your credit, have a credit that was never paid and charged off, have a judgment against you, or have declared bankruptcy or had a foreclosure or repossession in the last seven years, it is likely that you will have difficulty in obtaining a loan.

In some cases, a person has had a period of bad credit based on a divorce, medical crisis, or some other significant event. If you can show that your credit was good before and after this event, and that you have tried to pay back those debts incurred in the period of bad credit, you should be able to obtain a loan. It is best if you write an explanation of your credit problems and how you have rectified them, and attach this explanation to your credit report in your loan package. If you need assistance in interpreting or evaluating your credit report, you can ask your accountant or banker.

Research indicates that good personal credit history is one of the most important factors in identifying borrowers who will repay their commercial loans. Many loan programs require perfect personal credit in order to qualify. If you get turned down by one institution, that does not prevent you from going to another. I wanted financing for a real estate project once and had to go to seven lenders before I received my loan.

If you do not have the credit necessary to get yourself a loan with a lending institution, you may have to go to alternative financing sources discussed later.

Management Experience

A person who wants to open a business and has no experience in that business should not seek financing, let alone start the business, unless he or she intends to hire people who know the business or to take on a partner who has the appropriate experience. Regardless, the client should be advised to take some time to work in the business first and take some entrepreneurial training classes.

Equity

Equity is the difference between what is owed on a business and its actual worth. Financial institutions want to see a certain amount of equity in a business before they feel comfortable lending money. Most banks want to see that the total liabilities or debt of a business is not more than four times the amount of equity. Therefore, if you want a loan, you must ensure that there is enough equity in the company to leverage that loan. If the current debt to net worth is too great, it is unlikely that the business will be able to obtain additional financing.

Don't be misled into thinking that start-up businesses can obtain 100 percent financing through conventional or special loan programs. A business owner usually must put some of her/his own money into the business. The amount an individual must put into the business in order to obtain a loan is dependent on the type of loan, the purpose, and the terms. For example, most banks want the owner to put in at least 20 to 40 percent of the total request.

Detailed Business Plan

Before any lending institution worth doing business with will loan you money, you must provide a detailed business plan. We have discussed the two main functions of a business plan, which are

1. to give direction and purpose to an organization, and

2. to provide information to lenders and investors about the company's viability and vision.

The discussion about writing the business plan has already been completed. The discussion here will focus on the presentation. Be sure to do the following:

HAVE THE BUSINESS PLAN PROFESSIONALLY BOUND WITH MULTIPLE COPIES

It amazes me, the mentality of some people. They expect a lender to give them large sums of money, and they won't go to the expense of making a quality presentation. You want the business plan to have several hundred pages in a leather-bound binder.

PUBLISH THE BUSINESS PLAN WITH PLENTY OF TIME TO SPARE

You don't want a presentation with a lender to be postponed because you do not have your business plan available. Plan ahead; if you don't plan ahead, what are you telling your possible future lender? Be sure to take with you several copies of the plans, because you don't know how many decision makers may be at the meeting.

The Loan Process

The following questions are ones that need to be asked and answered by the management group looking to obtain a loan. The questions are structured as if a business is in operation. If you are looking at a start-up operation, then use future projections to answer these questions.

Can the Business Repay the Loan?

A lender wants to be sure the money it is loaning will come back. Do the numbers in your financial statement make sense? Do they show the business will do well, or do they indicate the venture might be a risk? Have you taken all things into consideration? Do you have current and future projections?

Can You Repay the Loan if the Business Fails?

The lender wants to be sure you have enough assets in your personal funds or collateral that you can cover the debt if the business can't. This is simple risk reduction by the lender. Most lenders will not require complete coverage of a business loan, but the more the borrower can cover, the lower the risk to the lender, and the more likely the loan will be approved.

Does the Business Pay Its Bills?

The business needs enough revenue to cover all expenses and have enough left over to make payments to the loan. If the company does not currently cover the expenses, what will happen once the loan payment comes due? If it is a start-up business, will the brokerage have enough income to pay its bills?

Are the Owners Committed to the Business?

Do the owners have their real estate license? Do the owners have an occupation outside real estate? Will it be hard or easy for the owners to walk away from this business? All these questions must be addressed before a loan is approved.

Does the Business Have a Profitable Operating History?

The company should show a profit and need money to expand operations to make more money. The borrowed funds should not go to a business that needs the money just to stay afloat. Desperation is not a good investment for a lender. If it is a start-up business, then show that the industry needs another competitor and that you can fill that void.

Are Sales Growing?

What are the trends for this business? The business should be able to show data that indicates a steady increase in profits. Any slumps or drops in profits need to be explained in detail. You need to indicate that the business has corrected any of the situations that created the drop in profit. You need to indicate you understand why you have increased the profit of the business and know how to continue that trend. If the trend is downward, the risk to the lender increases drastically. If it is a start-up business, give examples of others in the industry, their trends, and how you can improve on their business.

Does the Business Control Expenses?

Some brokers spend money on everything. They overspend for the best location in town. They buy the latest in technology, and they overpay their salespeople. All expenses should be analyzed to determine if any of the expenses could be reduced or eliminated. This is a difficult and time-consuming but necessary process. As a start-up business, you need to lay out the systems to control expenses.

Is There Any Discretionary Cash Flow?

The discretionary cash flow would demonstrate the ability to take on another payment—a loan payment. A real estate company that continually makes a profit will quickly get a loan to expand operations.

What Is the Future of the Industry?

The future of the industry should be strong. This includes both local and international markets. If the industry will not defend an expansion, the expansion should not be considered. I have seen brokers expand their operations to excess. They had real estate offices so big that the area could not support the volume of sales that the office required to stay viable.

Who Is Your Competition, and What Are Their Strengths and Weaknesses?

As you should have done previously, you should make sure of your competition and what they offer. To be caught sleeping and not notice what your competition has or is about to offer could be disastrous to your future. Your knowledge of your competition shows the lender that you are prepared.

Have You Filed and Paid All Income Tax Returns?

Lenders and government loan programs alike want to see that an individual has met his or her tax obligations for both filing and paying taxes. Many of the loan programs are in partnership with government agencies. These loan programs do not look favorably on individuals who have unpaid income taxes. Some brokers pay the taxes on the business last. The taxes should be paid first.

Does the Business Have the Ability to Repay a Loan?

If the brokerage is an existing business and it is profitable, then there are demonstrated profits to repay some amount of new debt. If a brokerage is not profitable, then it becomes very important to prove how it will be profitable in the near future so that a loan can be repaid.

If the brokerage is a start-up business, it is very important that you find as much data on comparable businesses or industry statistics as you can in order to "prove" the revenues you intend to generate and the expenses you anticipate incurring.

Does Your Business Have a Positive Net Worth?

The net worth (only applies to existing businesses) of the business should be positive. You need to have two net worth sheets: one for you personally, and one for the business. You can combine the two if you operate the brokerage as a sole proprietorship. The net worth statement helps the lender determine

- progress towards financial goals,
- plans for changes in assets or liabilities,
- ability to keep tax liability down, and
- ability to chart financial progress.

Be sure your net worth statement takes a look at all current assets. Current assets of a real estate brokerage are the pending contracts for sale. Examine your fixed assets—those items that your brokerage owns, such as copy machines and office furniture. The last analysis with respect to assets concerns the deferred assets, which are any investments the brokerage has made that cannot be converted to cash without a substantial penalty, such as a retirement plan.

Is Your Business Carrying Too Much Debt?

Existing businesses that have too much debt will find that their profits are directed at paying back loans and not building equity in the business that can fund future growth. Consequently, banks and government loan programs look more favorably at loan requests that do not add too much debt to the business. Banks often look for a debt to net worth ratio of four or less (total liabilities divided by equity).

Do You Have Enough of Your Own Money in the Business?

Most loan programs require that the business owner put his or her own money in the business. This owner equity injection shows that the owner believes in the business enough to risk his or her own money. Some loan programs require only 10 percent owner equity; other programs require at least 30 percent and will look more favorably on a loan request the more equity is in the business. A business owner who does not believe in a brokerage enough to risk his or her own money is a major blocking point for a loan.

Are You Willing to Personally Guarantee a Loan?

Most business owners are asked for a personal guarantee in order to obtain their first business loans. If the business fails, the lender can come after you personally. They do not lend to corporations unless the chairman or someone is personally responsible.

Does Your Business Have Qualified Managers and Advisors?

As existing real estate brokerages expand, they need more sophisticated management as it relates to strategic planning, marketing, record keeping, sales management, personnel, and so on. When you apply for a loan, your banker will consider the qualifications of your management team and advisors in order to determine whether they are capable of leading your business to the next level of growth.

If there are sectors of your business with which you need assistance, I strongly recommend that you attend entrepreneurial training classes, check out the NATIONAL ASSOCIATION OF REALTORS® online, visit a business assistance center or Small Business Development Center in your area, or contact your regional SBA office for information on local resources.

Do You Have Experience in Running Your Own Business?

For a new business especially, it is important for the business owner to demonstrate that he or she has experience in the real estate industry and/or entrepreneurial experience. If you have never owned or operated a real estate brokerage before, I strongly recommend that you do your research and take some college classes before opening your own brokerage.

If you cannot answer "yes" to all the questions above, then you may have difficulties obtaining financing at this time. Take the advice of business managers and realize that if you are in or attempting to open an enterprise that will not turn a profit, then you shouldn't do it. When I was in college, we evaluated a doll-making business to see if opening it was a financially feasible thing to do. The woman planning to start the business loved dolls. She would hand-make them and sell them out of her home. She decided that she wanted to take her savings and open an actual "doll shop." We proved beyond a shadow of doubt that the business would not make it. She didn't listen and opened anyway. Thousands of dollars later, she locked the doors. If you are going to seek out business advice, you may want to listen to it.

Preliminary Actions Before the Presentation

Now that you have your business plan and have answered all the previous questions positively, it is time to go for a loan. Before you show up at a lender's front door, there are a few things to do.

1. *Call.* Lenders like to be prepared for meetings, and showing up un- announced will only give you poor results. You will be asked to return at a better time or the meeting will stall without getting a decision. You need to build good relations with the lenders, and showing up and making them feel uncomfortable is not the way. Some lenders demand to see your business plan before they meet with you. They want to do that to be more prepared, but they could also eliminate you before you even get a shot to present. Do your best to avoid sending your business plan ahead of time, because you are not there to defend it.

2. *Write a proposal letter.* A proposal letter is simple a two- to five-page letter describing the need for the loan and the ability to pay the loan back. Be very specific in the letter about what you are actually asking for. Do you want a loan, or a line of credit, or a combination of both? Exactly how much money is necessary? Do not ask for too little because it will be evident that you cannot succeed without the funds necessary. Do not ask for too much because it will be perceived as imprudent on your part. The letter should not to go into details about your business or *how* you are to repay the loan—all that is found in the business plan. This is an expanded form of the Executive Summary in your business plan.

3. *Dress as if you were already a success.* Act like you have all the money in the world. I am not talking arrogance; I am talking confidence. Have

on a nice suit or business outfit and be there on time. Or even better, arrive about fifteen minutes early and rehearse in the car, but go in on time.

4. Have the following items with you:

- Two writing pens
- A notepad
- Your proposal and business plans
- Your business cards and business brochures

Calling on Lenders

Calling on lenders takes a little courage, but remember they want and need to make loans, or they are out of business; this is a relationship, but at the same time it is business. If they turn you down, there are other lenders.

Before you call your first lender, you should read through the following script:

Receptionist: "This is First Bank of Brittany, how can I direct your call?"

Broker: "Who handles small business loans?"

Receptionist: "That would be Bob Smith. Would you like me to connect you?"

Broker: "That would be great."

Loan Officer: "This is Bob Smith."

Broker: "Mr. Smith, my name is Dan Hamilton, and I would like to meet with you to discuss a business opportunity. Now, I am available later today, or would tomorrow be better?"

Loan Officer: "Well, how about 2:00 p.m. tomorrow? I could set aside some time then."

Broker: "Great. Now is there anything besides my business plan that you will need to see?"

Loan Officer: "Does your business plan cover your financial position?"

Broker: "Yes, it does."

Loan Officer: "Then that should be about it. See you tomorrow."

So you see, they aren't as mean as we like to think. They want these appointments because they never know which one is the moneymaker.

At the Appointment

Once you are in front of the loan officer, begin by making small talk. Mention that you like the way the bank is laid out. If you notice a picture of the loan officer's family, ask about them. Whatever you do, don't jump right into the presentation. Remember, you are building a relationship.

After a few minutes, you should begin your presentation. If the loan officer wants to take the lead, you can let him or her do so, but make sure you stay on track with your presentation.

The presentation should go through the following steps:

1. Ask the loan officer to sign a "Non-Disclosure Statement." Don't be intimidated; they actually expect you to ask for this, and if you don't have one, they might not consider you a player. If they refuse to sign it (I can't imagine why they would), then ask to speak to someone else in the organization. You don't want your idea stolen. I don't believe it would happen, but you need to protect yourself.

2. Ask the loan officer the "Preliminary Questions for a Loan Request," listed below. These questions are to determine if your loan is the type they actually do. Some lenders specialize, and if your business does not fall within their specialty, you will not receive a loan. They may not lend money in your amount; some lenders will not lend money in amounts of less than five million. If you are applying for $100,000, it won't work.

3. If you have determined that they *can* make the loan, go over your business concept. First, hand your business plan to the loan officer. Your discussion should center on your executive summary and/or your proposal. Remember, your proposal explains why you want the money, and the executive summary is all about your company and why you are a secure investment for the lender. You should mention the reasons for your business and what you expect a loan to do for you. Don't get into too much detail, and certainly do not have the loan officer flipping pages in your business plan. Lenders tend to be numbers people, so let them absorb your idea.

4. Ask the loan officer if he or she has any questions. If the answer is no, then ask for the loan. If the loan officer does have questions, answer them as well as possible and then ask for the loan. Do not leave without asking for the loan. Most loan officers cannot make a decision on the spot, so do not be concerned when the officer answers that he or she has to take this proposal to the loan committee for its approval. But you still must ask. Before you leave, ask the loan officer, "If there

is one thing about this loan request that would keep the loan committee from accepting it, what do you think that would be?" If he or she answers, you must be able to remedy that situation, or you're doomed.

5. If you have reached the time to leave, gather your things and ask when the next loan committee meeting will be. Ask how many business plans would they need, and politely excuse yourself.

6. The very first thing you do when you get back to your office is to write the loan officer a thank-you note and get it in the mail.

7. If you are turned down, go meet with another lender. Persistence is the key.

8. Some lenders have you mail your business plan to them, and they handle the entire procedure over the telephone or through the Internet.

The lending process and the type of loans those lenders make vary from lender to lender. The key is to find out as much information as possible about the lender before you make a presentation, so you can design the presentation to that particular lender. You also want to know you are not dealing with "predatory" lenders who would take you and your business. Watch for additions to your loan that allow the lender to be part of your business and take a share of the profits (called Shared Annuity Loans (SALs)).

Alternative Sources of Loans

Not all loans are from traditional lenders. Be sure of the quality of the lender before you originate a loan. A quick, uneducated decision could be the demise of your brokerage. The following are just a few lenders to which you could send a "loan request":

Partners

Taking on partners was a topic discussed earlier, but remember, the discussion here is about obtaining a loan. A loan can be paid off, and once that occurs there is no more liability on the part of the business. Be careful about taking on a partner, because you cannot get rid of them as easily. Taking on a partner is viewed as a business marriage. Once you take on a partner you cannot get rid of him or her, and if you do, it will cost you everything. Only take on someone like an accountant or an attorney who brings something to the table. Anyone else had better be only as a *last* resort. Why would you want to do all the work and have someone else share in the glory? So for the purposes of the following discussions, these ventures are considered to be loans.

Friends and Family

You can ask your friends and family for the loan; doing so could be a great source of funding, but it could also be a disaster on many levels. The plus side is that the relationship is already built, and the qualification process is probably extremely easy. A lot of your current relatives and friends have money right now that is just sitting in the bank. You could take that money and make everyone wealthy. The bad side is that if you do not succeed, you could lose not only your business but also your family. With a lender, if you go bankrupt, you can get on your feet again in a few years; if you use your friends and family, you only have one shot. If you lose their savings once, you will not get another chance. Not only that, but a lender is not at your family reunion or birthday party.

Business Partners

Business partners are the people you associate with in the real estate business. Hopefully, if you have performed as a real estate salesperson, these business partners know you and trust you. Some of these people have a great deal of money and are looking for a place to invest it with a better return than the bank is currently giving. You need to provide them with the same proposal you would a traditional lender. The good part, however, is that you already have a relationship built. Here is a list of some possible partners:

- Title attorneys
- Mortgage officers
- Inspectors
- Appraisers
- Structural engineers
- Real estate investors
- Surveyors
- Repair and remodel professionals
- Insurance salespeople

These people want you to succeed, because when you succeed, you could possibly help them with their businesses. Do not make a loan contingent upon your giving them business (that could be a violation of the Real Estate Settlement Act), even though they will want to be part of a growing company. If you know the owners of the company, go to them first. They probably have more discretionary income than those that work for them, and they probably started where you are today. Those people want to help you because they know what it was like to be hungry.

Investment Group

If the people you know cannot finance your project solely, think about forming an investment group. The investment group involves several individuals investing a specified amount in your business. These can be friends, relatives, or business partners. Each of them is paid back individually with interest. Separately, you will not have enough capital to begin a brokerage, but by combining several small investors, you can reach your goal.

Venture Capitalists

Venture capitalists are individuals, partners, or companies that have huge sums of money to loan to people who want to begin or expand their business but cannot obtain a loan from traditional sources. Venture capitalists generally specialize in pharmaceuticals and technology. However, there are some that specialize in the real estate industry. These people will give you money but want huge returns. The reason they want such a large return is due to the risk they are assuming. If you were such a quality loan, you wouldn't need them. They can be extremely valuable in the right circumstances, but use them only as a last resort.

Conclusion

The financing of a real estate brokerage can be a detailed and tricky undertaking. Great care must be used to get the loan officer the information that is required. To walk in and demand money is a fast way to leave without it.

Traditional banks are the major source of real estate business loans, but they are not the only source. A broker could turn to alternative sources such as partners, friends, family, venture capitalists, and investment groups.

It would be nice to be rich and have all the money to self-purchase a real estate brokerage company, but most of us need some help, and this chapter aims to aid in that process.

Chapter Fourteen Review Questions

1. What are the main assets of a real estate company?
   A. The land and building
   B. All the business equipment and fixtures
   C. The real estate salespeople
   D. The cash and cash equivalent funds held in financing institutions

2. Which of the following factors is of no interest to a lending institution?
   A. Your age
   B. Your collateral
   C. Your credit
   D. Your real estate background

3. _____ is anything of value that a lender could take to replace the loss of money in case of a default on a loan.
   A. Credit
   B. Collateral
   C. Cash
   D. Capital

4. What is the difference between what is owed on a business and its actual worth?
   A. Loan amount
   B. Equity
   C. Capital gain
   D. Value

5. What are the two main functions of a business plan?
   A. To give direction and purpose to an organization
   B. To isolate the true business clients and determine an adequate price for the services offered

    C. To provide information to lenders and investors about the company's viability and vision

    D. Both A and C

6. Which of the following is something you should do before a loan request interview?

    A. Have the business plan professionally bound in multiple copies

    B. Publish the business plan with plenty of time to spare

    C. You should do both A and B

    D. Neither will influence your chances of obtaining a loan. Loans are based on credit history and business viability.

7. Which of the following are questions you should be prepared to answer at a loan request interview?

    A. Can the business repay the loan?

    B. Can you repay the loan if the business fails?

    C. Does the business pay its bills?

    D. All of the above

8. Which of the following are questions you should be prepared to answer at a loan request interview?

    A. Are the owners committed to the business?

    B. Does the business have a profitable operating history?

    C. Are sales growing?

    D. All of the above

9. Which of the following are questions you should be prepared to answer at a loan request interview?

    A. Does the business control expenses?

    B. Is there any discretionary cash flow?

    C. What is the future of the industry?

    D. All of the above

10. Which of the following are questions you should be prepared to answer at a loan request interview?

    A. Who is your competition and what are their strengths and weaknesses?

    B. Have you filed and paid all income tax returns?

C. Does the business have the ability to repay a loan?

D. All of the above

11. Which of the following are questions you should be prepared to answer at a loan request interview?

A. Does your business have a positive net worth?

B. Is your business not carrying too much debt?

C. Do you have enough of your own money in the business?

D. All of the above

12. Which of the following are questions you should be prepared to answer at a loan request interview?

A. Are you willing to personally guarantee a loan?

B. Does your business have qualified managers and advisors?

C. Do you have experience in running your own business?

D. All of the above

13. A net worth statement would not be used to determine which one of the following?

A. Progress toward financial goals

B. The market price of services

C. Plan for changes in assets or liabilities

D. The ability to keep tax liability down

14. Which of the following best describes the current assets of a real estate brokerage?

A. Executory contracts

B. Liquid deposits in a financial institution

C. Petty cash

D. All of the above

15. Which of the following is not an example of a fixed cost of a real estate brokerage?

A. Copy machine

B. Current listings

C. Office furniture

D. None of the above

16. What type of an asset for a real estate brokerage is a "deferred asset"?

A. Cash

B. Licensed real estate salespeople

C. Sales that are in escrow and are pending

D. Retirement plan

17. Which of the following are preliminary actions before a loan request meeting?

A. Call the lender on the telephone and set the appointment

B. Write a "proposal letter"

C. Dress appropriately

D. All of the above

18. What things should be brought on a loan request meeting?

A. Two writing pens

B. A notepad

C. Your proposal and business plans

D. All of the above

19. At the appointment, your presentation should go through the following steps

A. Ask the loan officer to sign a "Non-Disclosure Statement."

B. Ask the loan officer the "Preliminary Questions for a Loan Request."

C. Go over the business concept.

D. All of the above

20. Which of the following is a good source of alternative funds for a real estate brokerage?

A. Partners

B. Friends and family

C. Investment group

D. All of the above

15 Starting Up a Real Estate Business

What does it take to start up your real estate business? Many factors we have discussed in this book are required; this chapter is to summarize all of that information. The first question we should address is, "Do you have what it takes to be a real estate broker?

Characteristics of Real Estate Brokers

Real estate brokers must be able to recruit, retain, research, analyze, negotiate, plan, and market. If you are considering becoming a real estate broker, you need to ask yourself this question: "What am I good at?" An honest self-assessment is a good place to begin before thinking about any career. The answer to this question is simple. It is easier to lie back and do nothing, but to be successful, you have to get up and take action.

By just setting up a doable plan and implementing it, you will be way ahead of most people in the world. The difference between your financial success and simply retiring flat broke is planning and taking action. Do you have any of the following issues?

1. I am lazy and just don't want to do it.
2. I think it will cost too much.
3. I feel like our real estate business is too small to have a plan.
4. I never seem to get any breaks.
5. It's too hard to actually do it.

If any of those issues sound like you, you are the only one that can change your beliefs.

Change Factors

People go through certain stages when there is any type of change in their life. If you plan to open yourself a real estate company, you can expect a great deal of change. Because this change is fast approaching, it is important that you possess the management skills necessary to lead your business to be a success. These skills include the ability to lead. Leadership is the ability to get others to believe in you and believe in your vision, and then to have them take action and follow you. The skills include the marketing and sales abilities that are extremely important in the real estate industry. The most important skill is the ability to communicate your ideas in a logical and understandable manner.

The first thing you will want to focus on is your leadership ability. Real estate companies continue to make the mistake of focusing too much on business processes and not enough on good, strong examples of leadership. To be an effective leader in the real estate industry, it helps if you do the following:

SET AN EXAMPLE

As the top person in your business, others look to you for direction, not only in terms of business needs, but also in relation to behavior, ethics, and standards. If you want others in your business to be professional, you must set an example for them to follow. You must adhere to the company dress code. I have seen brokers walk into their real estate office in a pair of shorts and a T-shirt on a weekend and then wonder why their salespeople show up during the week in shorts and T-shirts. You need to be to the office early and leave late. You need to be constantly busy. At company parties, never drink alcohol, or if you do, drink *very* moderately. If you think this isn't fair, then don't become a broker. You have volunteered to be the leader; now you must lead.

ALWAYS PROMOTE AN "OPEN DOOR" POLICY

Be available to your real estate salespeople. Never become too busy to listen to them and share time with them. The great real estate brokers of today interact more with their salespeople than in the past, and the salespeople expect it. These brokers interact by walking around and relating to their salespeople and learning about the problems they are facing on a day-to-day basis. Don't let a week go by without contacting each salesperson. Even more often is ideal, but sometimes that is not possible. If you are not in contact with your salespeople, then your competition will be.

BE GENUINE

As the leader, you must be as real and honest as possible in your interactions with others. Let others get to know you. Being a leader doesn't mean hiding your emotions. By interacting with your staff and salespeople on a one-to-one basis, you will build rapport and trust.

Being genuine also means making the tough decisions and sticking with them. Your salespeople need to know you are going to be genuine when you say something. There is no worse leader than one who is wishy-washy. No one knows what to believe.

HAVE PASSION

To be a strong broker, you must have passion in everything you do. Your passion is infectious to all those around you. If you believe in you, let others see that. I have stated many times that I can teach a broker everything except passion. If you don't have it, you need to find it, or you will find yourself out of the brokerage business. The brokerage business is tiring and drains energy at a very high rate, so make sure you are passionate about what you do.

Once your real estate brokerage company begins operating, it is very important to communicate on a regular basis with all those involved. Let your staff, salespeople, and clients know what is happening. Spend a great deal of time promoting yourself and your company. When you have successes, you need to communicate them. If you are featured in a local newspaper, you need to communicate it. If your communication skills are weak, develop a system for letting everyone know what is happening. By keeping everyone informed, you reduce the chances of low productivity and low morale that often accompany the opening of a new real estate company.

Phases of Change

It is important to realize that although you can use techniques to smooth the transition process, you will never be able to completely jump into the real estate brokerage business without experiencing at least some challenges. To reduce your frustration with this process, it helps to know the six phases people go through whenever they are experiencing any type of change, be it personal or professional.

ANTICIPATION

Generally, brokers talk with other real estate salespeople and get their commitment to join the new real estate company. Those real estate salespeople are now anticipating the opening of the new office. They really don't know what to expect, so they wait, guessing what the future holds. Any time someone is not sure of the future, they become anxious and can create more tension for the new broker/owner. When people become anxious, they can also become irrational. As a result, bad things can happen for the new broker. Communication is the key here. Keep every person informed, and answer any of his or her concerns.

CONFRONTATION

At some point the real estate salespeople begin to confront reality. At this stage, they are beginning to realize that the new office is really going to happen. They get excited and enthused. You think this is good, but it can be detrimental if they stop selling real estate because they feel your office will be opening soon. If there are delays in the actual opening of your office, the salespeople could lose a great deal of money.

REALIZATION

Once the new office is open for business, the people will usually reach the stage where they realize that nothing is ever going to be as it once was. This can be great news if the previous office was a horrible place to work. It can also be a rude awakening if the expectations were too great for any office to live up to, and that realization can oftentimes plunge people into depression.

DEPRESSION

Depression can be a necessary step in this process. This is the stage where a person mourns the past. Not only has he or she realized the change intellectually, but now he or she is beginning to comprehend it emotionally as well. This is where you as the real estate broker need to be careful that your salespeople do not regret their decision to join your company and decide to go back to where they came from.

ACCEPTANCE

This is the point where the people begin to accept the changes emotionally. Although they may still have reservations, they are not fighting them at this stage. Usually, they are beginning to see some of the benefits, even if they are not completely convinced.

ENLIGHTENMENT

In this phase, the people completely accept the new office, how you work, and the direction the company is taking. In fact, many wonder how they ever managed at their other office or their other career.

It is important to note that people in your company will move through the different phases at different rates of speed. One person may require only a short time and another may take months. By using the skills outlined above, you increase your chances of managing the new office environment as effectively as possible.

Leader or Manager

I have used these terms interchangeably, but they are in reality very different. Are you a manager or a leader? By learning whether you are more of a leader or more of a manager, you will gain the insight and self-confidence that comes with knowing more about yourself. The result is greater impact and effectiveness when dealing with others and running your business.

THE DIFFERENCES BETWEEN MANAGERS AND LEADERS

First of all, let's take a look at the general differences between a manager and a leader.

MANAGERS   Managers emphasize rationality and control; they are problem solvers; they focus on goals, resources, organization structures, and/or people; they are persistent; they are tough-minded, hardworking, intelligent, analytical, and tolerant; and they have good will toward others. Managers are good at following the direction of a leader and are excellent in a real estate corporate environment. Managers need to be held accountable by someone of higher authority.

LEADERS   Leaders are perceived as brilliant, but sometimes lonely; they achieve control of themselves before they try to control others; they can visualize a purpose and generate value in work; they are imaginative, passionate, non-conforming; they are risk takers. Leaders do not want to be micro-managed. They are self-starters. They lead by example and tend to work long hours. Leaders are harder on themselves than anyone else ever could be.

Managers adopt impersonal, almost passive, attitudes toward goals; decide upon goals based on necessity instead of desire and are therefore deeply tied to their organization's culture; and tend to be reactive because they focus on current information. They accomplish the goals the company sets, but rarely exceed those goals. Leaders tend to be active because they envision and promote their ideas instead of reacting to current situations; shape ideas instead of responding to them; have a personal orientation toward goals; and provide a vision that alters the way people think about what is desirable, possible, and necessary. Once they achieve the goals they have set, they are quick to expand those goals to new levels. Accomplishing their goals is extremely important to true leaders.

DIFFERENCES IN CONCEPTIONS OF WORK

Now let's look at managers' and leaders' conceptions of work.

MANAGERS Managers view work as an enabling process; establish strategies and make decisions by combining people and ideas; continually coordinate and balance opposing views; are good at reaching compromises and mediating conflicts between opposing values and perspectives; act to limit choice; and tolerate practical, mundane work because of a strong survival instinct that makes them risk-averse. They will do what is expected of them but are not that interested in doing more. They want situations in the real estate office to run smoothly and are good at delegating.

LEADERS Leaders develop new approaches to long-standing problems and open issues to new options. First, they use their vision to excite people, and only then develop choices that give those images substance; they focus people on shared ideals and raise their expectations; they work from high-risk positions because of a strong dislike of mundane work. They are frustrated with others who will not work all the time. They believe that only they can do the job well, and because of that are poor at delegating.

RELATIONS WITH OTHERS

Managers and leaders have very different relations with others.

MANAGERS Managers prefer working with others; report that solitary activity makes them anxious; are collaborative; maintain a low level of emotional involvement in relationships; attempt to reconcile differences, seek compromises, and establish a balance of power; relate to people according to the role they play in a sequence of events or in a decision-making process; focus on how things get done; maintain controlled, rational, and equitable structures; and may be viewed by others as inscrutable, detached, and manipulative.

LEADERS Leaders maintain inner perceptiveness that they can use in their relationships with others; relate to people in an intuitive, empathetic way; focus on what events and decisions mean to participants; attract strong feelings of identity and difference or of love and hate; and create systems where human relations may be turbulent, intense, and at times even disorganized.

DIFFERENCES IN SELF-IMAGE

The self-image of managers and leaders differ; for both, self-image is strongly influenced by the past.

MANAGERS Managers report that their adjustments to life have been straightforward and that their lives have been more or less peaceful; have a sense of self as a guide to conduct and attitude which is derived from a feeling of being at home and in harmony with their environment; see themselves as conservators and regulators of an existing order of affairs with which they personally identify and from which they gain rewards; report that their role harmonizes with their ideals of responsibility and duty; perpetuate and strengthen existing institutions; and display a life-development process which focuses on socialization. This socialization process prepares them to guide the real estate office and to maintain the existing balance of social relations.

LEADERS Leaders reportedly have not had an easy time of it. Their lives are marked by a continual struggle to find some sense of order; they do not take things for granted and are not satisfied with the status quo. They report that their "sense of self" is derived from a feeling of profound separateness. They may work in organizations, but they never belong to them. They report that their sense of self is independent of work roles, memberships, or other social indicators of social identity. They seek opportunities for change (i.e., technological, political, or ideological); support change; find their purpose is to profoundly alter human, economic, and political relationships; and display a life-development process that focuses on personal mastery and impels them to struggle for psychological and social change.

Development of Leadership

As you can see, managers and leaders are very different. It is important to remember that there are definite strengths and weaknesses in both types of individuals. Managers are very good at maintaining the status quo and adding stability and order to our culture. However, they may not be as good at instigating change and envisioning the future. Leaders, on the other hand, are very good at stirring people's emotions, raising their expectations, and taking them in new directions (both good and bad). However, like artists and other gifted people, leaders often have a tendency toward self-absorption and preoccupation.

If you are planning on owning your own real estate business, you must develop management skills, whether they come naturally or not. However, what do you do if you believe you are, in fact, a leader—a diamond in the rough? What can you do to develop as a leader? Throughout history, it has been shown again and again that leaders have needed strong one-to-one relationships with teachers, whose strengths lie in cultivating talent, in order to reach their full potential. If you think you are a leader at heart, find a teacher whom you admire—someone with whom you can connect and who can help you develop your natural talents and interests.

Starting Operations as a Real Estate Company

In real estate, as in other businesses, you must follow the rules and regulations of the land as set forth by the government. You must treat others with respect, and you must have a product or service that the public is willing to pay for. Specifically, before you begin operations as a real estate company, you must do the following:

A. *Obtain business name approval.* A start-up real estate company must have a business name approved by their state real estate commission. Most companies use a DBA (Doing Business As) and their own name. DBAs are filed at the county courthouse. Be sure to check your local regulations on how to handle this. Also be sure to check with your state real estate commission before filing the name of the company because some will not accept a proposed company name that may mislead the public into thinking they are not dealing with a real estate brokerage company.

B. *File legal paperwork.* The real estate company must file all the paperwork required by their state real estate commission. Don't take this lightly, because some of the filings can take a great of time.

C. *Create an evidence of trust account.* The principal broker applicant must submit documentation from a financial institution that is fewer than thirty days old verifying the applicant's trust account. The trust account is to be used in case of misconduct by the broker.

A real estate commission could require the broker to be bonded. Other real estate commissions set up recovery funds to compensate aggrieved persons if the real estate broker fails to do so.

D. *Pay appropriate fees for company registration.* I used to think it was quite odd for real estate brokers to fund the real estate commission to regulate us. But on further review, it would be worse not to have them do so. Their purpose is to protect the public against us. However, you do not have to worry about being in trouble with them if you handle your business properly.

After completing all of the above items, the entity must now act in accordance with the structure that was designed. Any major changes in owners or structure must be reported to the proper authorities before the changes occur.

Conclusion

Now you have a glimpse of what it takes to become a broker in a real estate office. With the complexities mastered and a thorough understanding of the processes necessary, you can now go out and open or expand your own operations.

Remember, no one book or course can tell you all of what it takes to succeed in the brokerage business, so keep yourself educated and keep this book handy for reference at all times.

Good business and great wealth to each of you!

Chapter Fifteen Review Questions

1. A real estate broker must be able to
   A. lie.
   B. cheat.
   C. recruit.
   D. steal.

2. Which of the following attitudes could be disastrous to a real estate brokerage?
   A. I am lazy and just don't want to do it.
   B. I think it will cost too much.
   C. I feel like our real estate business is too small to have a plan.
   D. All of the above statements can be disastrous.

3. Which of the following is not an important leadership skill?
   A. The ability to get others to believe in you
   B. The ability to get others to believe in your vision
   C. The ability to get others to ignore their personal ethics
   D. The ability to get others to take action and follow you

4. Effective leaders
   A. always promote an "open door" policy.
   B. are genuine.
   C. have passion.
   D. all of the above are important for effective leaders.

5. Which of the following is not a phase of change?
   A. Anticipation
   B. Realization
   C. Casting
   D. Acceptance

6. Which of the following are typically the risk takers?
   A. Managers
   B. Leaders

7. Which of the following typically need to be held accountable?
   A. Managers
   B. Leaders

8. Which of the following typically have a passion for setting and accomplishing goals?
   A. Managers
   B. Leaders

9. Which of the following tend to be the best at delegating?
   A. Managers
   B. Leaders

REFERRAL SALESPERSON CONTACT SCRIPTS

This script should be used get a referral group started.

BROKER: "Mr. Jones?

REFERRAL SALESPERSON: "Yes"

BROKER: "My name is Dan Hamilton, broker of Acme Realty. Did you receive the information that I sent to you on our exciting new program on how you can earn big money in real estate without ever selling or listing a home?"

REFERRAL SALESPERSON: "Yes"

BROKER: "Well, we've designed this dynamic, new program so that people like you, those whose licenses are on an inactive status, can potentially earn thousands of dollars more per year and work your own hours, from the convenience of your own home. Mr. Jones, let me ask you, if you could potentially earn $60, $70, $80 an hour or more, working part-time in real estate, and never have to list or sell, would you be interested in meeting with me at some time in the future to hear about our new program?"

Objection Handling Scripts

SALESPERSON: "Thanks for calling, but I'm happy where I am."

BROKER: "Understood and I am glad to hear that. Can I offer you the opportunity to attend an upcoming training event that could help you increase your production with no pressure or obligation to you at all?"

SALESPERSON: "I'm too busy to meet with you."

BROKER: "And that is exactly why you should meet with me. We can discuss not only how our company can help you make more money but how we can help you have more time to enjoy your success."

SALESPERSON: "Let me think about it, and I'll call you later."

BROKER: "I hope you do, because we can help your career. Hey, while I have you on the phone, can I offer you the opportunity to attend an upcoming training event that could help you increase your production?"

SALESPERSON: "I'm just not ready to talk about changing at this time."

BROKER: "I understand. A quick question, would an increase in your income with more flexible time for you be of any interest to you?"

SALESPERSON: "Why should I leave? I'm doing well here!"

BROKER: "That is exactly why you should leave. Let me explain. You are doing well because of you and your efforts. What I would like to show you is how our company can actually help you with your efforts. Our programs far exceed any in the industry. By simply meeting me and talking with me, you will see how you can take advantage of those services I am offering."

SALESPERSON: "Tell me what you have to offer over the phone."

BROKER: "If I could do that, I would suggest that you stay where you are. I am offering you countless services that will help you make more money and do it with less efforts to you."

SALESPERSON: "What will you do for me if I join you?"

BROKER: "Great question. I am glad you asked that. I would like to explain all the things we can do for you to increase your income with less efforts to you. Now we can meet later today, or would tomorrow be better?"

SALESPERSON: "Can I negotiate commissions?"

BROKER: "When we sit down and meet we will discuss all the opportunities that you have with our company to run your business. We can meet later today, or would tomorrow be better?"

SALESPERSON: "You're a training company."

BROKER: "Yes, we are, and thank you for recognizing that. Top quality training is one of the many benefits we offer to our people. I would like to discuss the many other services we also offer our salespeople."

SALESPERSON: "I don't want to pay franchise fees."

BROKER: "I wouldn't want it any other way. Do you know why? Franchise fees are used to give you services independent real estate companies cannot provide. National advertising is not cheap and name recognition is extremely valuable. Let me discuss with you the ways a small fee can return large profits."

SALESPERSON: "We've got more market share."

BROKER: "I truly am concerned about *you*, not your company. You are important, and within our company, we want our people to be successful and will sacrifice to ensure their success."

SALESPERSON: "I have a private office here."

BROKER: "How much money does having a private office actually make you per year? I ask because I can show you how our company can *actually* put more money in your pocket, and you can then spend it however you want; doesn't that make sense?"

RECRUITED AGENT CHECKLIST

NAME: _____

☐ Business cards ordered

☐ Keys to the office given

☐ Announcement to the Sphere of Influence

☐ Advertising for new or transferred listings coordinated

☐ Farm area chosen

☐ Name badge, desk plate, and door plate ordered

☐ Passcodes set up for copier, long distance, and security entry codes

☐ Name riders and car signs ordered

☐ Tour though the office with introductions

☐ Introduction to working the office equipment

☐ Location of forms and marketing materials

☐ Introduction to the staff and a description of their functions

☐ Gift for joining

☐ Letter from Broker or Manager sent to home address

☐ Introduced at office meeting

☐ ASSOCIATION OF REALTORS® MLS/notified

☐ Independent Contractor Agreement signed

☐ Personal photo taken

☐ Press release written and sent

☐ Real estate commission change/license sent

☐ Web site and e-mail address transferred or set up

☐ Telephone system orientation and direct line set up.

☐ Manager's coaching scheduled

CLOSING TECHNIQUES

BROKER: "If there were a way for you to have a better compensation plan, how would that affect your thoughts about a transition?"

BROKER: "If the bottom line dollars earned with your current company are actually less than what you could earn with our firm, would you think about the idea of a transfer?"

BROKER: "If your actual commission split with us worked out to be greater than what you currently have, with all of those costs and expenses, would it at least make sense to examine our program in detail?"

BROKER: "Did you sign a contract? For how long? What kinds of obligations and penalties does it contain if you choose to leave? Do you feel that is fair?"

COSTS ASSOCIATED WITH ASSOCIATING WITH A REAL ESTATE COMPANY

COMPANY:_____	COMPANY PAYS?	AGENT PAYS?
OFFICE COSTS:		
Telephone/Long Distance		
Business Cards (1,000)		
Desk Fees		
Copier Fees		
PROMOTIONAL ITEMS:		
Newspaper Advertising		
Internet Advertising/Web Page		
Property Brochures		
Marketing Campaign		
Magazine Advertising		
Just Listed/Sold Postcards		
Post/Stake Yard Signs		
Combo/Electronic Key Boxes		
Name Riders		
Direct Mail Printing/Postage		
MLS SERVICES:		
New Listing Insertion Fee		
Transfer Fee		
TRAINING:		
Sales/Legal Training		
Tuition Reimbursement Program		
TELEPHONE SERVICES:		
Long Distance Charges		
Answering Service		
Voice Mail Services		
High Speed Internet Access		
Facsimiles		
Total		

CHARACTERISTIC PROFILE

CHARACTERISTIC PROFILE				
Characteristic	Measured	Value	Scale	Total
1.				
2.				
3.				
4.				
5.				
6.				
7.				
8.				
9.				
10.				
TOTAL		100		
			Needs to be	700+

RECRUITING INTERVIEW QUESTIONS

1. Whom else will your decision affect?
2. Do you need a private office?
3. Do you have any special needs that are a concern?
4. How soon would you consider joining our company?
5. Must you settle any matters before making the decision?
6. Do you currently have any listings? Pendings? If so, when will they close?
7. Are you familiar with the procedures for changing real estate companies?
8. Have you interviewed any other offices that you liked?
9. Did you make any written agreements?
10. Are there any other real estate agents that may want to change?
11. Why are you thinking of changing?
12. What do you like best about your present company?
13. What do you like least about your present company?
14. Do you have any special interests or hobbies?
15. What do you (think you will) like most about being in real estate?
16. Do you (think you will) prefer listings or buyers? Why is that?
17. Where do you see yourself in five years? Ten?
18. How do you feel about the market?
19. What is your most successful marketing idea? or How do you plan on marketing yourself?
20. What's most important to you in a real estate company?
21. May I ask why you joined "Competitor Realty"?
22. Have the reasons why you chose the company then and the reasons why you are with them today changed at all?
23. What do you think of the company's overall office policies?
24. Would you like to see any of those polices changed or improved?
25. What are your primary and secondary motivations behind a change?

REAL ESTATE BROKERAGE VALUE PACKAGE

- Table funding
- Production awards
- Administrative help
- Marketing assistance
- Management expertise
- Team atmosphere
- Unparalleled training
- Top block service
- Career planning
- Ancillary business
- Accounting functions

- National company
- Professional ad writing
- Great location
- Advantageous compensation
- Family culture
- Private office
- Non-competitive managers
- Relocation business
- Social events
- Management advancement
- Community service

TRADE SHOW/CAREER DAY CHECKLIST

- ☐ Parking Pass and Directions
- ☐ Check In
- ☐ Payment
- ☐ Hotel Accommodations
- ☐ Maps of Area
- ☐ Printed Materials
- ☐ Laptop Computer
- ☐ Computer Power Cord
- ☐ Remote Mouse
- ☐ Extension Cords
- ☐ Data Projector
- ☐ Table Cloth with Company Logo
- ☐ Backdrop
- ☐ Refreshments
- ☐ Registration Forms
- ☐ Handouts
- ☐ Promotional Gifts
- ☐ Pens/Writing Pads
- ☐ Reserve Cash or Credit Cards
- ☐ Mobile Telephone

QUESTIONS TO BE ASKED BEFORE YOU
ACCEPT A SPEAKING ENGAGEMENT

1. What exactly is the topic to be covered?
2. How many people will be present?
3. How is the room arranged?
4. What audio-visual equipment will be on hand?
5. What is the speaking fee? Reimbursement for costs?
6. What time and for how long are you to present?
7. Are you the keynote speaker or a breakout speaker?
8. What type of audience will be there?
9. What does the audience expect?
10. When can you get to the facility?
11. Who is to pay for the printing of the materials?

CORPORATE CALLING LOG

	Date	Time	Number
Calls Made			
Proposals Sent			
Presentations Made			

RELOCATION SERVICES OFFERED

Here is a list of some of the services you could offer as a relocation specialist:

- Act as a recruiting partner for the company and promote the new location with the spouse while the company promotes the job opening with the employee.
- Provide a Newcomer's Packet with vital information on schools, housing, taxes, houses of worship, childcare, and much more.
- Offer individual and family relocation counseling.
- Offer assistance with mortgage pre-qualification through a preferred mortgage company.
- If the relocation person needs to rent before buying, provide rental assistance.
- Help with a job search for the spouse.
- Provide national and international assistance for all transferees.
- Provide basic real estate services, like being a professional and competent real estate person. You should provide assistance with selling and buying, plus the ability to manage and coordinate a number of related details, while always keeping open all communication channels.
- You should thoroughly know relocation management company operations.
- Be able to offer agency representation to their transferees.
- Make available discounts for their transferees on loans, temporary living, car rental, and hotels.
- You should be easy to communicate with—be accessible by phone, fax, and e-mail.
- Your company should have the financial ability to pay vendors up front on corporate listings.
- You should possess real estate expertise in the geographic area.
- There should be minimum qualifications for agents, such as the stipulation that they be full-time with at least three to five years' experience. They should have previous relocation experience, be available at reasonable times, be successful at assessing buyer's needs, as well as be detail-oriented and professional in appearance and conduct.

- Offer a home purchase program if the house doesn't sell in a given time frame.

- Help the transferee with the movement of household goods.

- Offer temporary living for those that have found a home but cannot move at this time.

- Provide home finding trips—destination assistance.

- You should present advice on tax implications of buying or selling real property.

QUESTIONS FOR SELECTING AN OFFICE

1. Do you have the funds to operate a real estate office? Do you have the funds to buy the infrastructure you need to start up a real estate enterprise? Do you have reserve funds necessary to continue operations for at least six months?

2. Do you have the expertise to manage a real estate office? Be honest with this one.

3. Do you want to operate a single office, or do you want to develop into a multi-office enterprise?

4. What type of real estate do you want to concentrate on? Residential? Commercial? High-end?

5. In which geographic areas do you want to specialize?

6. What do you predict as your office market share? Profitability?

7. What is the maximum number of salespeople you want in your office?

8. What are your office policies? Will you be strict or flexible?

9. Do you believe in a family atmosphere or a corporate structure? What type of reputation do you want to project?

10. What are your growth strategies for the business? Expansion? Franchise affiliation? Merger?

11. What type of training do you plan to provide?

12. Are you concerned about name recognition in the market? What will you do to address this issue?

13. Will your company offer ancillary services? Will you charge for these services?

14. Do you plan on being technology proficient, or do you plan to do things the old-fashioned way? How much are you willing to pay for technology?

15. Should you buy an existing real estate company or should you form your own?

16. Should you buy or lease a location?

17. What business equipment should you purchase?

EXPECTATIONS OF NEW SALES ASSOCIATES

1. KNOW YOUR OFFICE INVENTORY
   A. See all office listings.
   B. Plot active listings on map in prime market areas of office.
   C. Route homes by area, then make appointments and see no more than five homes at a time.

2. FARMING
   A. Choose a farm area.
   B. Compile all names, addresses, and phone numbers.
   C. Knock on all doors in the farm area.

3. CALL 100 PROPERTIES EACH WEEK
   A. Call all expireds every day.
   B. Call no more than ten for sale by owners per week.
   C. Call 25 houses on each side of office solds, new listings, and/or upcoming open houses.

4. HOLD TWO OPEN HOUSES EACH WEEK.

5. ATTEND OFFICE SALES MEETINGS AND TOUR.

6. ATTEND ALL TRAINING SESSIONS.

7. GOALS
   A. Put in writing production goals and discuss with broker.
   B. Put in writing those programs that are going to be implemented in the next thirty days.
   C. Make a weekly planner that details how the action steps will be accomplished.

EXPECTATIONS OF EXPERIENCED FULL-TIME SALES ASSOCIATES

Personal Production

1. Determine annual production goals and put them in writing.

2. Develop a personal marketing plan in alliance with personal goals. Review and adjust quarterly with manager's assistance.

3. Maintain a minimum activity level of five "Clear Cut" listing appointments per week.

4. Commit a minimum of $5\frac{1}{2}$ days to the real estate business per week.

5. Develop a follow-up system for contacting prospects and clients.

6. Set up a business farm area and consistently work it with mailings, phone calls, and personal contacts.

7. Invest in your business through personal or promotional advertising, mail-outs, giveaways, and so on.

8. Maintain a record of your sales and listing activity to determine your production levels and possible areas of improvement.

9. Meet with a manager each quarter to review activity and plan direction.

Office Participation

1. Conduct floor-time responsibilities professionally.

2. Tour all new office listings weekly.

3. Attend office meetings and company meetings regularly and on time.

4. Process all sales and listings accurately and immediately.

5. Continue calling:
   A. FSBOs
   B. Expired listings
   C. Finish with cold calls

6. Continue to upgrade skills and professionalism.

7. Present a professional image in appearance, attitude, and behavior.

POSSIBLE PEOPLE WHO MIGHT WANT TO BE IN REAL ESTATE

PERSONAL CONTACTS	CHRISTMAS CARD LIST
COLLEGE STUDENTS	PREVIOUS EMPLOYEES
AT HOME SPOUSE	INTEREST GROUPS
FRATERNITY MEMBERS	SPOUSE'S FAMILY
INVESTORS	INSURANCE SALESPEOPLE
SPORTING GOODS SALESPEOPLE	LUNCH PARTNERS
BEST FRIEND AND FAMILY	WEDDING PARTICIPANTS
SCHOOL TEACHERS	BOWLING TEAM MEMBERS
TRAVEL AGENTS	COMPUTER PROGRAMMERS
CHILDREN'S MUSIC TEACHERS	BANK PERSONNEL
NURSES	ATTORNEYS
GROCERY MANAGERS	VETERINARIANS
CAR SALESPEOPLE	APPLIANCE SALESPEOPLE
INTERIOR DECORATORS	HOME REPAIR PEOPLE
MILITARY	COACHES
APPAREL SALESPEOPLE	COSMETICIANS
AUTO REPAIR PEOPLE	CHURCH MEMBERS
NEIGHBORS	CIVIC ACTIVITIES
SPORTS OR HOBBIES	BRIDGE PARTNERS
FRIENDS	PTA MEMBERS
SCOUT LEADERS	CIVIC CLUB MEMBERSHIP
PHARMACISTS	SMALL BUSINESS OWNERS
HAIR STYLISTS	SPOUSE'S HAIR STYLIST
RESTAURANT MANAGERS	FURNITURE SALESPEOPLE
STORE OWNERS	PLUMBERS
DOCTORS	DENTISTS

IMPORTANT OFFICE INFORMATION

1. Identify All Major Roads:
2. List Any Special Geographical Features:
3. Name and Describe All Area Neighborhoods:
4. Demographics (by neighborhood):
   A. Age Levels:
   B. Income Levels:
   C. Lifestyles:
5. Location of:
   A. Board of Realtors:
   B. Local Government Offices:
   C. City Services:
6. Transportation:
7. Schools:
   A. Elementary Schools:
   B. Middle Schools (or Junior Highs):
   C. Secondary Schools:
   D. Colleges:
   E. Private Schools:
8. Commercial:
   A. Major Shopping Centers:
   B. Restaurants:
   C. Unique Specialty Shops:
9. Recreational Facilities:
   A. Golf Courses
   B. Parks
   C. Entertainment Centers

(YOUR OFFICE) TOUR SHEET

(To be given to each real estate salesperson who is on office tour)

Address: _____

What I noticed most about the property is_____

_____

The kind of person who should buy this property is_____

_____

I believe the price of the home should be_____

_____

Address: _____

What I noticed most about the property is _____

_____

The kind of person who should buy this property is _____

_____

I believe the price of the home should be _____

_____

ACTIVITIES FOR NEW REAL ESTATE SALESPEOPLE

1. Review office policies and procedures.

2. Schedule and attend any of your Board and MLS orientations.

3. Schedule and attend computer training.

4. Read your office's computer manual.

5. Familiarize yourself with the MLS computer program.

6. Attend MLS tours for your area.

7. Attend your office tour.

8. Sit in during "opportunity time" at your office's property desk. Learn the procedure.

9. Accompany one of your office's associates on an open house.

10. Research the supply room in your office—read the brochures and forms.

11. Complete envelopes to mail with notes for the announcement of your association with your new company.

12. Visit with a Mortgage Loan Officer.

13. Visit with an Escrow Officer from a neighborhood Title Company.

14. Visit your neighborhood Mortgage Company.

15. Check out tapes and CDs from your local Board office or from various Title Companies.

16. Preview all office listings in your market area.

17. Study a prospect profile form.

18. Complete Sample Contracts.

19. Compile a list of your Center of Influence.

20. Read any books about understanding people, their motivation, and so forth.

COMMITMENT EXERCISES

Full-Time Agents

"EDUCATION WITHOUT APPLICATION IS WORSE THAN WORTHLESS"—To help you practice the skills you have learned today, complete the following assignments during the next week and have your broker check each exercise as you complete it. When you have completed all of the exercises, have your broker sign at the bottom of the page.

1. Get a HUD key.

2. Three days this week make cold calls. Put each <u>lead</u> on a 4" x 6" card. Fill in the following chart as you call. You must call until you get a Clear-Cut listing appointment to count as a day.

	DAY 1	DAY 2	DAY 3
# OF CALLS			
TIME			

3. Have two outgoing referrals.

4. Schedule at least three listing appointments (Clear-Cut) by Prospecting.

5. Complete the independent contractor agreement.

6. Check out three books or cassette tapes on sales or real estate.

7. Role-play at least five times with another your Prospecting call.

8. Have your trainer monitor your Prospecting calls and give you feedback for fifteen minutes.

9. Put ten people on your Sphere of Influence. Put them on 4" x 6" cards. Bring the cards to class.

10. Answer these three questions:
- What do I want? Be specific, in writing, no limitations; dream.
- What will it take to get there?
- Am I willing to pay the price?

COMMITMENT EXERCISES

Full-Time Agents

"EDUCATION WITHOUT APPLICATION IS WORSE THAN WORTHLESS"—To help you practice the skills you have learned today, complete the following assignments during the next week and have your broker check each exercise as you complete it. When you have completed all of the exercises, have your broker sign at the bottom of the page.

1. Begin a business diary

2. Three days this week make cold calls. Put each <u>lead</u> on a 4" x 6" card. Fill in the following chart as you call. You must call until you get a Clear-Cut listing appointment to count as a day.

	DAY 1	DAY 2	DAY 3
# OF CALLS			
TIME			

3. Have two outgoing referrals.

4. Schedule at least three listing appointments (Clear-Cut) by Prospecting.

5. Complete a business budget

6. Check out three books or cassette tapes on sales or real estate.

7. Role-play at least five times with another your Prospecting call.

8. Have your trainer monitor your Prospecting calls and give you feedback for fifteen minutes.

9. Put ten people on your Sphere of Influence. Put them on 4" x 6" cards. Bring the cards to class.

COMMITMENT EXERCISES

Full-Time Agents

"EDUCATION WITHOUT APPLICATION IS WORSE THAN
WORTHLESS"—To help you practice the skills you have learned today,
complete the following assignments during the next week and have your
broker check each exercise as you complete it. When you have completed
all of the exercises, have your broker sign at the bottom of the page.

1. Find an investment prospect

2. Three days this week make cold calls. Put each <u>lead</u> on a 4" x 6" card.
   Fill in the following chart as you call. You must call until you get a
   Clear-Cut listing appointment to count as a day.

	DAY 1	DAY 2	DAY 3
# OF CALLS			
TIME			

3. Have two outgoing referrals.

4. Schedule at least three listing appointments (Clear-Cut) by Prospecting.

5. Develop a marketing manual.

6. Check out three books or cassette tapes on sales or real estate.

7. Role-play at least five times with another your Prospecting call.

8. Have your trainer monitor your Prospecting calls and give you feedback
   for fifteen minutes.

9. Put ten people on your Sphere of Influence. Put them on 4" x 6" cards.
   Bring the cards to class.

MY GOAL PLAN

Name: _____ Date: _____

1. Short-Term Goal (less than one year)

   _____

2. Mid-Term Goal (one year to five years)

   _____

3. Long-term Goal (longer than one year)

   _____

Steps to Reaching Short-term Goal	Timeline
1.	1.
2.	2.
3.	3.
4.	4.
5.	5.
6.	6.

Steps to Reaching Mid-term Goal	Timeline
1.	1.
2.	2.
3.	3.
4.	4.
5.	5.
6.	6.

Steps to Reaching Long-term Goal	Timeline
1.	1.
2.	2.
3.	3.
4.	4.
5.	5.
6.	6.

GOALS

Financial—_____

_____

Career—_____

_____

Family—_____

_____

Spiritual—_____

_____

Physical—_____

_____

Self-Improvement—_____

_____

PRACTICES OF CONDUCT

1. Do not divulge prices or terms of any previous or present offer.

2. Do not leave the office alone with someone if you are not sure about him or her. USE YOUR INTUITION.

3. Never present a contract without a signed agreement. Use a one-time listing form if necessary.

4. Never release a check to anyone without having him or her sign for it.

5. Never fail to give copies to buyers and sellers. Always give copies of anything someone signs. Remember to sign all listings, offers, and cancellations.

6. If you are the listing salesperson, request two keys; if not available, make two copies of keys. Make sure the keys fit. Use key boxes.

7. Never give out a key to an occupied house unless it is to another real estate salesperson. Request keys are signed out in logbook.

8. When showing a property, never leave doors unlocked unless you found them that way. Don't lock doors between house and garage if the owners use a garage-door opener. Leave the property in the same manner as it was when you arrived.

9. Do not commingle earnest money. Be careful of cash for which you are responsible. Give a receipt for all cash received.

10. Do not advertise real estate for sale, or purchase or sell property without signing "real estate salesperson" or "broker" behind your name or phone number. Remember: it's impossible to buy or sell property, even your own, without the company being liable.

11. Never talk real estate commissions with any real estate company or salesperson.

12. Never give out telephone numbers or e-mails of sellers.

13. Never talk to a seller about contracts, terms, his or her listing, and so forth, unless you are his or her listing salesperson.

14. Never make a verbal offer or present an offer by telephone.

15. You will need insurance to carry people. Be careful: you are responsible for accidents!!!

OFFICE POLICIES AND PROCEDURES

Responsibilities

1. Listing salesperson handles all seller activity.
    a. Estimate of seller charges
    b. Listing agreement
       All listing agreements and associated material must be turned in within 24 hours after the seller signs the listing agreement.
    c. The listing salesperson is responsible for establishing the file and verifying lot size, zoning, square footage, schools, and all other pertinent data.
    d. A Competitive Market Analysis should be included in the listing folder.
    e. The listing salesperson shall not enter any information that has not been verified with the seller. Any errors on the listing data sheet could result in the listing salesperson losing his/her listing commission. The listing salesperson must never underestimate the importance of a properly filled out listing-data sheet.
    f. Call the owner at least every week, starting the first week. Use MLS statistics as a reason to call and point out activity, competition, price reduction, and so forth; keep the owners informed of market activity.

    g. Furnish seller with advertising copy and comments each time property is advertised.

    h. Knock on doors in areas for the purpose of finding a buyer and/or to find other listing leads.

2. Buyer's salesperson handles all buyer activity.

3. Appraisers are handled by either the listing salesperson or the buyer's salesperson.

4. Repairs handled by both.

5. Closing handled by both.

6. Folder information sheet to be kept current and accurate by both.

7. Contract cancellations handled by buyer's salesperson.

8. Listing salesperson handles ads and listing renewals.

9. Broker/sales manager assists in listings upon request.

10. Buyer's salesperson closes out file.

11. Listing salesperson closes out MLS.

Floor Duty

Keep the floor covered for calls and drop-ins from 9 a.m. to 5 p.m. Monday through Saturday and 1 p.m. to 5 p.m. Sunday.

1. All agents shown on floor duty schedule are expected to work during the floor duty hours.

2. It is requested that the person on duty make no appointments during floor duty hours. If a listing or prospect call is received during the floor duty, then these calls should be serviced immediately. It shall be the responsibility of the "duty person" to notify the manager or another salesperson.

3. Floor duty gives you an excellent opportunity to secure prospects. Floor time can be profitable, even when there is little floor activity. It is a good time to bring listings up-to-date, to make telephone solicitation, or to plan work for the following day. It is recommended that on floor duty, salespeople:

    (a) Make cold canvass telephone calls

    (b) Contact expired listings

    (c) Contact "For Sale By Owners"

(d) Call sellers back for updates

(e) Call back current contacts

4. Advise office manager when sickness prevents fulfilling floor duty requirements.

5. COMPANY POLICY: NO SHOWING APPOINTMENTS AFTER DARK!!!!!

6. VACATIONS—Since the sales staff consists of independent contractors who receive no vacation pay, salespeople may regulate their own vacations; however, it is requested that the sales staff use judgment to assure that vacations do not overlap, leaving the office shorthanded. Salespeople must arrange for another salesperson to look after their business during vacations, illness, or extended absences.

7. USUAL OBSERVED HOLIDAYS: Mother's Day, Father's Day, Easter, Independence Day, Thanksgiving, and Christmas. Office is always open, but the staff will be off on these days.

8. To assure adequate parking space for our customers and clients, all salespeople and employees should park their cars the side of the building. Leave the spaces in front available.

9. The kitchen/dining area has been provided for the enjoyment and convenience of all salespeople who, on occasion, may want to remain in the office for a meal or snack. Keep the area clean.

Commissions

1. Commission will be negotiable unless otherwise approved by the broker or sales manager.

2. Reducing the commission from time to time may be necessary. In the event a salesperson finds it necessary to reduce a prior agreed upon commission *without management approval,* that reduction will be treated as offering a bonus and will be deducted entirely from the salesperson's share of commission.

GUIDELINES FOR REAL ESTATE PROFESSIONALS
TO HELP PREVENT CLAIMS

Real estate professionals do business in an intensely competitive world. In that world we must watch our backs because there are a *few* who would like to take our money. I don't believe all people are nasty, but the few can ruin your day or your career.

You have to be aggressive if you're a real estate salesperson or broker. But it's a good idea to try to move carefully, too. And while you can't really prevent a claim—since claims hinge on the client's perception of what you did or didn't do—there are still some concrete steps you can take to stop a claim from turning into a full-scale lawsuit or a major loss.

Written record keeping is one important measure. Accurate written records make up the only hard evidence you have to prove you acted professionally in a specific situation. Keep conversation notes in your computer file or write them right on the file folder.

DO HOMEWORK: First and foremost, say the experts, is to do your homework.

When you present a property, be sure you know and can point out the accurate properly lines or, better yet, have a survey. Make a check of your own listings and note the obvious defects. Explain these defects to the sellers, telling them that we must disclose these to the buyer. If the seller refuses to fully disclose, you may have to walk away from the listing. The seller should also complete a "Seller's Disclosure Form" that lists most things in a house and then note whether everything is working or not. It may sound like an unrealistic way to behave, but the alternative could be far worse. Case files disclosed to the courts have consistently held that brokers and salespeople have the obligation to know and communicate all pertinent facts as part of their professional responsibility. We are not inspectors, but we do have a standard of professionalism.

DELIVER SERVICE: The second guideline has to do with delivering on your promise of service. In other words, don't encourage your buyer to purchase on a whim, and don't push beyond the limits of reasonable sales-manship. It's not just good business, so make sure you have a satisfied buyer and a sale that will stick—it could help you ward off "buyer's remorse" claims.

Finally, be careful in what you say. When you don't know the answer to a question, say so. Find out the information as soon as possible, but don't guess. One apparently harmless remark during a busy afternoon of home tours could wind up as the basis of a misrepresentation claim letter.

SIXTY-DAY FITNESS REPORT

Name: _____

Thanks for selecting our company to assist you in developing for yourself a real estate sales career worth having. The letter of expectation that you have studied spells out what you can expect from our team and what is expected of you so that you can become a successful and important member of our professional real estate sales team.

The first sixty days of one's real estate career, as in most careers, are critical. This is normally the time frame when good work habits and professional ethics are established for the rest of one's career. We orchestrate the first sixty days and follow up almost daily as the agent progresses through the remaining thirty days.

This Sixty-Day Fitness Report is a detailed checklist of tasks that you should accomplish and goals that you should attain during this critical time in your career. It is **your** responsibility to make sure that each of these things is accomplished during the prescribed time. Let's develop a successful and profitable business for your and a career worth having. Use this actual checklist to check off accomplished tasks and to show to your manager and mentor for periodic review.

During the first sixty days, new salespeople should be physically prospecting or be at the office accomplishing the Sixty-Day Fitness Report tasks. New salespeople will work closely with their managers or mentors (if one is assigned), and other staff members to ensure that the first sixty days are PRODUCTIVE, COMPREHENSIVE, POWERFUL, and ENABLING.

Day 1

Manager *(normally accomplished in the morning)* [Administrative Assistants will review and make sure all paperwork is completed.]

☐ Complete Agent Profile Form

☐ Have Salesperson complete and sign Independent Contract Agreement

☐ Have Salesperson read Statement of Understanding

☐ Read and discuss Expectation Letter.

☐ Assign desk/workstation.

☐ Issue building key.

☐ Read and discuss "Also Insured" rider on auto insurance policy.

☐ Hand out Sales Meeting schedule.

☐ Hand out Floor Duty Policy.

☐ Get and complete MLS form.

☐ Provide training schedule and location.

(Normally accomplished in the afternoon)

☐ Have Salesperson complete Realtor Association Application.

☐ Have Salesperson complete Key Card Lease Agreement.

☐ Have Salesperson take Application and Key Card Lease Agreement to Association with a check and/or credit card and join board.

☐ Schedule Association Orientation and MLS Training.

☐ Get supplies for desk, map book, business calculator, and day planner, and so on.

☐ Set up desk/work station.

Management/Staff Review_____ Date:_____

Day 2

Staff Support

☐ Review Salesperson paperwork to ensure correct with Adminitrative Assistant.

☐ Explain Salesperson photo policy and where to order photos.

☐ Explain advertising policy.

☐ Explain office postage system.

☐ Assign mailbox.

☐ Order car signs.

☐ Order business cards and name tags.

☐ Explain printing needs/graphics system.

☐ Introduce to all support staff

☐ Issue telephone roster sheet.

☐ Explain forms wall.

☐ Demonstrate copier equipment use.

☐ Demonstrate fax machine use.

☐ Assign long distance code.

☐ Enter extension into phone system.

☐ Assist Salesperson in establishing voice mail prompts.

☐ Explain full capabilities of telephone system.

Manager

☐ Explain Property Management function.

☐ Explain web sites.

☐ Explain E&O Insurance and risk management.

☐ Explain Virtual Tours.

Salesperson

☐ Get desk supplies.

☐ Set up desk.

☐ Set up voice prompts on desk phone.

☐ Set up call forwarding.

Management/Staff Review _____ Date: _____

Day 3

Administrative Assistant

☐ Explain agent-billing system.

Manager

☐ Explain commission disbursement.

☐ Explain what happens if the Salesperson's bill does not get paid.

☐ Explain function and support of Marketing Director.

☐ Emphasize need to promptly turn in all listing/sales transaction paperwork.

☐ Referral procedures and qualifications.

☐ Explain referral assignment process.

☐ Explain corporate and third-party business.

☐ Explain agent-to-agent intra-office referrals.

Management/Staff Review_____ Date:_____

Day 4

Manager

☐ Explain auto insurance requirements.

☐ Read and understand all forms in Buyers and Listing Packets.

Allow a full afternoon for reading Policies and Procedures Manual.

☐ Read Policies and Procedures Manual and especially those policies noted below.

Confirm reading and understanding with initials on this form:

☐ Dress Code

☐ Floor Duty/Opportunity Time

☐ Listings

☐ Sales Reporting Procedures

☐ Commissions

☐ Referrals

☐ Property Management

☐ Goal Setting

☐ Operating Charges

☐ Termination

☐ Minimum Standards

☐ Established Agency

☐ Business Cards at Showings and Going Out of Town or Unavailable

☐ Tour

Management/Staff Review_____ Date:_____

Day 5

Manager

☐ Floor Duty Training
- Goals
- Procedures
- Dos and don'ts

☐ Role Playing for Floor Duty calls.

☐ Explain importance of Sphere of Influence (SOI) base.

☐ SOI homework: complete SOI list by Day 6 to include name, mailing address, work, cell, and home phone numbers, and e-mail address. Minimum of 25.

☐ Emphasize that the SOI is the best source of leads.

☐ Discuss importance of goals.

☐ Working with buyers
  ☐ Information on Brokerage
  ☐ Buyer's Representation Agreement
  ☐ Pre-qualify Mortgage Company
  ☐ How to show homes
  ☐ Closing the sale
  ☐ Writing, negotiating, receipting of the contract

☐ Working with sellers (listings)
  ☐ Elements of a good listing presentation
  ☐ Graphic aids
  ☐ Using laptop with marketing presentation
  ☐ Homework: develop initial listing presentation
  ☐ Develop notes/scripts/questions for Floor Duty callers

☐ Practice listing presentation

☐ Role-play for Floor Duty calls

☐ Introduce to MLS

☐ Explain CMA method

☐ Do CMA on computer

☐ Practice CMAs and general use of MLS

Management/Staff Review_____ Date:_____

Day 6

Manager

☐ Become familiar with real estate web sites

☐ Prospecting
    ☐ Floor Duty (company generated business)—role-play
    ☐ Sphere of Influence (SOI)—role-play
    ☐ Other types of prospecting
        ☐ Cold-calling
        ☐ Phone calls
        ☐ Walking neighborhoods, door hangers with just-listeds, Just-Solds, or other types of flyers
        ☐ Mail-outs—just-listeds, solds, flyers, newsletters, refrigerator magnets with calendars, recipes, sports schedules, and so on
        ☐ E-mail—short notes to multiple address lists or notes with attachments with all the above, including e-greetings
        ☐ Farming

☐ Homework:
    ☐ Write a trial offer on a house listed in the MLS.
    ☐ Use Buyer's Packet and fill out all necessary forms.
    ☐ Draft Introduction Letter to SOI list.

☐ Practice listing presentation with manager or mentor using a listing packet and filling out all necessary forms in packet.

☐ Role-play/practice for Floor Duty with manager or mentor.

Management/Staff Review_____ Date:_____

Day 7

Manager

☐ FSBO scripts and role-playing with other salespeople
☐ Expired scripts and role-playing with other salespeople
☐ Cold-calling scripts and role-playing with other salespeople

Management/Staff Review_____ Date:_____

Day 8

Manager

☐ Pre-qualifying by the salesperson for client wants and needs
☐ Pre-qualifying by Mortgage Company
☐ Cold-call for two hours

Management/Staff Review_____ Date:_____

Day 9

Manager or Mortgage Loan Officer

☐ Discuss various types of financing (VA, FHA, and Conventional).
☐ Discuss potential problems for qualifying.
☐ Discuss how to question clients about financing.
☐ Introduce the Mortgage Company.
☐ Prospect for two hours.

Management/Staff Review_____ Date:_____

Day 10

Manager

☐ Sale of Other Property Addendum

☐ Temporary Buyer Lease

☐ Temporary Seller Lease

☐ Back-up contracts

☐ Prospect for two hours

Management/Staff Review_____ Date:_____

Day 11

Manager

☐ How to conduct an open house

☐ How to advertise other listings

☐ Telephone prospect for two hours

Management/Staff Review_____ Date:_____

Days 12–18

Mentor

☐ Explanation of information on brokerage (agency)

☐ Schedule to attend an open house

☐ Conduct an open house (for another salesperson's listing)

☐ Goal-setting process

☐ Homework: telephone prospect for two hours daily

Manager

☐ Demonstrate how to do Net Sheets

☐ Homework: practice CMAs, Net Sheets on computer

Management/Staff Review_____ Date:_____

Days 19–25

Mentor

☐ Telephone prospect for two hours daily

☐ Drive about, learn areas, and team up if possible

Management/Staff Review_____ Date:_____

Days 26–32

Mentor

☐ Telephone prospect for two hours daily

☐ Drive about/learn areas and subdivisions

Manager

☐ Thirty-day follow-up

☐ First listing processed

Management/Staff Review_____ Date:_____

DAYS 33–39

Mentor

☐ Telephone prospect for two hours daily

☐ First contract receipted and in escrow

☐ At least twenty-five SOI names submitted to manager

☐ Drive about/learn areas and subdivisions

Management/Staff Review_____ Date:_____

DAYS 40–46

Mentor

☐ Telephone prospect for two hours daily

☐ Twenty-five more SOI names submitted to manager

☐ Drive about/learn areas and subdivisions

☐ Follow up on listings and contracts in escrow

Management/Staff Review_____ Date:_____

Days 47–53

Mentor

☐ Telephone prospect for two hours daily

☐ Discuss how to get more listings/sales

☐ Second listing processed

☐ Drive about/learn areas and subdivisions

Management/Staff Review_____ Date:_____

DAYS 54–60

Mentor

☐ Telephone prospect for two hours daily

☐ Follow-up interviews with management

☐ Drive about/learn areas and subdivisions

☐ Preview new homes

☐ Preview production

☐ Submit 25 more SOI names to manager

☐ Counseling

☐ Sixty-day follow-up with management

Management/Staff Review_____ Date:_____

NEW AGENT CHECKLIST

Sales Associate's Name: _____ Hire Date: _____

To be completed in the first week

Task	Contact Person	Due	Completed	Sign-Off
Learn Operation of Office Digital Camera	Administrative Asst.			
Learn How to Download Photos	Admin Asst.			
Learn How to Send E-Mails of Homes	Manager			
Input Your SOI into Your Computer	Agent			
Attend MLS Training	Agent			
Review Expectation Letter with Mgr	Manager			
Complete New Agent Application	Manager			
Complete Agent Profile	AA			
Sign Independent Contractor Agreement	Manager			
Complete IRS Forms	AA			
Complete Statement of Understanding	Manager			
RE Commission Sponsorship Form Signed	Manager			
Complete Business Card Application	AA			
Order Name Badge	AA/Manager			
Get Tour of Office and Key	Manager			
Discuss Personal Safety Guidelines	Manager			
Join Board of REALTORS®	Agent/Board			
Complete Key Card Lease Agreement	Agent/Board			
Complete Press Release	Agent			
Review Operations Manual	Agent			
Set Up Voice Mail	AA			
Learn Operation of Phone	Front Desk			
Learn Operation of Fax Machine	AA			
Learn Operation of Copier	AA			
Ensure All Paperwork Is Turned In	AA/Agent			
Send an E-Greeting from Internet	Agent			
Digital Photos for Advertising	AA			
Order Sign Riders	Agent/AA/Manager			
Order Car Signs	Agent/AA/Manager			
Complete Announcement Cards	Agent			
Discuss Office Meetings	Manager			
Discuss Office Tour	Manager			
Discuss the Office's New Agent Training	Manager			
Discuss How To Turn In Listing Package	AA			
Discuss How to Turn in a Sales Package	AA			
Discuss How to Turn in Status Changes	AA			

RELOCATION POLICY

1. All referrals will be directed to the Relocation Director or Manager.

2. Relocation Director will contact the client to determine wants and needs, and will place with the correct real estate salesperson best suited to work with the client based on the client's wants and needs and the salesperson's knowledge and service area.

3. Referrals will not be assigned on a rotation basis, nor will they be assigned according to which real estate salesperson is on floor duty at the time a referral comes in.

4. To qualify for incoming referrals a real estate salesperson MUST:
   A. Dress according to the Policy Manual.
   B. Maintain a clean car inside and out.
   C. Show only in areas the salesperson is familiar with. If the client desires to look outside of the salesperson's expertise, the salesperson must report to the Relocation Director for guidance.

5. The salesperson must attend appropriate, required training and become a certified relocation specialist.

6. The real estate salesperson must be willing to meet the client at the airport, make hotel reservations, and be of help in a broad range of services.

7. The salesperson must keep progress reports updated regularly. Keep Relocation Department updated monthly until contract, and then weekly.

8. If a real estate salesperson is unable to dedicate the necessary time or requirements of a referred client, the salesperson must report to the Relocation Director. Do not ever pass the referral to another salesperson.

TIME MANAGEMENT

1. Keep a written and prioritized to-do list.
   - ☐ It should flexible yet thorough.
   - ☐ Ask yourself: What is the most important thing I should be doing at this given moment?

2. Work at work, play at play, a corollary to work is work and home is home. Waste time honestly. If you don't feel like working, just admit it.

3. Have an assistant: If you don't have an assistant, you are an assistant, not a broker!

4. Work only 5½ days per week: this lessens burnout.

5. Handle paperwork only once: Do it, file it, and throw it away.

6. Use the phone, fax, mail, e-mail, and scan.

7. Combine activities.

8. Start the day early.

9. Never let your tank go less than half full.

10. Listen to educational CDs and always have educational books in your car.

11. Pay to have the things done that take up your personal time, like mowing, washing the car, cleaning the house or office.

12. Learn to say "NO." Refuse to do the other person's job.

13. Track your time.

Article	"Stop the Revolving Door: Treat Your Agents Like Customers"
Author	Rich Casto
Online mag.	Realty Times
Web address	http://realtytimes.com/rtpages/20040908_revolvingdoor.htm.
Published	September 8, 2004

Article	"Recruiting the Experienced Agent"
Author	Rich Casto
Online mag.	Realty Times
Web address	http://realtytimes.com/rtpages/20040420_experience.htm
Published	April 20, 2004

Article	"Why Agents Leave: It Isn't the Splits"
Author	Jon Cheplak
Online mag.	Realty Times
Web address	http://realtytimes.com/rtpages/20040324_agentsleav.htm
Published	March 24, 2004

Article	"Three Keys to Recruiting Better Agents"
Author	Terri Murphy
Online mag.	Realty Times
Web address	http://realtytimes.com/rtpages/20030225_recruiting.htm
Published	February 25, 2003

Article	"Errors and Omissions Insurance for Real Estate Agents"
Author	Janet Wickell
Online mag.	About
Web address	http://homebuying.about.com/cs/errorsomissions/a/errors_omission.htm
Published	no date

Article	"How Do You Measure Up?"
Author	Robert Freedman
Online mag.	Realtor Magazine Online
Web address	http://realtor.org/rmomag.NSF/pages/HowDoYouMeRobArchive1999Sep
Published	September 1, 1999

Article	"The Future of Real Estate Brokerage"
Author	Ellen P. Roche, PhD., Kate Anderson
Online mag.	Realtor.org
Web address	http://www.realtor.org/Research.nsf/files/futurehighlights.pdf/$FILE/futurehighlights.pdf
Published	no date

Book | *The Vault Real Estate Career Guide*
Author | Raul Saavedra
Publisher | Vault, Inc.
Address | 150 West 22nd St., New York, NY 10011
Published | November 2003

Article | "How to Make a Valuable Office Policy Manual"
Author | Tracey Velt
Online mag. | Planet Realtor
Web address | http://www.planetrealtor.com/Florida/FLRealtorMagazine/
BookSmart0605.cfm
Published | 2005

Article | "Will Your Recruits Fit In"
Author | Michael Abelson
Online mag. | Realtor Magazine Online
Web address | http://www.realtor.org/rmomag.NSF/pages/
forbrokersJune03?OpenDocument
Published | June 1, 2003

Article | "Make Your Recruiting Mirror Your Market"
Author | Laurie Moore-Moore
Online mag. | Realtor Magazine Online
Web address | http://www.realtor.org/rmomag.NSF/pages/
MakeYourReLauArchive1998May?OpenDocument
Published | May 1, 1998

Article | "Do a Reality Check on Your Recruiting Costs"
Author | Laurie Moore-Moore
Online mag. | Realtor Magazine Online
Web address | http://www.realtor.org/rmomag.NSF/pages/
DoaRealityLauArchive1998Sep?OpenDocument
Published | September 1, 1998

Article | "Which Brokerage Is Right for You?"
Author | Mariwyn Evans
Online mag. | Realtor Magazine Online
Web address | http://www.realtor.org/rmomag.NSF/pages/feb03brokerage
Published | February 1, 2003

Article | "Recruiting the Best"
Author | Chris Heagerty
Online mag. | Texas Realtor Online
Web address | http://www.texasrealtoronline.com/issues/0900/recruiting/
recruiting.html
Published | September/October 2000

Article | "Effective Meeting Tips"
Author | None given
Online mag. | Meeting Wizard

Web address http://www.meetingwizard.org/meetings/effectivemeetings.cfm
Published   2001–2005

Article   "What's in a Name?"
Author   David Avrin
Online mag. The Visibility Coach
Web address http://www.visibilitycoach.com/newsletter/april05.html
Published   April 2005

Article   "The Approachability Philosophy"
Author   Scott Ginsberg
Online mag. Front Porch Productions
Web address http://www.hellomynameisscott.com
Published   no date given

Article   "How to Start a Kiosk Business"
Author   none given
Online mag. Entrepreneur.com
Web address http://www.entrepreneur.com/article/0,4621,309713,00.html
Published   July 18, 2003

INDEX

Index